RADICAL APPROACHES TO ADULT EDUCATION:
A Reader

LIBRARY
DEVELOPMENT STUDIES
KIMMAGE MANOR

D1336099

RADICAL FORUM ON ADULT EDUCATION SERIES
Edited by Jo Campling, Series Consultant: Colin Griffin

113041

Radical Approaches to Adult Education: A Reader

Edited by
TOM LOVETT

ROUTLEDGE
London and New York

bermann Library Kimmage

113041

Radical approaches to adult

bermann Library Kimmage

First published in 1988 by
Routledge
11 New Fetter Lane, London EC4P 4EE

Published in the USA by
Routledge
in association with Routledge, Chapman & Hall, Inc.
29 West 35th Street, New York NY 10001

© 1988 T. Lovett

All rights reserved. No part of this book may be reprinted or·
reproduced or utilized in any form or by any electronic, mechanical or
other means, now known or hereafter invented, including photocopying
and recording, or in any information storage or retrieval system, without
permission in writing from the publishers.

British Library Cataloguing in Publication Data

Radical approaches to adult education.
   1. Adult education — Political aspects
   I. Lovett, Tom
   374   LC5219

   ISBN 0-415-00561-2
   ISBN 0-415-00620-1 (Pbk)
Library of Congress Cataloging-in-Publication Data

ISBN 0-415-00561-2
ISBN 0-415-00620-1 (Pbk)

Printed and bound in Great Britain by
Biddles Ltd, Guildford and King's Lynn

Contents

PART I

PERSPECTIVES - HISTORICAL AND THEORETICAL

Contents

PART II

CONTEMPORARY INITIATIVES

vi

Contributors

MYLES HORTON was born in Savannah, Tennessee in 1905. He is the founder of the Highlander Centre in that State. Myles still lives in the Centre's campus near Knoxville and, although in his 80s, travels the world sharing his knowledge and experience with those involved in movements for social change. He is the co-author with Frank Adams of Unearthing Seeds of Fire: The Idea of Highlander.

TOM LOVETT is Professor of Community Education in the Department of Adult and Continuing Education at the University of Ulster and founder member and chairman of the Ulster People's College. In 1985 he was awarded the J. Roby Kidd International Award by the International Council for Adult Education for his work in adult education in Northern Ireland. His publications include Adult Education, Community Development and the Working Class (2nd edition, University of Nottingham Press, 1982); Adult Education and Community Action - with C Clarke and A Kilmurray (Croom Helm, 1983) and Working Class Community in N. Ireland, with Peter McNamee (Ulster People's College, forthcoming).

RICHARD JOHNSON became director of the Centre for Contemporary Cultural Studies at the University of Birmingham in 1980, after teaching social history at the same university since 1966. He has written and edited books and articles on nineteenth-century British history, on the sociology and contemporary history of education, on cultural theory and on representations of the past.

PAUL ARMSTRONG studied sociology at the Universities of York and Essex. He has taught social studies and adult education in further education and at the University of Hull, from where he is on secondment until December 1988 to the Further Education Unit to carry out research on the Youth Training Scheme.

SALLIE WESTWOOD teaches in the Department of

Adult Education, University of Leicester. She is the author of All Day Every Day; Factory and Family in the Making of Women's Lives (Pluto Press and University of Illinois, 1985). She is currently researching health issues with the Black Mental Health Group in Leicester.

PAULA ALLMAN was educated in the USA and received her doctorate in education in 1972. She was Social Science Staff Tutor/East Midlands for the Open University from 1975-1979. In 1979 she was appointed lecturer in the psychology of adult development in the Education Division of Nottingham University. Since 1983 she has been the Course Tutor for the Diploma in Adult Education at Nottingham.

ROLLAND G. PAULSTON is a professor in the Department of Administrative and Policy Studies at the University of Pittsburgh. His doctorate is from Columbia University and his professional and scholarly work has focused on problems of education in development effort. Research findings have been reported in the following publications: Other Dreams, Other Schools (University of Pittsburgh Press); Conflictive Theories of Social and Educational Change (UCIS); Changing Educational Systems (World Bank); Nonformal Education (F. Praeger); Society, Schools and Progress in Peru (Pergamon); and Educational Change in Sweden (Teachers College Press).

RICHARD J. ALTENBAUGH, a twentieth-century social historian, completed his Ph.D. in the History of Education at the University of Pittsburgh in 1980. He has served as a faculty member of Indianna University, the University of Pittsburgh, and the University of Louisville. Mr Altenbaugh is currently an Assistant Professor in the Department of History at Northern Illinois University. He has published articles and reviews in the History of Education Quarterly, Paedagogica Historica, Theatre Journal, Educational Studies, and the Journal of American History, among others. Mr Altenbaugh has just completed a booklength manuscript, "Education and Worker Struggle: The American Labor Colleges of the 1920s and the 1930s".

BUDD HALL is currently Secretary-General of the International Council for Adult Education which is based in Toronto, Canada. Budd has worked in the US, Nigeria, Tanzania, and England before taking a position as research officer with ICAE in 1975. He is best known for his work in promoting participatory research and for his contributions linking adult educators around the world. He is married with two sons.

JANE L. THOMPSON is a Lecturer in Adult Education at Southampton University. Her publications include Adult Education for a Change (Hutchinson); Learning Liberation: Women's Response to Men's Education (Croom Helm) and with the Taking Liberties Collective, Learning the Hard Way: Womens Oppression in Mens Education (Macmillan).

BRIAN MARTIN was born in 1947, received a B.A. from Rice University (Houston, Texas) and a Ph.D in theoretical physics from Sydney University. He then worked for 10 years in applied mathematics at the Australian National University. His technical scientific papers are mainly in the areas of stratospheric modelling, numerical methods, wind power and astrophysics. He has also written widely on the critique of science and technology, nuclear power, war and peace issues, and social action, including the books The Bias of Science (1979) and Uprooting War (1984). He has been active for many years in environmental, peace and radical science groups. In 1986 he joined the Department of Science and Technology Studies at the University of Wollongong.

JOHN FIELD ex-welder, active in the British rail-workers' union; worked at Northern College, Barnsley, from its foundation in 1978 until 1985, when he moved to the newly-established Department of Continuing Education, University of Warwick. Publications include Education for a Tolerable Society: working class education in the Dearne Valley, 1918 - 1945.

RICHARD TAYLOR (b. 1945) is Director of Extramural Courses and **KEVIN WARD** (b. 1946) Co-ordinator of Pioneer Work, at the Department of Adult and Continuing Education, University of Leeds, where they have worked closely together over several years in the development of community-based adult education, particularly with unem-ployed adults, within the extramural provision of the department. In 1986 they co-edited Adult Education and the Working Class: Education for the Missing Millions (Croom Helm). Richard Taylor is also co-author of University Adult Education in England and the USA: a Reappraisal of the Liberal Tradition (Croom Helm, 1985). Both have written widely on adult education issues.

FRANK ADAMS has been learning to be an adult educator since 1959, first in unions, then subsequently in the civil rights, anti-Vietnam War, Appalachian and worker-ownership movements. He is the author (with Myles Horton) of Unearthing Seeds of Fire: The Idea of Highlander, and co-author of Putting Democracy to Work: A Practical Guide for Starting Worker-Owned Businesses, and To Know for Real: Royce S Pitkin and Goddard College.

RETTA ALEMAYEHU played important roles in directing and co-ordinating adult education programmes in his capacity as Research Associate in the Education Research Centre (now Institute) and Assistant Dean of Continuing Education at Addis Ababa University in Ethiopia. At the national level, he was member of the Supreme Council of the National Revolutionary Development Campaign and Central Planning where he also served as member of the Executive Body of the National Literacy Campaign Co-ordinating Committee. Currently he is working on his doctoral degree specializing in adult education at the Ontario Institute for Studies in Education, University of Toronto, Toronto, Canada.

Acknowledgements

I would like to thank my students on the MA in Continuing Education course at the University of Ulster for their assistance in helping me develop the original idea for this book. I would also like to thank all the contributors for their faith in the project and their individual efforts. Last but not least, I would like to thank Shirley Scott for her patience and hard work in typing the final draft.

Foreword

The Workers Education Programme developed by the British Labour Movement in the latter part of the nineteenth century has been an important influence on radical adult education, especially in the western world.

Learning from the experiments of the Chartist Movement, the Mechanics' Institutes and Workers' College, the growing labour movement set up an educational programme consisting primarily of lectures on Marxism. The intention was to demonstrate the connection between theory and practice and to prepare the members for taking power. As taking power became less imminent, attendance at the lectures declined, and they were replaced by tutorial classes and residential colleges such as Ruskin.

Although a great deal of radical adult education has been patterned after the British model, it is not always appropriate. In some countries the labour movement is a single-purpose organisation and does not embody the elements of worker organisation, political party, cooperatives and socialist philosophy that characterised the early British movement.

A labour movement in partnership with capitalism is not in a position to deal with many of the concerns of the working people as a whole or the poor or minorities. These problems have to be addressed by educational programmes connected with other organisations. Consequently, radical adult education programmes have to be developed to deal with these problems.

In the United States, for example, where the labour movement is weak and there is no Labour Party, radical adult education programmes were set up outside the labour movement and usually took the form of labour schools whose aim was to enlarge the union membership and make it more democratic by strengthening the rank and file.

Some of these schools were connected with the Socialist or Communist Party. Some were sponsored by the

Catholic Church; others were independent. But they all had in common the desire to help working people understand their world and the institutions that affect their lives. They put forth a vision of a more just society and attempted to help their students discover ways to make that vision a reality.

Most radical educational activities today are not limited to working with organised labour but encompass, rather, work with a wide variety of organisations involved in issues of social justice, such as minority rights, health care, cultural empowerment, protection in the workshop, cooperatives, and international concerns.

The choice or organisations and movements to work with is often based on evidence that (1) the organisation is moving in a radical direction or providing a radicalising experience; (2) is demanding structural reforms; (3) is involved in a continuous learning process; and (4) has the potential for multiplying leadership for social change.

More recently radical adult education has been informed by the educational philosophy of Paulo Freire and by the spread of popular education programmes in Central and Latin America. This model of adult education involves the exploited in a critical analysis of their own social experience which leads to collective transforming action.

Reading this book there can be no doubt of the vitality and creativity of radical adult education which is making new history.

Myles Horton

Introduction

Tom Lovett

All serious educational movements have, in
England, been also social movements. They have
been the expression in one sphere - the training of
mind and character - of some distinctive
conception of the life proper to man and the kind
of society in which he can best live it.

(R.H. Tawney)

The historical roots of many contemporary adult education
movements and organisations lay initially in a concern for
social justice and radical change. As Tawney's statement
affirms, they were, in many respects, radical movements
concerned with a new view of man and society. There are
examples like Frontier College and the Antigonish
Movement in Canada, Highlander and the Labour Colleges in
the USA, the Folk High School Movement in Scandanavia,
Società Umanitaria de Milan in Italy, the WEA and NCLC in
England. The links between these different initiatives, and
their influence on each other, was more important than we
often assume.

That tradition of linking adult education to movements
for social change is re-emerging as adult educators grapple
with the social, economic, political and moral issues facing
people in a complex, violent, unequal and rapidly changing
society. In their reactions to the issues and problems facing
us all in the latter part of the twentieth century many
governments now place a high value on adult education.
Terms such as 'continuing', 'permanent', 'recurrent', 'lifelong' are increasingly used to signify a new concept of adult
education which will rise to meet the challenges of the
1980s.

Already in line with these developments there is more
emphasis on linking adult education more effectively to the
needs of the economy, concentrating on 'clients needs'
'coordinating resources', 'effective delivery of services'.

Introduction

Increasingly we are told that we are all learners now; that education is a life-long process; that we must be educated for change; that we must learn to make better use of our increased leisure hours - particularly the unemployed!

These developments are indicative of the fact that adult education is becoming less marginal to the mainstream of education and the major preoccupations of the state. Whilst it was marginal it was allowed the space to be more critical of existing institutions and structures, less concerned with the needs of the system in narrow economic terms. This liberal adult education tradition is now itself under threat, subject to cost-effective analysis, asked to become more 'relevant' to the needs of the state.

However, the same tradition has also been criticised by radical educators for its failure to respond effectively to the continuing and widening inequalities in our society. Much of the criticism has arisen during the past decade as it has become increasingly obvious to concerned adult educators that the social engineering of the post-war period (of which the liberal adult education movement was an important part) has failed to create a more just and equitable society.

The active involvement of adult educators in various contemporary issues and movements (i.e. women, community action, peace, the environment, the unemployed, Third World development) has provided them with the experience to challenge that tradition. They wish to reaffirm the radical tradition in adult education, stressing its concern with linking education to social movements; constructing alternative adult education organisations and movements; emphasising a collective perspective concerned with individual and collective advancement.

That tradition has historically been involved with movements for social change, e.g. cooperatives in Denmark; Scandinavian study circles with Scandinavian social democracy; American Land Grant Colleges with rural development in the USA. The Società Umanitaria of Milan founded in 1893, convened the first European conference on unemployment; the first on adult education; set up the first labour exchanges in Italy; the first cooperative housing scheme; the first institution for the rehabilitation of the unemployed; trained cooperators; had a large 'People's Theatre'; started the Italian People's Universities; started the first adult education unions; promoted People's Libraries

- all before 1910![1]

It's interesting to note that, although there are obvious echoes here of recent adult education initiatives in this country, Gramsci, the Italian Marxist, was very critical of the People's Universities comparing them to English merchants handing out 'trashy baubles to African negroes in exchange for gold'.[2] For him such exercises, although radical in <u>method</u>, were essentially reformist. They would not succeed unless there was a strong link between such institutions and the masses and unless 'they had worked out and made coherent the principles and the problems raised by the masses in their practical activity, thus constituting a cultural and social bloc'.[3]

The contrast between the liberal and radical approaches in this educational tradition of active involvement in social, economic and political problems and issues is evident in North America where the European Folk High School movement was an important influence in numerous education movements. In Denmark, it had been closely associated not only with the cooperative movement but the growth of Danish nationalism and culture in the nineteenth century. However, in other Scandinavian countries it had close links with the labour movement. In the USA both were important influences in workers' education in the early part of the century. In 1907 a Work People's College was established by Finnish socialists in Minnesota.[4] It was an important influence on the Labour College movement which blossomed in the USA during the 1920s. It provided workers with hard intellectual education, within a Marxist perspective, and training in practical skills. The knowledge and experience gained in strikes and other industrial activity were not regarded as interruptions of school work but as genuine education as a result of which 'students and teachers alike bring wiser judgement and a keener sense of reality to their classes'.

In some schools students and staff had to work, as well as study together, often reversing the usual roles. Special importance was attached to art and drama in the work of the schools. Students wrote, directed, produced and acted their own plays and the skills associated with drama production were included in the curriculum. The aim of the many Labour College courses is summed up in the following statement of objectives from the Work People's College - 'The school recognises the existence of class struggle in society and its courses of study have been prepared so that industrially organised workers, both men and women, dissatisfied with conditions under our capitalist system can more effectively carry on an organised struggle for the attainment of industrial demands and ultimately the realisation of a new social order'.[5] The Work People's College, and the American Labour College Movement, played an important role in the American Labour Movement up to the 1930s when it eventually fell victim to pressure from conservative trade unions and government.

However, another initiative influenced by the Danish Folk High School tradition, the Highlander Folk School in Tennessee, which was established in the 1930s by a radical Baptist minister, Myles Horton, has survived to this day. Highlander played an important role in the growth and development of the trade union movement in Tennessee in the 1930s and more recently it played an important educational role in the Civil Rights Movement. Although Highlander was also committed to active physical involvement in the problems and issues facing people in that depressed region of the USA, it was not so ideologically rigid as the Work People's College and the Labour College movement referred to above. It was deliberately vague about the exact meaning placed on its governing concepts - brotherhood, democracy, mutuality, concerted community action - letting the time and the people define them more precisely. It quickly learnt that ideology, no matter how firmly rooted in objective reality, was of no value if it was separated from a social movement of struggling people.

Its axiom was 'learn from the people and start education where they are '. It sought to educate people away from the dead end of individualism into the freedom that grows from cooperation and collective solutions to problems. Its goals were the release of the potential and energies of the people not the relief of those problems. Like the Labour Colleges it placed great stress on culture and art, particularly local working-class culture. However, there was less stress on hard intellectual effort and more on education for the will and imagination and creative human relationships. Information and training were provided by linking action to intensive, short-term, residential workshops. This was supplemented by research support for local activists. Highlander suffered from attacks by the Ku Klux Klan and other reactionary elements in the South. In 1961 the State of Tennessee seized the school's property and revoked its charter. However it was quickly reorganised and rechartered under its present name, the Highlander Research and Education Centre, and continues its work on a new site in New Market, Tennessee.

At the other end of this continuum from the revolutionary Marxist approach of the Work People's College, through the radicalism of the Highlander Centre is the Antigonish movement of Nova Scotia in Canada.[7] This was a programme of adult education, self-help and cooperative development which became world famous during the 1930s. Again, as with Highlander, the Folk High School movement in Denmark was an important influence and the leading figures were clergymen, Father Moses Coady and Father Jimmy Tompkins. Coady was the intellectual figurehead of the movement, operating from the Extension Department of St Francis Xavier University. Tompkins was the fieldworker building the foundations of the movement amongst the poor people of the region in the 1920s.

Antigonish believed that reform would come about through education, public participation and the establishment of alternative institutions, i.e. cooperatives and credit unions. For Coady adult education was an aggressive agent of change, a mass movement of reform, the peaceful way to social change. It was a populist movement, strongly anti-communist but with a vision of a new society. This was the foundation of its educational philosophy and approach. It drew no fine distinctions between action and education. The movement was involved in actually creating cooperatives and credit unions linking them closely with a system of education support which was wide-ranging including mass meetings, study clubs, radio discussion groups, kitchen meetings, short courses, conferences, leadership schools and training courses.

Although it did not embrace the Marxist analysis of the American Labour College Movement or the radical political philosophy of the Highlander Centre, the Antigonish movement did succeed in engaging large numbers of workers in an extensive educational programme linked to social action which even today would be regarded as too radical by many adult education institutions! In fact, it appears that St Francis Xavier University was not particularly happy with this active community involvement. When Coady died in 1959 the movement effectively died with him. As so often in such cases the university effectively 'institutionalised' the movement establishing a Coady International Institute to train people from the Third World in Antigonish methods, whilst remaining somewhat aloof from the continuing problems of poverty and injustice in its own region.

In Great Britain this tradition of active involvement in social movements is historically associated with the National Council of Labour Colleges. The latter, which grew out of the Plebs League and the disagreement with what was seen as the academic and reformist attitude of Ruskin, the workers' college at Oxford, was in some respects similar to the American Labour College Movement. Up until 1929 it had its own residential college and close links with the trade unions. However, echoing the American experience, as these unions became more right-wing they became more a hindrance than a help! It also appears that the rigid Marxist teaching approach of the NCLC was less successful with students than the WEA's more traditional liberal approach, particularly during the 1930s when students were interested in the causes of unemployment and practical solutions.[8] The WEA although less dogmatic and more 'objective' was more democratic and flexible in its teaching methods, developing a more critical, analytical approach in its students. The NCLC was a revolutionary educational movement with some very 'conservative' educational methods and techniques which often succeeded because of the high motivation of the students and their commitment to the political philosophy of the NCLC. The WEA was essentially a reformist movement.

However, both organisations trained successive generations of leaders for the trade union and labour movements, although they were less actively involved in seeking practical solutions on the ground than the initiatives in Europe and North America, discussed above. The WEA has survived as the main provider of working-class education. It placed greater stress on seeking state support for its work against the emphasis placed on independence by the Labour College movement. A recent article on the WEA and the NCLC argues that this was the right approach; that it is unwise and unnecessary to ignore the possibilities of using the resources of the state; that such support did not, as the supporters of the Labour College movement argued, weaken its (the WEA's) commitment to the labour movement.[9]

That view has, until lately, been generally accepted. It has its origins in developments in workers' education in the late nineteenth and early twentieth centuries which stressed the need to demand equal access to educational facilities provided by the state. This became the main feature of popular liberal politics and then of the Labour Party's educational stance. The debate between the WEA and the NCLC in the early part of this century was thus, in some respects, the final battle in an older debate about independence and incorporation in workers' education which reaches back into the early part of the nineteenth century.

There was in fact a popular radical education tradition in the early nineteenth century which was closely associated with the radical political movement and sharply oppositional to all provided and centralised education, including the Mechanics' Institute.[10] Benjamin King, a Chartist, commenting on the latter said: 'Mechanics' Institutes were not intended to teach the most useful knowledge but to teach only as might be profitable to the unproductive. He trusted, however, we should now get working men to inquire how the produce of their labour was so cunningly and avariciously abstracted from them, and thence go on to the attainment of truth, in order to obtain, before long ... happiness and community.'[11] This movement was much more informal, flexible and undogmatic than the Labour College movement of the early twentieth century. Educational activities, eg. communal readings, discussion groups, travelling scholars, newspapers, were closely related to other activities in the family, neighbourhood and work. There was little distinction between education and non-education. The emphasis was on really useful knowledge and collective enterprise. The strategy was one of establishing alternatives. It was opposed to rigid dogma. Thus there were few organisational orthodoxies, little bureaucracy and little division between officials and the rank and file. It found in the life of the masses the source of the problems it set out to study and resolve. It was undogmatic because there was nothing but experience from which theory could spring. All it had was its popularity. Thus the informal and unacademic character of the education. However, education was seen as essentially political, part of a political movement, and the movement conducted an internal debate about education as a means of changing the world.

This book is an attempt to provide some practical examples of work in this radical collective tradition, to place it within the context of earlier, historical, initiatives in this field and to examine the influence of some of the important theorists. It will, I believe, serve to illustrate the fact that modern concerns are often an echo of past debates and experiences. It will also assist in the process of clarifying the problems and contradictions involved in radical adult education today, pointing the way forward in terms of possible new alternative initiatives.

The first section of this book offers the reader an opportunity to undertake an intellectual journey back to the roots of this radical education tradition in the early nineteeth century, through to the debates about workers' education and the role of women in the late nineteenth and early twentieth centuries. It then looks at the influence of contemporary theorists on the practice of radical adult education and finishes with an outline of a typology which attempts to provide a link between theory and practice.

The second part of the book then examines some examples of contemporary practice, particularly education linked to social movements, i.e. community action, the women's movement, the peace movement, trade unions, the unemployed, worker cooperatives and the Third World.

Many of the problems and contradictions facing the latter find an echo in the earlier accounts of radical adult education in the nineteenth and early twentieth century, i.e. the search for really useful knowledge; the conflict between the demand for collective education for individual development and collective education for individual and collective development and advancement; the demand for access to educational institutions as opposed to the concern for local space for, and control over, their own educational resources; the tension between concern with method as against an emphasis on content.

My own interest in this radical tradition (and the possibility of establishing radical alternatives in adult education) is a journey which began over twelve years ago when I took a group of Protestants and Catholics from Northern Ireland to a Folk High School in Bergan, Holland. I thought it would be useful for them to get away from the 'troubles' at home and to reflect quietly on the issues and problems facing them in their divided communities.

We were assisted in this process by Louis Kools, a tutor in the Folk High School. Everyone enjoyed and benefited from the experience. They were particularly struck by the friendly atmosphere and informality of the Folk High School and its programme of outreach work in the community.

Louis told me the story of Highlander in the USA where he spent a year's study leave. He had written a book about his experiences. Unfortunately I could not read Dutch. However, he lent me Frank Adam's book, Unearthing Seeds of Fire. I was so impressed by the story of Highlander and my experience in the Folk High School that I decided to visit Highlander and, if possible, set up something similar in Northern Ireland.

In 1979 I was able to make such a visit and met Myles Horton and the staff at Highlander. About the same time I had read about the Antigonish Movement and the American Labour Colleges. Combined with my own personal experience of the WEA, the NCLC and Ruskin College (I had been a student at one time or another at all three!), and my involvement in community education and community action in England and Northern Ireland, I developed a proposal for an Ulster People's College - an alternative radical adult education centre.

It received a very enthusiastic response from radical adult educators and activists in Northern Ireland and eventually, with their support and financial assistance from trusts and charities, the College was established in Belfast in 1982. This is just one practical example of the importance of linking present concerns with past initiatives. There are many others. Hopefully this book will stimulate more.

REFERENCES

1. P. Du Sautoy and D. Waller, 'Community Development and Adult Education', in The International Review of Community Development, No.8, 1961.

2. Q. Hoare and G. Smith (eds and trans.), Selections from the Prison Notebooks of Antonio Gramsci (London: Lawrence and Wishart, 1973), p.330.

3. Ibid., p.330.

4. See Chapter 5, 'Adult Education in Radical US Social and Ethnic Movements'.

5. Ibid.

6. F. Adams and M. Horton, Unearthing Seeds of Fire - The Idea of Highlander (N. Carolina: J.F. Blair, 1975).

7. J. Lotz, 'The Antigonish Movement', in Understanding Canada: Regional and Community Development in a New Nation (Toronto: N.C. Press, 1977).

8. See Chapter 2, 'The Long Search for the Working Class: Socialism and the Education of Adults, 1850-1930'.

9. Ibid.

10. See Chapter 1, 'Really Useful Knowledge, 1790-1850: Memories for Education in the 1980s'.

11. Ibid.

PART I

PERSPECTIVES - HISTORICAL AND THEORETICAL

'Really Useful Knowledge' 1790-1850:
Memories for Education in the 1980s

Richard Johnson

MEMORIES

The educational practices of early nineenth-century English radicals first interested me in the early 1970s. Researching this topic was a way of changing myself, from conservative Cambridge history to social history and Marxism. I wanted to get closer to popular experiences, to write history 'from below'. I followed Edward Thompson, Brian Simon and others in reading new sources; the books popular in the movements, the autobiographies of activists, above all the radical press. I gave the first version of this paper at a History Workshop and published it in Radical Education.[1]

This first enthusiasm was mistaken in some ways. It will not do to identify popular or working-class attitudes with those of the most articulate radicals. One of their commoner ironic self-descriptions was that of 'schoolmaster' - though, as Barbara Taylor has shown, there were 'schoolmistresses' too.[2] The image reminds us how radical leaders, though often obscure local people, did not merely express popular views, but tried to shape them. Moreover this band of schoolteachers had many disagreements, almost as many as their students. Even so, I still believe that the radical leaderships were closer to popular experiences than the 'educationalists' of the time: professional middle-class enthusiasts who were bombarding gentry, clergy and urban bourgeoisie with arguments for intervention, and whose writings still dominate educational histories today.[3]

Another unexpected thing happened when I started to write about 'really useful knowledge'. The early nineenth-century examples set up some extraordinary resonances with the present, my present. I do not think I was equipped to understand this at the time. I was too much the historian. I thought that the object of history was 'the past' and that history was an act of reconstruction. Politically the thing to do was to choose your scene; like so many social historians of the time, I wanted to follow Edward Thompson in 'rescuing' popular struggles from historical condescensions. I think now that historians always work on a past-present relation and that history is a public form of memory,[4] in which the emotional or intuitive resonances provide main motives for study. Like memory, history is as much about forgetting as remembering. I blush now to think how much I overlooked in my sources especially in the light of recent feminist histories.[5] Historical agenda grow out of today's preoccupations. Where else could they come from?

So I approach 'really useful knowledge' today, as something I want to remember. Remembering remains hard work, of course: it is important to recall events, values, feelings, to do historical research in detail, at length, carefully. But the most useful memory-work also faces up to the present, and self-consciously so. It asks: so why these episodes? Why remember this today? And, in this context, why have I this recurrent interest, indeed fascination, in episodes 200 years ago?

Is the fascination a matter of parallels? Are there warnings here about what to avoid? It may be that differences are just as important. The recognition of great discontinuities may shock us into thought. This makes us look at past episodes more historically, but may also re-historicise the present. We learn that modern conditions are not that necessary; they are as transient as the past conditions are. So we can change them.

FEATURES

Radical education was essentially an oppositional movement, gaining energies from contesting orthodoxies, in theory and practice. The first criticisms of the sorts of schooling which were provided were formed in the period up to 1820, under the shadow of a counter-revolution. The early schooling enterprises - Sunday Schools of the more conservative-Evangelical kind, the monitorial day schools were seen as coercive and knowledge-denying. When more liberal schemes were put forward in the 1820s and 1830s - Mechanics' Institutes, the Useful Knowledge Societies, infant schools, plans for state education - they were opposed too, though more conditionally. Before the 1860s there was not enough working-class support for state education to overcome the opposition of its Tory-Anglican opponents.[6]

Criticism was not limited to opposition. Alternatives were proposed. Education was differently defined. It was partly a matter of religion. Radical education tended to be secular and rationalist; it drew on Enlightment ideas of an expanding human nature.[7] But there was a polarisation within Christianity too. Philanthropic educators inherited a Pauline, Hebraic, Puritan-Evangelical view of human nature as finite, limited and flawed. Since social evils like crime, riot, pauperism, 'vice' and even epidemic diseases were 'moral' at root, moral and religious education was the answer.[8] Religion was a source of order, in society and in individuals; God was a kind of policeman in the sky. Radicals by contrast, developed the legacy of natural theology (God known only through Nature), and of Christianity as a morality of cooperation among equals. The morality of 'that good man' Jesus Christ was turned against inequality and injustice. There was also a real excitement about secular knowledges, especially as solvents of dogmatic religion and as keys to understanding society and human nature.[9]

A third feature was a preoccupation with education and politics, knowledge and power. Educating yourself and others, especially in a knowledge of your 'circumstances', was a step in changing the world. Knowledge was a natural right, an unconditional good. The typical middle-class argument - that only the 'educated' should be able to vote - was angrily dismissed. Yet there were differences around education and politics within radical movements too. Some groups, the Owenites for instance, were more likely to adopt 'schoolmastery' attitudes than others; the others always insisted on some moral or physical force. It was genuinely difficult to know which educational practices were for the here and now, as strategies for change, and which could only be enjoyed once the changes had come. This tension between education as a strategy and education, or the educative society, as an ideal grew stronger as the movements weakened in the 1840s.[10]

Finally radicals developed a varied, vigorous educational practice of their own. In a sense this was 'adult education'. Yet this label misleads, reading back our modern separations anachronistically. Rather child/adult differences were less stressed than they are today, or than they were in the contemporary middle-class culture of childhood. This was just one feature of the relative informality of the characteristic solutions.

So radical education challenged the educational

5

enterprises of 'Church Christianity' and the liberalism of the urban middle classes. It mounted alternatives in its philosophy, pedagogy and institutional arrangements. It was not merely a critical or oppositional movement, but counter-hegemonic, threatening to construct a whole alternative social order.

The success or failure of such an enterprise depended on all the relationships of force in early Victorian society, including the sheer weight of economic impositions and the control of military force. It did not depend on education alone, but on the contexts of the educational struggle.

CONTEXTS

The most obvious context was the growth of schools and school-like institutions. The massive institutionalisation of knowledge is one great discontinuity between the early nineteenth century and today. It is from this period that we may date the great transformation in the conditions of learning. Of course, there had been schools before; but public schooling in eighteenth-century England had been about the charitable rescue of degraded children, or about sponsoring a promising few. The ambition of getting all children into school, voluntarily at first, was new. The form of schools testified to this ambition; with the monitorial school we enter the era of mass schooling. Achieving universality was a very protracted process. Up to the later 1830s the growth of the new day schools was geographically uneven and proceeded in fits and starts. Then there was a marked change of gear, fuelled by the fear of popular knowledges, and by a triangular rivalry of Church, Dissent and the state. By the later 1840s the pattern of 'voluntaryism' had emerged: Anglican dominance, the subordination of Dissent, the state's assumption of supervision, especially over teacher-training, buildings and standards. A network of public day schools was formed, not universal, but spanning most localities by the 1860s.[11]

'Public' is a keyword here.[12] As the archaic English usage of 'public school' suggests, public did not imply (as in America) a civic, secular, non-proprietorial institution. For English philanthropy, 'public' meant 'properly supervised'. The form of supervision might vary - trustees, benefactors, committees of subscribers, a clergyman or minister - but there must be some connection with fit and proper persons, members of a local elite. If a school lacked such connections it was deemed 'private'. If its pupils were working-class it was particularly suspect. The growth of mass schooling involved the hegemony of this public model. Since private schools were popular with working-class parents, the promotion of these institutions of the bourgeois public was as much about control, regulation and monopoly, as about 'filling in gaps'.

Schooling was only one side of an impulse towards moral regulation, though it became a kind of metaphor for the whole process. 'The schoolmaster' was needed everywhere where there were new relations to learn. Again and again customary knowledges proved inadequate to new situations. The schoolmaster appears as the workhouse master educating out pauperism, as the reforming magistrate closing down communal sports, as the Victorian paterfamilias laying down public rules for private practices, and also as the radical journalist, demagogue or lecturer. The extraordinary explosion of print and of public speech, creating whole new media and audiences, was part and parcel of this missionariness and the popular foment it was designed to combat. Again, the education of adults was paradigmatic: the most famous and perhaps the founding use of the schoolmaster metaphor was Henry Brougham's 'The Schoolmaster is Abroad' speech which launched the Mechanics' Institutes in 1823.[13]

Popular movements must be seen in relation to ruling strategies, divided as these were between a Conservative-Anglican repertoire, rooted in a landed social order, and a Liberal dissenting or secular option based in the industrial bourgeoisie, the cities and the metropolitan intellectual groupings. When magistrates and millowners breached customary practices, they forced innovations in popular defences. These then became signs of emergency to the ruling groups and, latterly, forced them to innovate again, often with good reason. Social historians have shown the remarkable creativity of popular political culture in this phase, though they differ as much as ever on the significance of the findings.

For Marx and Engels, newly based in Britain in the 1840s, popular movements marked the beginning of the end of an epoch. The crescendo of popular agitation -Jacobinism in the 1790s, followed by Luddism (Thompson's 'revolutionary underground'), post-war radicalism, the battles over press freedom, trade unionism, Poor Law and

Factory Acts in the early 1830s, then Owenism and Chartism - presaged a revolution. Surely these were stages in the formation of a revolutionary class. Later historians, critical of this Communist Manifesto framework, have stressed, none the less, the formation of a new working-class identity. Thompson's classic study still makes sense of the extraordinary diversity in terms of class formation, elaborating its cultural and political side. In the debate that has followed, a new consensus is beginning to emerge among those impressed by his findings, but doubtful about the overall thesis.[14] Here was a vigorous popular politics certainly, but in what sense was it 'working-class'? It did not arise from conditions that were already proletarian: the typical figure (if there was one) was 'the artisan', or semi-independent small producer. These were the struggles, rather, of small producers becoming proletarians. The movement had a strong proletarian admixture certainly, but had many others, including non-class elements as well. In fact it has been precisely this social range that has fascinated the new-left critics of a flattened post-war socialism, including the feminist historians.

It may well be that the modern resonances depend on this 'transitional' nature of the period. Some modern dilemmas and conditions were beginning to form, but they did not seem inevitable yet. Contemporaries encountered them as particularly new and oppressive, and so they can be made visible to us today. So the creativity of responses at that time was not altogether exhausted in their own day, but speaks to us now.

TRANSFORMATIONS

So what were the modern conditions that were imposed and resisted at the time? I would not start with the imposition of schooling. Schooling was too marginal to daily life in this period to be the central site of change. It needs to be decentred in modern explanations too. It may be that schooling emerges as a solution to problems first posed elsewhere.

Changes at the place of waged work might be thought a better starting-point. The proletarianisation of the worker was deeply formative. Like Thompson, we might think of this in terms of an initial loss: sometimes as erosion, sometimes as sudden theft of spaces for autonomy or self-activity. Marx stressed the loss or alienation of conscious sensuous human labour in the production of commodities for capital: the reduction of the worker to operative or 'hand'.[15] Thompson sees the loss as wider, including a deeper regulation of time and public spaces for instance.[16] Feminist historians have brought whole new features of this transition into view, features equally central to educational change.[17] Deepening proletarianisation was accompanied by changes in the sex-gender arrangements of society. It sounds odd, but accurate I think, to speak of the formation of modern genders as well as classes; and so to explore the relation between the two.

We can think of gender formation, too, as deepened polarisation or heightened difference, in this case between men and women in a model of heterosexual monogamy. The polarisation of gender positions involved further privileging men in particular ways. Within the bourgeoisie and professional middle class, men and women were assigned to the 'separate spheres' of public life and domestic nurturance. Child-adult differences were given greater force as well.[18] This was most graphically seen in the physical divisions of household space.

In public discourses about the family (and much else besides) this patriarchal arrangement was heavily preferred. It involved an intense focus on the socialisation of children as a specialised and separated activity, not necessarily involving school, but always some domestic division of labour.

There were similar transitions in working-class households, but with rather different results. The changes in production often involved a similar separation of the household from the place of waged work. Yet the division of labour was less complete. The characteristic destiny of the working-class woman was the double shift (some form of earning and domestic labour). The privileging of the working-class man was as the main breadwinner. Similarly, partly for reasons of space, partly for family income, the child and adult worlds could not be so sharply segregated, though compulsory schooling itself was to bring this pattern nearer. By the 1860s one can certainly see in philanthropic commentary, the figure of the 'respectable' working man, usually a skilled worker, often a trade unionist and follower of the Liberal Party. He keeps his wife at home and he sends his children to school. He bases his industrial strategies on the family wage (and often the exclusion of women) and

9

favours state education, compulsory, secular and free. Yet this experience was only a sectional one within the working class as a whole, not easily universalised.[19]

Any adequate detailed account of the contest of radical education and provided forms (which we still lack) would have to take account of this shifting ensemble of relationships: the combined forms of class, gender and age-rank relations. I shall argue later that the provided forms of schooling won out because they were better adapted to the new conditions, and its relationships of time, space, or power, or so it seemed, in the short run. At the same time rupturing of older patterns was so severe, and the popular legacies were culturally so rich, that alternative possibilities for learning and living could emerge and be sustained for several decades.

DILEMMAS

Radical education revolved around a complicated and layered dilemma. Radicals valued 'the march of mind' for many different reasons. As in all periods of change there was a tension between conservation and transformation in popular responses. It was necessary actively to learn new ways because the older common senses were not enough any more; yet customary skills and cultural inheritances seemed all the more precious because they were threatened. Issues around literacy are a case in point. The ability to read was especially valued because its transmission was threatened in communities drastically affected by industrial change, handloom-weaving districts for example. Elementary accomplishments like reading and knowing how to sign your own name did decline in some areas in the early Industrial Revolution.[20] Yet the desire to read and write was also very actively stimulated by the new conditions, especially by the great surges of popular political activity, with their extensive presses and expanding reading publics.

There was a heightened sense too of the educational condescensions of the rich and the powerful. The charge of popular ignorance, from Edmund Burke's 'swinish multitude' to later liberal cajolings was deeply resented, especially as a way of blaming oppressions on the poor themselves. As William Cobbett put it:

The tyrant, the unfeeling tyrant, squeezes the

labourers for gain's sake; and the corrupt politician and literary or tub rogue find an excuse for him by pretending, that it is not want of food and clothing, but want of education, that makes the poor starving wretches thieves and beggars.[21]

Positively, radicals looked to their own education to remove superstition and combat the ideological resources of authority. Sometimes, not very consistently perhaps, they waxed as philosophical about the evils of popular ignorance as their liberal counterparts. These different ways of valuing knowledge ran right through the movements from Jacobinism to Chartism.

Jacobinism's key texts, Tom Paine's, The Rights of Man and The Age of Reason, introduced what were to be recurrent themes to radical readers: the dependence of aristocracy, monarchy and tyranny in general on popular ignorance, the complicity of religion in this, the optimism, therefore, about popular enlightenment, and the ultimate value of intellectual independence, of making up your own mind about things. Very similar themes are to be found in later phases including the rather unreasonable faith in Reason. Even the titles and mastheads of the radical press signal educational commitments:

Knowledge is Power. (The Poor Man's Guardian)

Knowledge and Union are Power. (The Cooperator)

Developing the principles of the rational system of society. (The New Moral World)

The Change from Error and Misery to Truth and Happiness. (The Crisis)

The Midlands County Illuminator. (which 'illuminated' Leicester under the editorship of Thomas Cooper)

As the revolutionary Chartist orator, Julian Harney, put it in 1842, 'We tell these puny Canutes that despite their bidding the ocean of intellect will move on!'[22]

At the same time radicals were acutely aware of educational difficulties, an awareness often enforced by personal experience.[23] Sometimes these were a poverty of resources: lack of books, teachers, time, energy, peace and quiet. In the best radical writing about education, that most in touch, I think, with the pressures on most working people,

11

enlightenment ambitions meet a powerful sense of imposed constraints, material and cultural. Sometimes the conditions are portrayed as absolutely incompatible with any education at all. Such insights were widespread in the later years and in movements based on the industrial North and Midlands. One longish example must do. The writer is probably James Morrison, editor of the Owenite, trade union newspaper, The Pioneer, but it is interesting that his wife, Frances, also wrote for the paper.[24] Did they write this poem of everyday life together?

Now mark the toilsome artisan: the bell arouses him from slumber; - and soft ease invites him to another nap, but jerk must go the eyelids, - the half-stretched limbs must spring, - on go the vestments, - up lifts the latch, - and with a hurried step he hastes to work. A few short minutes past the time, provokes a reprimand; - that reprimand must not provoke reply. To work, toil, toil, till strength requires a breakfast - thanks if the cupboard holds one; - a demi-hour allowed to gulp it down. To work again till hunger calls for dinner, - a scanty meal, - and off again to labour until night. Night comes, and now for peaceful leisure. - A book perchance - a book! a noisy brat to nurse; a scramble for a loafs small dividend; a cry of pain; or half-a-dozen little feet held up, petitioning for shoes; fit scene for quiet musing. A cluster round the homely hearth, scrambling for scanty rays of heat. A pretty picture, that - fine opportunity for useful training! The mother half wornout, her temper chafed, too busy far to rear the tender thought, - a rap 'o the head more like, eliciting a charming chorus. O, what a wretched catechism is that between a labourer's child and his poor jaded mother! Their little souls grow full of brambles; their health depends on fickle chance; their wanton playfulness has no room to sport in; and these are but the sweets of poverty...

Having portrayed household circumstances in this way, the writers turn on the privileged with an angry torrent of wrongs:

Pooh! cry the rich, it is the lot of poverty - there

> must be rich and poor - the poor are naturally
> ignorant... Wrapped up in vile conceit, and ever-
> ready with the admonition, ye, too, do join the cry,
> the crafty cry of overabundant wages; the
> hackneyed slang respecting rights of capital; the
> enormous wrong of scorning our base origin; the
> wicked partiality of law; the sordid crippling of our
> light amusements; the maw-worm whine of puffed
> up charity; the tract, the soup, the caps and
> tippetts, and little leather breeches...[25]

Then point out the basic injustice of it all: 'just let our noisy
brats enjoy a turn in your trim nurseries'. Were conditions
really equalised, they argue, there would be no more charges
of ignorance or brutishness.

As if this were not enough, the growth of provided
education after 1830 brought further twists to the dilemma.
First you were excluded from learning by the absence of
resources or household conditions. Then, once available, the
proferred knowledges turned out to be wildly inappropriate.
Far from promising liberation, this knowledge threatened
subjection. At best it was a laughable diversion - useless
knowledge in fact. At worst it added, to the long list, yet
another kind of tyranny. Announced by Tom Paine and lesser
radical luminaries like William Godwin or George Ensor this
theme - of knowledge as subjection - also reverberates
through the movement.[26] Cobbett, for instance, the original
de-schooler, had no doubts about the objects of the
monitorial school:

> They wish to make cheap the business of learning
> to read, if that business be performed in their
> schools; and thus inveigle the children of poor men
> into those schools; and there to teach those
> children, along with reading, all those notions
> which are calculated to make them content in a
> state of slavery.[27]

Like many writers Cobbett drew analogies with industry and
with police to describe the schoolteacher:

> He is their overlooker; he is a spy upon them; his
> authority is maintained by his absolute power of
> punishment; the parent commits them to that
> power; to be taught is to be held in restraint and,

13

as the sparks fly upwards, the teaching and the restraint will not be divided in the estimation of the boy.[28]

He also wrote his own Sunday School hymn:

Let dungeons, gags, and hangman's noose,
Make you content and humble.
Your heav'nly crown you'll surely lose,
If, here, on earth, you grumble.[29]

By the 1830s the new forms of provided education had appeared, some of them less obviously knowledge-denying than older forms. Yet a critical distance was maintained, especially from the Society for the Diffusion of Useful Knowledge and its Penny Magazine. There was a host of jokes on all possible permutations of 'useful knowledge':

In conformity with the advice of Lord Brougham and the Useful Knowledge Society, the Milton fishermen, finding their occupation gone, have resolved to become capitalists forthwith.[30]

'Why', it was asked, 'did not the lass Victoria learn really useful knowledge by being apprenticed to a milliner?'[31] 'What', asked The Poor Man's Guardian 'is useful ignorance?' Why, 'ignorance useful to constitutional tyrants', of course.[32] One editor of the unstamped illegal press even produced a one-off issue of a little number entitled 'The Penny Comic Magazine of an Amorous, Clamorous, Uproarious, and Glorious Society for the Diffusion of Broad Grins'.[33]

So, despite the jokes, dilemmas deepened. It was 'really useful knowledge' that was wanted; 'education-mongers' offered its opposite. This was so clearly not education, that Cobbett was forced to try to find a new word for it: 'Heddekashun'.[34] So how was the genuine article to be obtained? How were radicals to educate themselves, their children, their class, their brothers and sisters, within all the everyday constraints? Overwhelmingly the answer, in this period, was we must do it ourselves! That way, independence could be preserved, and real knowledge won. We can understand radical education best, perhaps, as the story of these attempts.

RESONANCES

Where, in the early 1970s, had I heard this before? Not 'historically', I mean, but in some present time. There were certainly some similar themes in the personal confessions in the student occupations in the late 1960s; and in the brief ferment around 'deschooling' in the early 1970s, selling The Little Red Schoolbook outside the local comprehensive with the Schools Action Union. All that work, all that personal investment, some of the student voices said, from infant school, to primary school, to secondary school, to college, to university; yet I still have not found what I really wanted to know.

I would go further now. When the new system was forming, in the early nineteenth centry, educational dilemmas were expressed with a peculiar poignancy and force. I really think, however, that the dilemmas expressed then were the typical problems for all subordinated groups subsequently facing institutionalised educational systems. Schooling typically produces these dilemmas again and again. Most often the dilemmas have been hidden or unspoken. They have acquired a public voice when a particular group, faced with educational exclusions has demanded access, and then or later, also faced the problem of 'content'. The dual dilemma has arisen for women who have had a long battle to fight since the mid-nineteenth century against exclusion, limited subject choices, and informal subordination in the classroom. It has arisen for those excluded on racial or ethnic grounds who are then faced with the ethnocentrism or outright racism of existing curricula. The dilemma has been a continuous aspect of working-class educational experiences, particularly powerfully posed by adult or 'mature' students. First there is the struggle to 'get in'; and then all those struggles with teachers or tutors about what we want to know and they are prepared to teach.

All this is made incredibly complicated by the responses, even some of the more typical responses, of teachers and learners to the basic conditions. Of course, people always try to win advantages, individual or collective, from the contradictions they are caught in. They also defend themselves against the pain and damage involved. These resistances and defences may in turn appear to be the problem, especially from the teachers' point of view. They may also divide the students themselves, or redivide an already divided group. Not all resistances are really transformative.

Perhaps the commonest response has been to handle the pain of exclusion or humiliation, or irrelevance, by cutting and running. The personal investment has been minimised in different ways. There is a long history of working-class pupils leaving school as early as possible. Evidence of student resistance within the school is almost as extensive, from monitorialism to the comprehensive. In these options - early leaving or the school counter-cultures - the common preference is for common sense and customary knowledges against the knowledges of the school. Though this is certainly a form of resistance, it may carry high costs and lead to conservative outcomes. The forms of resistance may oppress other pupils, as the 'lads' school counter-culture does, seal off commonsense knowledges from potential development, and block off individual opportunities for learning.

A second strategy has been to invest in school or college, but only up to a point, treating knowledges externally, as a matter of performance only. The investment is really in certification and its assumed benefits, including the self-esteem it may bring. In a way, the contents of knowledges is irrelevant, so long as they are good to certify with and go through your paces. A particular way of learning is necessary. The learner must make an abstraction of the 'useful' exam-passing, teacher-pleasing parts. Knowledge is torn away from any connection it may have with the practical life of the knower, except as an instrument or means. Again, there are high personal costs in inhabiting knowledge-forms like this. As a teacher of 'successful' pupils, including PhD candidates, I am still surprised at the levels of pain and of ambiguity that personal problems to do with knowledge continually reveal.

If you put these two strategies together - cut-and-run and instrumental use - they are conservative in a deeper, social, sense. They produce again, in each new generation, the social divisions and contradictions which are the source of dilemmas in the first place. The first strategy puts the subordinated group back 'where it belongs', not really 'ignorant' or 'stupid' of course, because the commonsense knowledges are real, and not necessarily accepting either; but subordinated none the less. The second strategy allows a selective recruitment to the middle classes especially to those sections where qualifications are the main currency.

What have been the main collective strategies for untying so formidable a tangle? If we look at the history of the popular politics of education, we find that demands for access, on behalf of excluded groups, has been by far the commonest strategy at least from the 1850s.[35] Sometimes, especially in the late nineteenth and early twentieth centuries, this has retained a 'counter-educational' edge. Questions about who controls the education system or what is taught there have been raised. More commonly, especially latterly, such questions have been left to politicians and professional teachers. This politics does not really shift the contradictions I have tried to describe. Indeed it may deepen them. Particular social alliances, often involving a section of the working class, and almost always the educational professionals have demanded 'education for all'. In so far as this is conceded, it has returned to the majority as much as an imposition as a gift, and with all the old ambiguities. The more exalted the expectation of change, the fiercer the realist backlash. The outcome, unpopular education, has been a gift to those social conservatives who never wanted popular education anyway, but only, at most, a pacified working class.

We have to place the counter-educational strategy within this context of dilemmas, defences, resistances and forms of politics. Maybe we shall then see why it resonates so. Is it because it seems to offer a way out of the traps, seems to step clear of the ambiguities? It brings dilemmas fully to view, and then resolves them? If this is so, it must be said that this clarity is rare. As a widespread solution, counter-education outside the educational institutions seems a feature of periods of exceptional political excitement: in Britain there have been counter-educational revivals in the socialist and feminist agitations before World War I, with continuing traditions into the inter-war period;[36] during World War II especially in the forces;[37] and among the college-going radicals and feminists in the 1970s. Perhaps it was this last moment that was the source of all my 'resonances'. Perhaps it is worth pursuing the pattern of similarities and differences a little further. What exactly does early nineteenth-century education offer us by way of solutions? And what does the later history of the movement tell us about its limits?

FORMS

The key feature was informality. Certainly, radicals founded their own institutions. In the late 1830s and 1840s there were even schemes for a whole alternative system. The Owenite and Chartist mainstreams, however, looked askance at the more ambitious projects.[38]

Typically, then, radical education differed from the provided kind in its actual organisational principles. Education was not separated out and labelled 'school'. It did not happen in specialised institutions. Even when Political Unions, Chartists and Owenites formed their own secular Sunday Schools, or newspaper reading rooms or Halls of Science, these were part of the cultural politics of the branch. The frequent emphasis on a meeting place of your own had less to do with specialised uses than escaping from the control of magistrate or publican (and perhaps from domestic space?) and having a physical focus for local activity. The crucial division that radicals refused, of course, was that between education and politics: hence their contestation of the 'no politics' rule in Mechanics' Institutes, and the occasional secessions to form a political forum of their own.[39]

Solutions were highly improvised, haphazard and therefore ephemeral. From one point of view - the building of a long-term alternative - this was a weakness, but it had strengths too. Education remained in a close relation to other activities, was even inserted into them. People learned in the course of their daily activities, and were encouraged to teach their children too, out of an accumulated and theorised experience. The modern distinction between education (i.e. schooling) and life (everything outside the playground walls or off campus) was certainly in the process of production in this period. Philanthropy espoused the public school as a little centre of missionary influence in an alien social world.[40] Radicals breached this distinction, however, all the time, often quite self-consciously. As George Jacob Holyoake put it, 'Knowledge lies everywhere to hand for those who observe and think.'[41] It lay in nature, in the social circumstances of daily life, in the skills of labour, in conversations with friends, in the play of children, as well as in a few much-prized books.

It is often hard to separate radical initiatives from the inherited cultural resources of the people more generally.

18

There were complex interleavings and dependencies here. It is not sensible to see the working-class family, neighbourhood or place of work as a part of radical education. Yet these were - or had been - the main educational spaces for working people. Radicals occupied them accordingly, often giving them a new twist. They taught their children to read and to think politically. They became accepted as the local 'scholar' of the neighbourhood. They led workplace discussions on 'the hardness of the times'. Similarly, when they became private schoolteachers, often more out of necessity than choice, they occupied one node of educational networks indigenous to working-class communities. Radicals did not invent the proto-profession of travelling lecturer, but they certainly expanded and politicised it: hence the travelling demagogues of Chartism, the Owenite 'social missionaries' and the women lecturers who found a place in Owenism through its religious heterodoxy, critique of conventional marriage and commitment to gender equality.[42]

Some radical writers, in some ways the more conservative ones, made a great point about using the old forms and rejecting the new-fangled resources like schools. Cobbett epitomises this view, though I think he was a symptomatic as well as, certainly, an idiosyncratic figure. All Cobbett's descriptions of learning emphasise the inseparability of education and practice: learning hurdlemaking by helping father at work in a Hampshire copse; teaching children to write letters and manage a farm through the medium of a hamper from a prison cell; the daring image of the Sandhill, a childhood game to set against the philanthropic ban on play.[43] His own children, he boasted, were taught 'indirectly'. Things were made available - ink, pens and paper - 'and everyone scrabbled about as he or she pleased'. So 'the book-learning crept in of its own accord, by imperceptible degrees'.

What need had we of schools? What need of teachers? What need of scolding or force, to induce children to read and write and love books?[44]

This is all very winning, but note how much the whole strategy of building on an inherited culture depended on the daily autonomies, relatively leisurely or unsupervised patterns of work for instance. Aside from wondering where Mrs Cobbett was in all this, we might set Cobbett's old-style patriarchy against Morrison's 'toilsome artisan' and the considerable evidence for the involvement of Chartist and Owenite women in the more school-like radical solutions.

For radicals also added some inventions of their own. The simplest addition was the meeting place or reading room, stocked with radical newspapers.[45] More ambitious and continuous radical branches organised a whole calendar of events, including lectures and classes, plus one-off special events like big public meetings or the public confrontations with the clergy sought especially by Owenites.[46] The most important radical invention of all was the press. It was not the respectable 'Fourth Estate' that created a popular newspaper-reading public, but the law-breaking, speculative journalists of the radical press.[47] With some exceptions – particularly the Chartist Northern Star – 'newspaper' is rather a misnomer. Really we are talking about argumentative, opinionated little magazines, essentially concerned with commentary and analysis, often in support of particular movements. Most were saturated with an educational content. Even The Northern Star carried regular adverts and reviews of radical literature, publicised lecturers with Chartist appeal, monitored the 'education-mongers', reported radical sunday schools, and sustained a weekly commentary on political events.[48]

As a form these 'newspapers' were very versatile. Some parts, like the Poor Man's Guardian's expositions needed pondering over and discussing. Other parts, like Cobbett's or Feargus O'Connor's addresses, could be declaimed aloud in pub or other public place. Radical newspapers were not bought and read individually at home, but were passed from hand to hand and discussed in a pattern of multiple if not communal readership.[49]

The preference for collective forms seems a general feature. Here the progressions of autobiographies are very interesting. They often start, these little narratives of knowledge,[50] with quite individual and sometimes isolated childhood patterns. Later, in adolescence or early adulthood, a more communal pattern is set, though it may not yet involve a movement. Soon, however, the individual educational progress is indistinguishable from the political culture of the movement, which autobiographers often document. Later these collective patterns fall apart and we are back to 'individuals' again.

CONTENT

Perhaps the phrase 'really useful knowledge' is the best starting-point. Much more than a parody of the Society for the Diffusion of Useful Knowledge, it stressed all the key radical themes. It expressed the conviction, first, that real knowledge served practical ends - ends, that is, for the knower.

> This knowledge will be of the best kind because it will be practical (The Cooperator)[51]

> It is a wrong use of words to call a man an ignorant man, who well understands the business he has to carry on...[52]

Statements like these were partly a protest against mere book-learning. From this point of view it was possible to be 'extremely enlightened' and have 'a facility for words', but have no knowledge! Radicals often stressed, in Cobbett's phrase, 'how to do as many useful things as possible'. For Cobbett this included gardening and cottage economy, but also book-learning of different kinds, especially grammar, arithmetic, history and geography.[53]

'Practical', however, meant a lot more than this. It was not an invitation to a vague pragmatism. The key discriminator was practical for what? And for whom? When 'practical' was specified more tightly all this came into view:

> All useful knowledge consists in the acquirement of ideas concerning our conditions in life. (The Pioneer)[54]

> A man may be amused and instructed by scientific literature but the language which describes his wrongs clings to his mind with an unparalleled pertinacity. (Poor Man's Guardian)[55]

> What we want to be informed about is - how to get out of our present troubles. (Poor Man's Guardian)[56] (emphasis added)

So 'practical' implied a particular point of view: practicality depended on your social standpoint and political purpose. One person's useful knowledge was another's useless ignorance. As Benjamin Warden, an Owenite and Chartist put it:

> Knowledge was very differently understood in its application to the people generally. Brougham and others summed it up as little more than honour and obey the King, and all who are in authority under him. 'You may get practical science', say they, 'but it is only to make you better servants'. Their views expressed a limited range, while our own are founded on all known facts. Mechanics Institutes were not intended to teach the most useful knowledge, but to teach only as might be profitable to the unproductive.[57]

Practical knowledge was knowledge from the point of view of 'the people' or 'the productive classes'. But this popular point of view was not just a novel descriptive angle, producing new facts, nor was it just a question of learning how to cope or have realistic expectations. The real point, the real practicality, was learning how to change your life. Really useful knowledge is 'knowledge calculated to make you free'.

So this notion of 'practical' was especially rich. We might look at one more example. When a reviewer in The Pioneer exhorted readers to get help from 'men of talent' in 'the highest branches of science', he met this editorial rebuke:

> No proud conceited scholar knows the way – the rugged path that we are forced to travel; they sit them down and sigh, and make a puny wail of human nature; they fill their writings full of quaint allusions, which we can fix no meaning to; they are by far too classical for our poor knowledge-box; they preach of temperance, and build no places for our sober meetings... but we will make them bend to suit our circumstances.[58]

I love this quotation. There is so much going on in it. There is a resistance to 'scholars' who assume knowledges which most people lack; yet there is also a sense that they have something to offer: otherwise why 'make them bend' etc. In a way, it seems the scholars are quite ignorant, and impractical too. We (the people) know more than they, especially about 'rugged paths'. Yet we also lack something ('poor knowledge-box') which they appear to possess. The solution seems to be to make 'them' (the scholars) work for 'us' (the people) - on our agenda, our circumstances, perhaps in our language too. So two important traps are avoided: being intimidated by academic pretensions, and collapsing into a self-satisfied lauding of common sense. 'Practical' does not exclude learning: a productive relationship is sought between common sense and systematic knowledges or philosophies. Practice has implications for knowledge, but knowledge has implications for practice too.

Radicalism's preferred knowledges - I have called them 'spearhead knowledges' elsewhere - provide examples of these general features. These knowledges had a pressing immediacy and were very much for the here and now. They were indispensable means of emancipation, directing practical actions. Their most usual expression was in practical forms, in exposing this or that instance of tyranny, or illuminating an area of daily experience. As critical theories they were capable of infinite application.

By the 1830s there were, perhaps, three main components in radical theory.[59] For the radical mainstream, 'political knowledge' retained its pre-eminence from the days of Tom Paine. Later versions find their richest elaboration in the pages of the Poor Man's Guardian and in the writing of Bronterre O'Brien. Radical political theory was a blend of the belief in natural rights, the commitment to 'extreme democracy' (typically manhood suffrage with considerable ambiguity about women's rights), and a critique of the exclusive, propertied nature of the state. The state was seen as a thoroughly partisan institution, heavily loaded towards the interests of property of different kinds. From this all kinds of evils flowed: unjust laws, unfair taxes, the suppression of movements to redress grievance, the basic unfairness of the lack of popular representation. Political knowledge was, therefore, an attempt to explain everyday experiences. Why doesn't government protect us? Why does the law penalise the poor person's attempts to gain redress? Why does reform favour only the propertied? How might we secure our democractic rights, and in doing this, change the direction of policy and law?

Radicals also developed their own economic analysis. Common justice and a sense of the importance of labour prescribed that the labourers should enjoy the full fruits of their toil; 'labour economics' or 'moral' or 'cooperative political economy' was an attempt to explain why this did not happen. Capital stole a proportion of the product in a kind of tax called profit. Lacking an analysis of exploitation in capitalist labour itself, such theories were still an attempt to make sense of the daily fact of poverty amidst the extraordinary productiveness that was all around.

Both these kinds of knowledge had, we might note, the same form. Moral economy and political knowledge incorporated criteria of political judgement - economic justice or natural rights - at their very heart. They did not pretend to neutrality. They also contained a theory, or principle of explanation. Owenite 'social science' or 'the science of society'[60] shows a similar structure. The Owenite's central moral value was 'cooperation' or 'community'. It was this, a secularised version of Christian neighbourliness, that would characterise 'the new moral world'. Social cooperation among equals-in-circumstance was the only enduring source of social progress and happiness. The Owenites' main explanatory idea was the educative force of 'circumstances' especially of certain social institutions. Often this came down to a farily mechanical environmentalism, posing great difficulties for a theory of change or revolution. Yet Owenism greatly extended the radical analysis. It represented capitalism as necessarily competitive, disharmonious and violent, but focused especially on the socialising weight of three institutions: the family, the church and the school. Analysis was extended into domestic arrangements and the private sphere and, thence, to the 'formation of character' more generally. It was therefore possible to speak publicly, often for the first time, of evils silently suffered in private, especially by women. The growing division between public and private spheres was partially broken. Taboo-breaking, especially on religious and sexual issues, became an Owenite profession, not least in relation to Owenite feminist attacks on the partiality of religion in gender terms, and the exclusions operating against women within radical movements themselves.

'Really useful knowledge' meant one or other or all of these knowledges, usually with further additions. From the popular point of view, this did indeed easily transcend anything which philanthropy offered. We can see, perhaps, why the recreational fare of Mechanics' Institutes, or the very limited curricula of schooling looked so trivial and oppressive. Radicalism embraced, after all, a theory of the class nature of the state, a theory of economic exploitation, and a theory of cultural domination. It even stretched, in Owenism, to a theory of 'character' or of what we would call 'subjectivity' or 'personality' today.

So the radicals were right when they argued that their conception of knowledge was wide, comprehensive even. It was comprehensive in at least two senses: it was, or should be, universally available, but was also 'liberal' in that it was wide-ranging, critical and open. Again, The Poor Man's Guardian summed this up:

> Self-reformation is the only reform that will establish the happiness of mankind. Man must be taught to know what are, as well as what are not his rights; he must learn the dependence of his happiness on the happiness of his fellow-creatures... he must be made to love, instead of feating - to pity, instead of blaming - to reason instead of listening - to be convinced, instead of believing - and, above all, he must know his weakness as an individual, and his strength in proportion as he UNITES and co-operates with others.[61]

LIMITS

The shift of strategy to the demand for state education occurred in the middle decades of the nineteenth century.[62] By the 1860s a section of the skilled organised working class had joined the Liberal agitation for a compulsory state system, while insisting on a secular curriculum, and some measure of state control. Although a proper history is needed, perhaps I have said enough about contexts to suggest how this change came about. I would give a central place to the material changes that formed the proletarian household, closed down some of the previous autonomies around the place of work (household and workshop), and forced some critical separations: home/waged labour, work/leisure, education/living, child/adult. As the need for a separate educational sphere developed, religious and philanthropic agencies supplied it, in a highly regulated, but never uncontested form. Though latterly radical education reached for more and more school-like solutions of its own, its particular strength had been its connection with pre-proletarian patterns, and, perhaps, the artisanal strata of the old working population. Schooling corresponded to the new conditions: regularised work patterns for adults and the intensification of capitalist control of labour especially. But schooling also had its own effects: especially in accentuating the child-adult distinction, favouring the more bourgeois family forms and divisions of labour including the marked gender separations, and, in its indirect effects, competing with indigenous educational resources, especially private schools and family and neighbourhood-based learning more generally.

Recognition of this double process is important in solving some conundrums in the social history of education, especially the difference between those who insist on 'social control' or schooling as an imposition, and those who point to working-class 'demand'.[63] The growth of schooling was certainly not merely a matter of institutional or ideological imposition. But the idea of 'demand' (and the whole model of motivations implied) is actively misleading. Historians who argue this way, just like the modern politicians, fail to see that economic relations and changes may also coerce, transforming the very framework of choice and intentionality. What was sensible and feasible under one set of conditions, ceases to be so under new ones. The main virtue of the model of 'demand' is that it has a place for active popular agency, albeit extremely individualistically. As we have seen, the pattern of popular strategies - of resistances and defences - was altogether more complex than this. Counter-education was one of these strategies; the use of provided schooling, quite extensively before compulsion, was another. Radical education died, splintered or changed into other forms both because powerfully-backed 'solutions' were offered, and the underlying social conditions became more and more adverse.

TODAY

Is radical education recoverable, as more than a memory? This is partly, I am sure, a matter of underlying conditions. It may be that radical education always depends, minimally, on widespread political excitement, and especially the expectation of major social change, and the existence of educational resources, including time free from necessary labour. This points to the need to analyse the existing situation of different social groups in our own society, to see what spaces and resources already exist. The 1970s movements are suggestive here, but may also point to quite a pessimistic conclusion. These movements have been strong precisely among those groups with the most extensive experience of formal education, especially in its more autonomous spaces in and around colleges and universities. The professionals, students and intellectual producers who have often supported them most strongly have shared rather 'artisanal' conditions of work. Could it be that my own 'resonances', and those of other writers on the subject depended mainly on our own conditions of life, as teachers who were looking for some larger justification for our work? Our response, which was often also a response to the interest of successive generations of students, was to try to build some counter-educational dimensions into our practice as professional educators. But is that all there is to our memories? Do they have a wider social relevance? Is this an experience that can be generalised?

If my analysis is right, many of the original dilemmas remain, even or especially for much wider social groups than those with a professional stake in learning. We are entering a period of deep educational reaction, or merely useful knowledge, to coin a phrase. In the perpetual English ping-pong between utilitarian and academic conceptions of knowledge, we are up against utility with a vengeance. Your average Owenite, time-travelling today, would have no difficulty in recognising the Manpower Service Commission as a new Society for the Diffusion of Useful Knowledge. She would see very clearly that the project of this and many other schemes is to make human nature finite, by reducing education to training and training to coping with the world as it is, according to a business point of view. I think she would be as angry as I am at this attempted reduction of youthful possibilities to someone's instrument, this attempted closure of our whole social future. The insults offered, especially to young working-class people, include the familiar one of blaming them (their lack of 'skills') for systematic social evils, especially unemployment.

Yet merely useful knowledge has plausibility, for most people, against conspicuously useless kinds. Actually academic knowledge forms do have social uses. They seem, so far, the most appropriate forms for reproducing social elites and adding an educational justification for inequalities. They have also harboured, so far, opportunities for critical thinking, albeit divorced from popular experiences. Together these two failed forms reproduce each other. In their current deployments - academic forms for would-be climbers into a shrinking elite; training for the rest - they deepen social divisions. The continuing appeal of really useful knowledge is that it cuts across the division, and the personal dilemmas produced by it. Critical knowledges, which look beyond the bourgeois and patriarchal horizons, can be both practical and wide. Their practicality is not fatalistic, based on the notion that history and fundamental social change stopped somewhere around 1976.

Alternatives already exist, in curricula and ways of working. They are scattered, disorganised, often conforming to the separations of the division of labour and the formal institutions. They exist in the good sense of people who suffer under the major oppressions and have developed their own real knowledges about this. They exist in some of the new philosophies - and in some revisions of the old. I know that in fits and starts a new critical social theory is developing, inheritor, in many ways, of Marxism. The question of connections is therefore posed very sharply. Who, among the more popular elements will make the new philosophies 'bend to suit our circumstances'. Who, among 'the scholars' will learn to start out from the good sense of subordinated groups, and turn it into spearhead knowledges? Where, in what spaces, with what organisational forms will this happen; or is it happening already?

Some difficulties about this happening have been explored already, on the more popular side. Resistances and defences against academic, school and expert knowledges may block out critical knowledges too, the more so the more they take academic forms. 'Proud conceited scholars' have their defences too - even though their work depends, in the end, on some popular alliance. Typical, in my experience, is the search for some additional guarantee aside from the value of knowledges as shown in practice. Scholars want to find some internal criterion for really useful knowledge, failing to see its deeply contextual nature. So they search for criteria of objectivity or hard science, or cling to some particular theory which is preferred, for a while, within their own particular group. There are, most likely, some fashionable ephemera like this within the new philosophies. As usual these defences prove to be someone else's oppressions. They evoke, in turn, all the more popular resistances - and so the splits continue.

Who produces the knowledges and for what reasons was a central issue for nineteenth-century radicals. Their answer was very clear: in the end it is the people's knowledges that change the world. This means that self-education, or knowledge as self-production, is the only knowledge that really matters. Others may be resources here, but in the end you cannot be taught, you can only learn. Really useful knowledge occurs only in an active mood, and must have its active centre among subordinated social groups, the equivalents of 'the people'.

So, on this side of the great divide, how far can this happen, if at all, within the formal educational institutions? To some extent it is happening already - there have always been literal radical schoolteachers too. Possibilities differ by time and place. But it is often possible, still, to have a counter-educational element in formal education, minimising the pressures of assessments and requirements, engaging students' real interests, inciting self-education. I realise now how 'really useful knowledge' has always appealed as reflecting back some aspirations in my own daily practice. More subtly, perhaps, my account of it took the pressure off current desires.

Such attempts will always be very deeply contradictory. They run against the grain of the dominant individualism of assessment and certification. Compromises are continually necessary to hold a space for counter-education at all. As conditions once more worsen and autonomies shrink, the terms of compromise may become less and less acceptable, if anything of the original project is to survive.

So I doubt, in the current history, that the sites of formal education will be decisive, even in the educational struggle. I think we must look to see new forms of politics, rather, where change is not understood as a mechanical, lever-like process, but as a transformation of self and others. Until there are more contexts of this kind, which also cut across the usual social differences, I do not think that today's really useful knowledges will emerge in their most politically-pointed, mobilising forms. Instead, we shall continue to be stuck with today's 'quaint allusions' and an obstinate popular pragmatism which refuses all but the most conservative of its lessons.

REFERENCES

1. Ruskin History Workshop, May 1976; '"Really Useful Knowledge": Counter Education - The Early Working Class Tradition 1790-1848', Radical Education, Nos 7 & 8 (Winter and Spring 1977). The longest and most detailed presentation of the research is in '"Really Useful Knowledge": Radical Education and Working-Class Culture' in John Clarke, Chas Critcher and Richard Johsnon (eds), Working-Class Culture: Studies in History and Theory (Hutchinson, 1979). Cited hereafter as RUK.

2. Barbara Taylor, Eve and the New Jerusalem: Socialism and Feminism in the Nineteenth Century, (Virago, 1983). I found that reading this book made me want to rethink, more radically than I have been able to do so far, the framework within which I approached early nineteenth-century education. This would have required redoing or supplementing a lot of the research as well.

3. For a discussion of some typical sources for educational history see Richard Johnson, 'Elementary Education', in Gillian Sutherland et al., Government and Society in Nineteenth-Century Britain: Commentaries on British Parliamentary Papers (Irish University Press, 1977).

4. This theme is explored in various essays in Richard Johnson, Gregor McLennan, Bill Schwarz and David Sutton (eds), Making Histories: Studies in History-Writing and Politics (Hutchinson and University of Minnesota Press, 1982).

5. Especially Taylor, Eve, and the work of Catherine Hall, cited below, note 17.

6. This argument is developed in Richard Johnson, '"Educating the Educators": "Experts" and the State, 1833-39', in A. Donajgrodski (ed.), Social Control in Victorian England (Croom Helm, 1977).

7. Especially through the writings of Tom Paine and, to a lesser extent, William Godwin. See especially Thomas Paine, The Rights of Man (Penguin, 1969); Thomas Paine, The Age of Reason, ed. Moncure Daniel Conway (London, 1896).

8. The classic text is J.P. Kay, The Moral and Physical Conditions of the Working Classes Employed in the Cotton Manufacture in Manchester (Manchester, 1833). But this feature is pervasive in the social commentary of the time.

9. This is discussed in the major histories. See especially E.P. Thompson, The Making of the English

Working Class (Gollancz, 1963); Harold Silver, The Concept of Popular Education (MacGibbon and Kee, 1965); Brian Simon, Studies in the History of Education 1780-1870 (Lawrence and Wishart, 1960).

10. One example was the tension within Chartism over the Collins/Lovett plan for a whole alternative education system (See RUK, p.99).

11. For these chronologies, and for a good listing of the relevant histories see Michael Sanderson, Education, Economic Change and Society in England 1780-1870 (Macmillan, 1983).

12. The public/private division as described here was certainly established by the mid-nineteenth century and was used by the Horace Mann Education Census of 1851. It had already been used and elaborated by the Statistical Societies of the 1830s.

13. Henry Brougham, Practical Observations upon the Education of the People (19th edn, London, 1825).

14. See especially Gareth Stedman Jones, 'Re-Thinking Chartism', in Languages of Class: Studies in English Working-Class History 1832-1982 (Cambridge University Press, 1986); C. Calhoun, The Question of Class Struggle (Basil Blackwell, 1982); Perry Anderson, Arguments within English Marxism (Verso, 1980); RUK, pp.100-2.

15. The fullest and most complex statements of these themes are to be found in Marx's earliest work, especially The Economic and Philosophical Manuscripts of 1844, but the theme of 'dispossession' or 'alienation' informs the whole subsequent critique of capitalism.

16. E.P. Thompson, 'Time, Work-Discipline and Industrial Capitalism', Past and Present, No. 38 (1967).

17. See, especially, Catherine Hall, 'Private Persons versus Public Someones', in Carolyn Steedman et al. (eds), Language, Gender and Childhood (RKP, 1985); Elizabeth Whitelegg et al. (eds), The Changing Experience of Women, Part I: 'The Historical Separation of Home and Workplace' (OU/Blackwell, 1982); Catherine Hall, 'The Early Formation of Victorian Domestic Ideology', in S. Burman (ed.), Fit Work for Women (Croom Helm, 1979).

18. There is an increasing, interesting and important literature around the constructedness of childhood generally, from which it is clear that the late eighteenth and early nineteenth centuries were, for the middle classes, a point of change here too. See especially, Carolyn Steedman et al., Language, Gender and Childhood (cited

above, note 17): Jacques Donzelot, The Policing of Families (Pantheon, 1979).

19. Michelle Barrett and Mary Macintosh, 'The Family Wage', Capital and Class, II (Summer 1980), for a useful summary of literature and issues.

20. E.g. , Michael Sanderson, 'Literacy and Social Mobility in the Industrial Revolution in England', Past & Present, No. 56 (August 1972).

21. William Cobbett, Rural Rides (Penguin, 1967), pp.265-6.

22. R.C. Gammage, History of the Chartist Movement, 1837-1854 (Merlin, 1969), p.216.

23. For an expansion of this argument, with more examples see RUK, pp.94-7.

24. Taylor, Eve, p.96.

25. Pioneer, 16 November 1833.

26. For Godwin, see K. Codell Carter (ed.), Enquiry Concerning Political Justice by William Godwin (Oxford UP, 1971); George Ensor, an interesting Irish educational radical, see George Ensor, On National Education (London, 1911).

27. Political Register, 7 December 1833, quoting from Long Island Register, 21 November 1818.

28. William Cobbett, Advice to Young Men (London, 1906, from 1829 edn), p.264.

29. Political Register, 7 December 1833, p.603.

30. The Poor Man's Guardian, 18 May 1833.

31. Ibid., 22 June 1833.

32. Ibid., 24 September 1831.

33. Listed in Joel H. Wiener, A Descriptive Finding List of Unstamped British periodicals 1830-36 (Bibliographical Society, London, 1970).

34. William Cobbett, Cottage Economy (London, 1850 edn), p.4.

35. The paragraph that follows is based on the early chapters of Centre for Contemporary Cultural Studies, Education Group, Unpopular Education: Schooling and Social Democracy in England since 1944 (Hutchinson, 1981).

36. See the following article in this volume by Paul Armstrong. Also the important studies by Stuart MacIntyre, A Proletarian Science: Marxism in Britain 1917-1933, (Cambridge UP, 1980) and Jonathan Ree, Proletarian Philosophers: Problems in Socialist Culture, (Oxford UP, 1984).

37. Neil Grant, 'Citizen Soldiers: Army Education in World War II', in Formations of Nation and People (RKP,

1984).

38. For the politics of all this, more complex than can be explored here see RUK, pp.94-100.

39. Again, reactions to Mechanics' Institutes were complex and ambiguous, more ambiguous perhaps than to any other middle-class initiative. See RUK, p.78 and note 13 above.

40. For this conception of the 'public' school, see Richard Johnson, 'Educational Policy and Social Control in early-Victorian England', Past & Present, No.49 (1970).

41. G.J. Holyoake, Sixty Years of an Agitator's Life (London, 1892), Vol. 1, p.4.

42. Taylor, Eve, esp. Ch. 5.

43. Political Register, 21 September 1833, p.735; William Reitzel (ed.), The Autobiography of William Cobbett (Faber, 1967), pp. 123-5; Rural Rides, (Penguin, 1967), p.41.

44. Advice to Young Men, pp.247-55.

45. E.g. Thompson, Making (1963 edn), pp.717-20. And for the later period, Dorothy Thompson, The Chartists: Popular Politics in the Industrial Revolution (Wildwood House, 1984), esp Ch. 2. and pp.158-72, especially interesting on the mix of different kinds of meeting places.

46. For a very full discussion of Owenite branch life, see Eileen Yeo, 'Robert Owen and Radical Culture', in S. Pollard and T. Salt (eds), Robert Owen: Prophet of the Poor (Macmillan, 1971) and cf. J.F.C. Harrison, Robert Owen and Owenites in England and America (RKP, 1969), for rather different readings of the 'religious' character of the movement. For women's place in branch life see Taylor, Eve, esp. Ch. 7: in Chartism see Thompson, Chartists, Ch. 7.

47. For the radical press generally, see Thompson, English Working Class; Patricia Hollis, The Pauper Press (Oxford University Press, 1970); Joel H. Wiener, The War of the Unstamped (Cornell University Press, 1969); Thompson, Chartists, Ch. 2; J.A. Epstein, 'Feargus O'Connor and The Northern Star', International Review of Social History, vol. 21, part 1 (1976).

48. E.g. Northern Star, 5 May 1838, 2 June 1838, 28 July 1838; 25 August 1838; 6 and 13 January, 10 and 13 March, 21 and 29 April 1838; 9 June 1838; 13 and 20 April 1844.

49. For Cobbett, see Thompson, English Working Class esp. p.749; for O'Connor, see Epstein, cited above note 47, p.84.

50. For expansions of these points, see RUK, pp. 80-3.

51. The Co-operator, 1 January 1830.

52. Political Register, 21 September 1833, p.731.

53. For references and an expanded discussion of Cobbett's educational views see RUK, pp.88-91.

54. Pioneer, 31 May 1834.

55. Poor Man's Guardian, 25 October 1834.

56. Ibid., 14 April 1834.

57. Ibid., 14 April 1832.

58. Pioneer, 25 January 1834.

59. For a fuller summary see RUK pp.86-8. And see the analyses in Stedman Jones, Languages; Hollis, Pauper Press; and Thompson, English Working Class.

60. For Owenism specifically, see Harrison, Owen and Owenites: Thompson, esp. pp.779-807; Taylor, Eve, passim.

61. Poor Man's Guardian, 26 February 1831.

62. What follows draws on RUK, pp. 99-102 and the early chapters of Unpopular Education. See also Richard Johnson, 'Education and Popular Politics', Open University Course Unit, E353, unit 1 (1981).

63. These debates are discussed in Sanderson, Education (cited above note 11).

2

The Long Search for the Working Class:
Socialism and the Education of Adults, 1850-1930

Paul F. Armstrong

During the summer of 1983, Britain's Channel 4 broadcast a series of three programmes written and introduced by Jeremy Seabrook based on a book of the same title, What Went Wrong?, published some two years earlier. The book is subtitled 'Working People and the Ideals of the Labour Movement', and this was reflected in the concern of the television series to examine 'the hopes and ideals of people who gave their lives to the Labour Movement and its struggle for a better life for working people, and the working out in practice of those visions and dreams'.[1] Seabrook's thesis is that 'something went wrong'. That is, 'something faltered between the dream and its realisation'. In his analysis of 'what went wrong', Seabrook posed many questions about the nature of our 'consumer society', capitalism, the welfare state, the labour movement itself, the role of the Labour Party, trade unions, the problem of unemployment and changing employment structures, the decline of the working-class communities and their sense of identity as a class. Seabrook also, having analysed the nature of the problem, pointed to a solution, 'what can still be done'. He has identified as the central issue the erosion of working-class solidarity, which subsequently expressed itself in the weakening of ties with both the trade unions and the Labour Party. His strategy was to argue for the development of new forms of solidarity, to strengthen the resistance against consumerism and exploitation.

It is not the intention of this chapter to provide a comprehensive critique of what is in many ways a peculiarly romantic socialist perspective offered by Seabrook, nor an evaluation of his particular analysis. Rather, taking seriously his question, it shall be argued that any answer to the question must take into account the historical relationship between the eriosion of working-class consciousness and the development of formal education, and the unresolved contradiction or paradox contained within the development of education for (or of) the working-class. Certainly, in Seabrook's own writings, there is a recognition of the role of education in the development of the labour movement and its socialist consciousness, but he fails to give this a central explanatory focus in his analysis. Several of the people he interviewed made reference to the significance of education as a vehicle for upward social mobility, an 'escape route' from the working class. Indeed, this is a common theme of many working-class people's autobiographies, as Johnson has pointed out in Chapter 1, and this poses a contradiction, which is conveyed by the title of Roy Greenslade's edited collection of upwardly-mobile working-class academics' autobiographies, Goodbye to the Working Class,[2] which can be contrasted with those life histories which refer to 'informal educational culture':

> Read any autobiography of almost any active trades unionist, socialist, campaigning feminist or secularist published since the last war and the early chapter or chapters will amost certainly be taken up with describing the influence of that informal educational culture.[3]

Here Worpole goes on to quote extracts from the autobiographies of Jennie Lee, Harry Pollitt and Robert Roberts[4] to reinforce the point. He could equally have referred to novels such as the semi-autobiography, The Ragged Trousered Philanthropists, in which one of the characters observes: ' "In my opinion there's too much of this 'ere eddication, nowadays," remarked old Linden. "Wot the 'ell's the good of eddication to the likes of us?" '[5] Such accounts are either individually or collectively recognising the contradiction or dilemma for socialism, which has a clear expression in the ideal stated by Harrison, that the aim of worker's education should be to enable the student 'to raise, not rise out of, his class.[6]

In more contemporary writings, Freire refers to this as the problem of 'education for liberation' and 'education for domestication'.[7] We have to begin to recognise that the contradiction or paradox is contained by the fact that these are not part of a dichotomy, not polar opposites but contradictory forces bound up in the dialectic, in the same way that education as social change is not an alternative analysis to education as social control.

The contradiction can be expressed in the form of a

question: is it possible for working-class people to receive education or be educated without, at the same time, becoming middle-class? Sociologists have pointed to three aspects of education that would suggest that the answer to this question is pessimistic.

First, education operates as an agency of socialisation, generally referred to as a secondary agent of socialisation, serving to reinforce those dominant values, attitudes and appropriate behaviours being taught in the world outside education, in the family and in the community, through the media, and so on. This analysis has been extended in more recent theoretical contributions by Marxist theorists, particularly Gramsci and Althusser, seeing education as either a form of hegemonic control or as part of the ideological state apparatus, acting to reproduce rather than challenge existing social and cultural inequalities.

Second, and this can be seen in the autobiographical accounts, education is a vehicle for social mobility, and has been for the past century in industrialised nations. As such it is particularly attractive to reformists, who naively believe that if enough working-class individuals were to become upwardly socially mobile through educational opportunities then society must be transformed. Such a view is over-optimistic, for history tells us that the idealism of writers like Harrison is misplaced in so far as the history of working-class education, far from being the history of the introduction of a socialist society, is the history of migration from the working class to the middle classes, as, thirdly, these upwardly-mobile, working-class intellectuals are incorporated into the dominant cultural values, norms and life-styles of the bourgeoisie. Historically, therefore, education has been part of the seduction rather than the liberation of the working classes.

The study of the historical development of working-class education would seem to confirm this pessimism, particularly since 1850, when socialist movements appeared to be losing their way. However, the study of history is also intended to generate optimism; for only by understanding the historical failure to resolve the paradox or contradiction can we get to its core, from within which we can begin to transcend the dilemma and make progress. The study of the history of education for socialism is the study of lessons to be learned.

In examining the historical failure of socialist education to generate and develop working-class consciousness, it is difficult to know how far back we need to go. In many ways, the history of adult education in Britain is an integral part of the history of socialism. A dominant concern in adult education has always been how to reach the working classes. As Blackwell and Seabrook have put it:

> One of the prevalent themes in adult education has always been how to reach the working class. From the struggle in the 19th century over the control of the Mechanics' Institutes, through the angry polemics between the Workers' Educational Association and the Labour College Movement at the beginning of this century, to the agonisings of the Russell report in the early 1970s, the whole debate about adult education has been an ideological argument, sometimes covert, sometimes open, about the power of education to shape or remould the working class.[8]

It is not possible here to trace the history of adult education and socialism throughout the whole of this period, from the late eighteenth century to the post-Russell era. Fortunately, a detailed analysis of the education of the working classes in the early period has been well provided, particularly in the work of Simon[9], and of course by Johnson in Chapter 1 and elsewhere.[10] Johnson has pointed out that up until 1850 very little was specifically written about <u>adult</u> education, because at that time the child-adult distinction was itself less stressed, and no great difference between the education of 'children' and 'adults' existed, for such distinctions were to be later socially constructed.[11] This construction actually took place in the latter part of the nineteenth and early twentieth centuries, which is the period with which this chapter is primarily concerned. But before we move on to consider this period, there are a number of points we shall need to bear in mind about the pre-1850 era.

First, this early period of working-class education was based on either nonconformist religious movements, such as Methodism, or on early socialist movements, such as Chartism. A distinguishing feature of socialist education was that it was seen unambiguously as a political strategy, a means of changing the world, without the liberal concern for objectivity which was to develop in the later period. But even so, as Johnson has argued, the dilemma of such 'radical' forms of education was obvious.

A second distinctive feature of working-class education in this pre-1850 period was that it was concerned with self-education rather than what Johnson referred to as 'provided' education. An example of 'provided' education in this period was the creation of ideological institutions, which were places where working-class children were taught the correct values and moral practices which they were not being taught in their own families or communities. That is, they were explicitly about socialisation or hegemonic control. Most often the basis of these ideological institutions was religious philanthropy. Paradoxically, by the 1830s, the Mechanics' Institutes were being 'provided' because intelligent members of the working classes were no longer satisfied with religious answers to their questions, and so secular institutions had to be devised to provide a scientific basis to social issues, and thereby act as agencies of social control as much as 'Sunday' or day schools for children.[12]

In contrast to 'provided' education, working-class and socialist education during this period, as self-education, was informal, and stressed the need for 'independent' working-class education, which was to be a prominent demand for the remainder of the nineteenth century and into the first two or three decades of this century. The importance of being independent from either the state or the church was recognised by the Chartist leader, Ernest Jones, who said, 'A People's education is safe only in a people's hands.'[13]

By the beginning of the second half of the nineteenth century, educational provision for the working classes was described by Johnson as 'improvised', 'haphazard' and 'ephemeral', and it is therefore perhaps not surprising that in the second half of the nineteenth century, there was increasing state intervention in the provision of bourgeois education, to resist and suppress the development of proletarian education. That there was a fear of the potential power of such education is apparent in this Times editorial published in September 1851:

The education of the people has for years past been made a constant theme of discussion, and has proved unfortunately as constantly a subject of bitter dispute and fierce animosity. Great alarm has been evinced lest improper instruction should be imparted to the labouring population. ... While this dispute has been going on the power of the State, which might be beneficially employed in furtherance of popular instruction, has been paralysed. Scattered, and therefore feeble means, have been used to impart knowledge to the poor - jealousy and intolerance checked every endeavour - and thus the great body of the labouring classes have been left to their own exertions and such chance assistance as the benevolence of individuals might supply.[14]

The editorial proceeds to warn that whilst the state was arguing with the Church over who should provide education for the working classes, they were providing their own 'evil instructors' who got on with their 'mischievous endeavours' while the attention of the 'unwary shepherds of the flock' was diverted. In other words, the great mass of the population were being taught by 'the very worst possible teachers' whose 'evil teaching' recommends a 'new state of things':

Systems the most destructive of the peace, the happiness and the virtue of society are boldly, perseveringly, and without let or hindrance openly taught and recommended to the acceptance of people with great zeal, if not with great ability. Cheap publications, containing the wildest and most anarchical doctrines are scattered broadcast over the land, in which religion and morality are perverted and scoffed at, and every rule of conduct which experience has sanctioned, and on which the very existence of society depends are openly assailed; while in their place are sought to be established doctrines as outrageous as the maddest ravings of furious insanity - as wicked as the most devilish spirit could by possibility have devised. Murder is openly advocated - all property is declared to be robbery - the rules by which marriage is declared sacred and inviolate are treated as the dreams of dotage, obedience of every description is denounced as a criminal cowardice; law, as at present constituted, is asserted to be a mere device for enslaving mankind; and morality is described as an efficient auxiliary to law, for the same mischievous purpose.

The ignorance and 'happy indifference' of the middle classes has to be overcome in a 'wise, generous and tolerant spirit' to oppose these 'real enemies of truth and virtue': 'Let a prudent spirit of conciliation enable the wise and the good to offer to the people a beneficial education in place of this abominable teaching.' Given such forthright views it is hard to accept the myth propagated by many left-wing educationalists, especially those who claim to speak on behalf of working-class organisations, such as the Labour Party and the trades union movement, that the gradual introduction of a state education system in the second half of the nineteenth century was a 'working-class achievement'.

Alongside this idea that education is a 'good thing', is a second myth - that state education was the result of philanthropy, handed down 'from above' because of the benevolence of the bourgeoisie. It was not the fear of a proletarian revolution in the mid-nineteenth century, nor the threat to the growth of industrial capitalism, but because working-class people were too ignorant or too immoral or too apathetic or too poor, to provide educational opportunities for themselves or for their children, that state education had to be provided. Not only does such a myth hide from view the ulterior motives of the bourgeoisie, but in an ethnocentric way, is denying the validity of the educational schemes that were innovated and initiated by the working class and socialist movements.

A third myth as to why state education developed was to do with the technological need for an educated workforce, to make a positive contribution to the development of industrial capitalism. This functionalist account, lacking the paternalism of the second myth, was perhaps the most seductive of all, in arguing for what was later to be called a 'correspondence' between the needs of individuals and the needs of an industrial economy, which if they were to 'fit' together would be of benefit to all. Whilst one cannot deny that all groups have benefited from the development of industrial capitalism, although by no means equally, the lessons of history would deny that there has ever been such a correspondence.

Such myths were not products of retrospective interpretation by twentieth-century educational theorists, but were genuinely believed at the time, and as such had real consequences. In part, this was permitted by the growing disillusionment with socialism by the mid-nine-teenth century, which had lost its grip on working-class

41

consciousness. As the above _Times_ editorial suggests, and as others have confirmed, even the Chartist movement was becoming overtly less political.[15] Through trade union organisations, the labour movement began to press for social and political reforms, and with changes brought about on electoral reform, factory legislation, public health and housing, the working classes were being seduced into believing that social and political reforms were significant social transformations. Chartist principles were being left behind, and through the introduction of the state education system, following Forster's Education Act of 1870, together with a promise of a major reform of the university sector,[16] this seduction of the working classes was very nearly achieved, although it was to be another 75 years before this was completed with the development of a welfare state. These developments were not guided by the principles of socialism, but by those of liberal reformism. To be fair, these were not that far removed from the ideas of Chartism, which can, in any case, be understood as a reformist rather than a revolutionary movement. Chartism saw social change as gradual, piecemeal and evolutionary, and accorded a central role to education in the process of social transformation rather than violence. In writing about liberal educational ideas of the nineteenth century, Reeder sugests that a distinctive feature of the Chartist programme was its emphasis upon education with the aim of intending to 'help the working classes secure and make effective use of the vote'.[17]

So, it could be argued that as early as the 1830s, the working-class movements and organisations on the road to socialism had already lost their way. Of course, the potential was there right up to and beyond the end of the nineteenth century, which was a concern for Reeder who saw that there might come a time when 'moral force Chartists' could lose their faith in the efficacy of education and then take to revolutionary ideas.[18] For this to happen, socialist educationalists had to recognise and transcend the paradox contained in the provision of state education. We can begin to understand why the 1870 Education Act was seen by some as a 'victory' for the working class. The dilemma is clear, for although it might be part of the seduction, this may have been necessary for the working classes to realise what was going on, in order to give direction to their programmes of action:

Wanderings in the educational wilderness were inevitable so long as the working population was for the most part illiterate in the crudest sense of that term. Not until after Forster's Act of 1870, whereby elementary education was made compulsory in Britain could there arise the first intimations of a movement in favour of Independent Working-Class Education.[19]

Within this 'educational wilderness' were a number of false routes as well as a few 'oases'. One of the false routes, according to Eden and Cedar Paul, was cooperative education. As the Cooperative Movement was an independent working-class movement, it might be expected that cooperative education would be instrumental in establishing a revolutionary proletarian culture, but again this appears to have lost its direction in the mid-nineteenth-century period. This was to be confirmed later on in the century when, in 1885, the Cooperative Union's Central Educational Committee was established in order to give direction and coordination to its work, specifying two main aims: 'technical' education for cooperation, and the training of cooperators. It appeared that the aim was to train cooperators to become 'useful reformers within the existing order' and there was 'not a word about social revolution'.[20] The attitude of the Cooperative Movement remained uncertain for many years, hovering somewhere between demanding from the state 'increased educational facilities' of the ordinary kind, and the provision of independent education aimed at the formation of cooperative character and opinion. The actual educational work undertaken independently by the Cooperative Movement was comparatively small.

What went wrong? According to Eden and Cedar Paul, the dominant economic system proved too strong for the Cooperative Movement; they were not able to escape the dominant hegemonic influence of bourgeois ideology. Furthermore,

> ... co-operators are not class conscious but only co-operator conscious ... the co-operative movement would seem to be useless because it is not animated with the spirit of revolution. The co-operation is a co-operation between the slaves and the machine which drives them. Such co-operation

is no more than a lubricant easing the chafe of the chains, but incapable of loosening those chains. To be co-operator conscious is not enough. Revolutionary class consciousness is essential.[21]

A similar criticism could be made about the establishment of working-men's colleges which were also alien to any revolutionary spirit. One of the earliest established was in London in 1854. Whilst this was, in part, the direct result of the energy of the Chartist movement, with an emphasis on self-help and independent education, such bodies were supported by middle- and upper-class philanthropists, such as F.D. Maurice. As a result,

> there was no breath of that vivifying atmosphere of the class struggle which sweeps like a draught of fresh air through the early trade-unionist movement. Though called working men's colleges, they were in no sense whatever a spontaneous product of the working-class spirit, a manifestation of the demand for a distinctively proletarian culture.[22]

One particular aspect of the dilemma posed by such colleges was the role of the teacher. As Harrison has indicated in his history of the London Working Men's College, it was never intended that the tutors employed would be university professional men, but that ultimately - it was hoped - the tutors would be raised up from among the working classes.[23] Even today this is a 'living tradition' which has enabled the College to retain its financial independence, except that it uses volunteer teachers, following in the footsteps of men like Thomas Hughes, Lowes Dickinson, John Ruskin, G.M. Trevelyan and James Laver. In recent years, some of the many students who prepared for university entrance there have returned to the college as teachers, thus maintaining the ideal of mutual service described by Maurice in 1854 as the privilege of helping people to educate themselves.[24] Harrison quotes one of the founders, Ludlow, writing in 1861, who points out that teachers with university degrees are not necessarily the most appropriate, for only 'working men' can understand the educational needs of other working men.[25] As to the teachers' specific role, critics point to the 'subtle and subconscious flavour of patronage', quoting Furnivall as saying, 'I urged every teacher to have his class to tea at his own room, if possible', and commenting:

> Could the gospel of 'Climb out of the working class', as opposed to the gospel of 'Expropriate the expropriators and install the classless common-wealth', find more ingenuous expression?[26]

The same remark could be made about the development of Ruskin College, a residential institution for adult working-class students, founded in Oxford in 1899, and where within a very few years there was to be a head-on collision between those who believed that state education was an entitlement and a 'victory' if achieved, and those who believed that proletarian education should remain independent. But to understand this dispute we need to go back to 1873, the year when the university extension movement was pioneered by James Stuart, a history which has been thoroughly researched and written about.[27] But a few observations need to be made in order to make sense of what was to happen in Oxford a few years later.

The 'extensionist' movement did not seek to develop an autonomous, independent proletarian education, but rather to bring university education to the general mass of the population. Stuart's analysis was that the educational system, as it had developed, was class-based and was in danger of perpetuating the 'grievous class distinctions', and whilst one could not argue with this, the proposed solution was apparently to try to blur or play down these class divisions, to provide an education not specific to a particular class; in other words, a kind of 'comprehensive' university education in which 'rich and poor, men and women' could be taught together. This is confirmed in the writings of the time which suggest either that university adult education would break down 'intellectual caste' and create a 'new class'[28] or they deny the significance of social classes altogether.[29]

At this time, there was general agreement that the university extension movement had become almost exclusively middle-class[30] in both outlook and the students who were enrolling for their courses. Perhaps it was just as well that their financial arrangements were such that student fees were forced up and would have excluded the majority of working-class people in any case, if the education they were to receive had little to do with socialism. This is clear from the attempt to sweep the class issue under the carpet. The emphasis of this education was social harmony, liberal humanism and an impartiality that would enable students to rise above the mundane material and social concerns of the time. From this the liberal tradition was born, but as important, as Simon says, was the link established between universities and working-class audiences.

Ruskin College was part of this link. By establishing the College at Oxford, the benefactors had a clear philanthropic aim to bring working-class people to the University. Because of the failure of the extension movement to make much progress with the working classes, it was thought necessary to work through organised working-class movements such as trades unions, cooperative societies, working-men's clubs, and so on. The trade union movement in particular gave support to this institution, selecting students from their own membership to be sent there to study.[31]

Not long after Ruskin College was established, in 1903 Mansbridge introduced to working-class education the 'Association to Promote the Higher Education of Working Men', principally to organise and teach a programme of university-level courses throughout the country. The association was soon to be renamed the Workers' Educational Association (WEA), which was to lead the way in workers' education for the next eighty years, initially as a coordinating federation of working-class and educational interests, and subsequently as a 'responsible body' of state-financed adult education. Very much part of the liberal tradition of extension work, the WEA had little to do with socialism in a revolutionary sense, even though it has been supported by many left-wing politicians and social theorists such as R.H. Tawney and G.D.H. Cole. Its emphasis has been on democracy, reform, improving existing machinery, increasing equality of educational opportunities and above all the necessity for impartiality or objectivity in its teachings and provision. Furthermore, the rift was widened when Mansbridge was able to secure the promise of state funding, which has been described as one of his 'greatest achievements',[32] but not for socialism, nor for the working class, for there is no doubt that such sponsorship entails the loss of a degree of control.

It was this issue of control that was the centre of the dispute at Ruskin College, though not so much financial as ideological. Throughout the first few years of the century, the trustees of the College were seeking closer links with Oxford University, but from the students' point of view this would interfere with their education, particularly the curriculum. Already there had been some difficulties with both the content of the curriculum and the way particular subjects, especially economics, had been taught, to the extent that at one point the students were boycotting all lectures (except Dennis Hird's lectures on sociology), and organising their own study groups instead. The students were making the criticism that the curriculum bore little relevance to their own needs and that the growing emphasis on objectivity was alien to their socialist principles. The students were particularly critical of the WEA and its efforts to coordinate an inter-class programme of tutorial classes, which they saw as a tool of the governing classes, and their view was reinforced by the fact that the WEA sought financial suport from the state. But the conflict was deeper than financial control, as Raymond Williams once pointed out by saying that any educational organisation cannot expect to be financed and academically controlled by universities, and still carry out a programme for the working class.[33]

For what both Ruskin and the WEA were also seeking to do was to foster the relationship with universities, and this emerged in the publication of a joint report between the WEA and the university authorities in 1908, entitled Oxford and Working-Class Education. This brought to a head the conflict that had been building up at Ruskin for 'By 1908 the student body was frankly socialist in colour, predominantly marxist in outlook, and a thorn in the side of the university.'[34] The report made specific proposals for closer links between the university and Ruskin, which aroused deep hostility among these Ruskin students. The details of the conflict are recorded in detail elsewhere,[35] but what came out of the conflict was the polarisation of working-class education viewpoints between those, on the one hand, who followed the WEA's liberal, impartial education instead of 'socialist propaganda', and on the other, those who reaffirmed the socialist claim for an independent working-class education.

This was the beginning of an institutional rivalry, which Blackwell and Seabrook refer to as 'the angry polemics between the Workers' Educational Association and the Labour College Movement at the beginning of the century',[36] which was to go on for more than fifty years.

This was not just an ideological split, because in 1908 a group of students at Ruskin College formed the Plebs League to promote independent working-class education, and after a strike in 1909, broke away from Ruskin to establish the Central Labour College, which was to give impetus to the labour college movement for the next twenty years, as providers of independent education. By this stage, it was clear what 'independent' meant - free from state financial control, university influence, from capitalist interests, and from those 'who would swing the reactionary rod over the mental life of the working class'.

Up to this moment in time, adult education had promised much for the development and spread of socialism in Britain, but had achieved very little. Eden and Cedar Paul summarise this by saying that historically the provision of adult education had been little more than 'graduated doses of bourgeois culture'. In particular, the WEA was guilty of an 'unconscious bias in favour of institutions of the bourgeois state'.[37] The particular criticism was that the WEA, the university extension movement, working-men's colleges, and other 'wanderings in the educational wilderness' had failed to develop either proletarian culture or working-class consciousness, which were so necessary, according to Marx's analysis, if a social revolution was to occur. The only 'oases' in this educational wilderness were the Plebs League and the Labour College Movement.

The Plebs League remained convinced of the need to provide independent working-class education, and saw its aim to equip workers for the struggle against capitalism, through organisations that were in the exclusive control of the proletariat, with the object being to 'develop and increase the class consciousness of the workers, by propaganda and education, in order to aid them to destroy wage-slavery and win power'.[38] As such it was blatantly propagandist, and this was to be the basis of the critique of attempts to provide independent education for the next twenty years or more, particularly that critique emanating from its main rival, the WEA. The following quote is said to be a response to the Plebs League attack on the WEA, which it viewed as a 'disguised capitalist agency':

> Some WEA'ers enjoy denouncing the wickedness of the Plebs League as a perverter of the mind, teaching the workers not to think freely for themselves, but to imbibe certain doctrinaire

opinions supposed to be a guarantee of rectitude in the class struggle.[39]

The case for 'socialist progaganda' has been put forward, though perhaps with insufficient conviction. As the Horrabins pointed out, it is difficult to maintain the distinction between 'education' and 'propaganda', and frequently, even today, anything associated with socialism is seen as propaganda, and anything which supports the cultural hegemony is considered to be 'educational'.[40] Some degree of support for the Horrabins' argument is to be found in Cole's writings, who though a supporter of the WEA never denounced the Plebs League nor the Labour College movement. He did, however, believe that it was possible to distinguish education and propaganda. Cole once confessed that in political and industrial work, he was a 'propagandist' persuading others to accept his opinion, but in education, he was a 'midwife, trying to help them bring their own ideas to birth'.[41] But, argues Brown, this did not mean that Cole accepted the notion of impartiality, and offers the following extract from the Students Bulletin of April 1925 in support:

> ... we must clear our minds of the cant of impartiality and academic superiority. There is no such thing as an impartial teacher. Every teacher is bound to teach the facts by the light of his interpretation of them. Nor can a good teacher honestly suppress his own interpretation, or keep it in the background.[42]

For the Plebs League, class bias in teaching was not only unavoidable, but a necessity, for

> schemes for non-partisan education movements which pretend that the educational activity is neutral, contain nothing but a snare for the working class. The high-sounding shibboleths of 'humane education for the workers', 'opening of universities to the working man', 'the merging of class with class' are the last relics of an ideology incompatible with the historic mission of the workers.[43]

Two points emerge from this. First, there is the possibility that other agencies of adult education, by claiming impartiality, were actively <u>reducing</u> class consciousness. This coincides with a point made by Simon who said of the WEA that it appeared 'to be providing a diversion, to be weakening rather than advancing the working-class cause'.[44] Second, the notion of 'last relics' was over-optimistic, since it was this liberal tradition that was to maintain its strength, and the demand for an independent, partisan, working-class education which was to weaken and all but disappear over the next half-century. Perhaps at the time there was cause for optimism, given the resurgence in socialist thinking not only in Britain but throughout Europe since the 1880s, and the fact that the working classes were more homogeneous and better organised than at any other point in their history.

Again, we have to ask what went wrong. The Plebs League, in attempting to resist the hegemonic control over working-class education, broke away from Ruskin College and set up an independent labour college in Oxford, the Central Labour College, in 1909. Once more, the history of this college and its subsequent demise have been well documented.[45] The major difficulty in establishing such an enterprise was to remain both financially and ideologically independent. The Central Labour College did get some support from a minority of trade unions, the most prominent of these being the Amalgamated Society of Railway Servants (later the National Union of Railwaymen) and the South Wales Miners Federation. Such support was far from adequate, and after an abortive attempt in 1910 to merge with a revitalised Ruskin College, the college was moved to London in 1911, and four years later, severe financial problems led to its management being taken over by the two unions from which it drew its main support. An immediate positive effect of this was that it now had to be recognised along with Ruskin College by the Trades Union Congress, which had previously given its support to Ruskin alone. But by now the First World War was disrupting its activities, although the Plebs League's work was maintained, if not stimulated, as it was able to provide a programme of provincial classes, using economic and political education, and at the same time remaining faithful to its basic principles of raising class consciousness and emphasising political agitation and propagandist work.

After the armistice in 1918, the Central Labour College was able to resume its activities in London, attempting to consolidate and build on the progress made by the Plebs

League during the war. To facilitate this, it was felt that a national coordinating body was required to oversee the development of the Labour College movement, and so the National Council of Labour Colleges (NCLC) was set up in 1921. In part, this also has to be seen as a response to an initiative taken by the WEA, which soon after the war finished, joined with the Iron and Steel Trades Council to set up the Workers' Educational Trade Union Committee (WETUC), which used the WEA administrative machinery to negotiate directly with trade unions wishing to provide classes and courses. In the same year, the WEA was given state recognition by the Ministry of Reconstruction's Adult Education Report of 1919. It is not surprising, therefore, that the conflict between the WEA and the independent labour college movement intensified through the next decade, primarily going through the same debates as previously. The NCLC, like the Central Labour College and the Plebs League was seen as a Marxist propaganda body, not educational, whereas the WEA was even more seen as an organ of state control. Such ideological and financial support given to the WEA and the Tutorial Class movement by the state and the trade union movement, 'gave structural confirmation of the ideological marginality and isolation of the NCLC's Marxist orientation'.[46] Nevertheless, this did not mean that there was nothing radical about the WEA. In some of its regions, most notably Yorkshire, the WEA 'managed to evade most of the regulations designed to keep the WEA in the straight path, and the workers do control their own education'.[47] However, their similarities played down and their differences emphasised, the NCLC chose to maintain a consistent opposition to state and local authority funding. Brown suggests that this was due to necessity rather than choice; in any case, the labour college movement was not free of all constraints. Indeed, as its sponsoring unions shifted their political views to the right, Brown argues that the NCLC had to shift also to keep its 'right-wing patrons happy' and therefore were probably under as many, if not more, constraints than the WEA.[48] Brown goes on to suggest that here is one of the contradictions that the labour college movement failed to get to grips with, for the bourgeois, capitalist ruling class has to make concessions 'even to institutions, such as the WEA'.[49] This, it is arguable that the WEA managed to obtain financial support form the state, universities, local authorities, and so on, without 'seriously compromising the content of its work'. We might need to be cautious here, however, as contemporary debates concerning the historical significance of the WEA may not be directed by sophisticated theory, and the issue of hegemonic control may be either neglected, misunderstood or played down. For example, in the issue of the WEA News that celebrated the 80th anniversary of the WEA, Fieldhouse suggested that

> Establishment support for the new adult education movement after 1908 reflected a genuinely liberal belief in the value of education as an aid to human self-fulfilment, but it also reflected the desire to contain the growing power of the labour movement and to ensure that it adopted a liberal-individual-istic ideological framework rather than a Marxist-socialist one. The prospect of working class political power awakened in the ruling class a new enthusiasm to educate the workers in responsible democratic citizenship.[50]

To which the then president of the WEA responded:

> The only paper with which I am not in general sympathy is Roger Fieldhouse's ... in my view the picture he paints of Establishment patrols probing the WEA perimeter to keep the Association within bounds is both inaccurate and misleading. Overt pressures were firmly resisted. Of course limits existed, and still do, but they were defined by the WEA itself. The Association was not forced to embrace objectivity, balance and thoroughness in study, it chose to do so.[51] (Emphasis added)

The fact that the WEA set its own parameters and chose to adhere to a liberal ideology is a clear example of the way in which hegemonic control has infiltrated the consciousness of WEA leadership and membership throughout its eighty year history. When the WEA was celebrating its 21st anniversary, in 1924, the Plebs Magazine sent the following fraternal greetings:

> ... it is no fault of ours that you have reached your twenty-first anniversary; we should be much happier to attend your funeral. ... You exist to extend the benefits of University culture to the

working man that you patronise. We show our
readers that your education, and all education that
is not based on the central factor of the class
struggle, is false history and false economics.[52]

In fact, within five years, the NCLC had attended the
funerals of both the Plebs League and the Central Labour
College. The Labour College movement had never been on a
secure financial footing, and during the economic recession
of the 1920s it became much more difficult for the
movement to survive. Unable to sell very much of its
literature or many copies of its magazine because workers
were either unemployed or on strike, the Plebs League
disappeared into the NCLC in 1927, although its spirit was
said to have lived on. Less than two years later the crisis
overcame the Central Labour College, when the National
Union of Railwaymen withdrew financial support due to the
economic circumstances of the time. According to Craik's
account,[53] however, the NCLC were to blame, because of
the division and conflict that it generated between itself
and the Labour College after 1924.

And so with the closing in 1929 of what was then the
'only Trade Union residential college in the country', it was
the end of an era of hope and optimism for the development
of socialism. Of course, it was not the end of the story. The
NCLC continued until 1964 when it was taken over by the
Trades Union Congress. In the 1930s, the NCLC had begun
to lose support and credibility due to growing anti-
communist feeling among trade unions. After the Second
World War, the NCLC's commitment to Marxist theory was
only superficial as its views moderated to make its ideology
virtually indistinguishable from that of the Labour Party and
the TUC. The demise of the NCLC was ironically paralleled
by the strengthening of the WEA, which by this time had all
but lost its sense of socialist purpose.

What lessons are to be learned from this period of
history? In asking 'what went wrong?', this chapter has
focused on the failure of adult education to contribute to
the development of a socialist class consciousness and to
establish a counter-hegemony. In spite of the enormous
efforts made by both working-class organisations and
individuals, the theory and practice of socialism has not
been very far advanced through adult education. This failure
to establish an independent working-class education movement, capable of challenging the dominant hegemony,

reveals the power of the ruling class to control ideas, not least through the necessity of any educational organisation to obtain funding or financial support. The dilemma that we are confronted with is that education, even at its peak in the nineteenth century, reached only a very small percentage of the working population. We should take heed of Johnson's warning that we cannot assume that the attitudes of radical leaders and writers were those of 'the workers'; they were not necessarily speaking on their behalf.[54]

Resistance may require rethinking the organisation of a socialist education for adults. History lessons tell us that in part the failure of the working-class movement to develop its own educational provision was that it took on bourgeois models of educational organisations and attempted to recreate them, but with distinctive curricula and pedagogical styles. Perhaps something more radical is required in terms of how that curricula and pedagogy are to be organised. The chapters in the second part of this book give some illustrations as to what form these radical initiatives might take.

By studying the history of the labour movement, we can see that the working classes have always been fragmented and divided. Rarely in history have the working classes been united in a common cause. The sectarianism, internal in-fighting, and conflict so much a characteristic of contempory left-wing politics is clearly nothing new, but was a distinctive feature of working-class life throughout the nineteenth and twentieth centuries and of such conflicts and disagreements were carried on through and between educational organisations. Education has therefore failed to develop that degree of class consciousness that the 'oases' in the educational wilderness promised, but lost in their long search for the working class. Perhaps contemporary conspiracy theorists would be able to 'blame' external agencies such as the state or the media for deliberately creating and encouraging these divisions between working-class organisations. But such analyses are relatively naive.

It is probably fair to say that the socialist theories subscribed to during this historical period were crude and unsophisticated. Marx's own writings were only just beginning to appear in English at this time. The patriarchal nature of this period of socialism reflects this lack of sophisticiation. The emphasis of the Plebs League on oppression was inevitably crude and neglected the more powerful analyses that are now developed concerning the nature of bourgeois democracy, hegemony, and the role of the state with respect to the ruling classes. Their view of the state as merely an agent of the ruling class and oppression led the Plebs League and the NCLC to adhere rigidly to a principle of resisting state control that ultimately turned out to be foolish. As we have said, they were not free from constraints, and nor did they resolve the paradox of hegemony and whether proletariat education was less imbued with this than bourgeois education. Bourgeois hegemony does not exist only in financial control nor overt control over the curriculum, but operates in much more pervasive and subtle ways, such as the creation and satisfaction of needs, the acceptance of the faith of the experts and professionals, and so on.[55]

Fundamentally, it comes down to whether the energy for social transformation can develop within existing structures or whether it has to come from outside and be imposed. To work within existing structures always runs the risk of incorporation, but at the same time can be seen to be engaging with the dialectic of the contradiction, and it is in this process, the development of an antithesis, that praxis begins to take shape. Understanding 'the other side of the case', the presentation of alternative views are character-istics of the liberal tradition, and principles espoused in the teachings of the WEA, but at the same time, they are necessary if a counter-hegemony is to be constructed. Praxis is not possible in an ideological vacuum, nor is it best developed in a totally oppositional way. This tendency of the working-class organisations to dismiss everything bourgeois has the danger of not recognising the potential of some aspects, such as educational institutions, which might be useful to socialists, providing they remain critically aware of the dimensions of hegemony and the possibility of incorporation.

REFERENCES

1. J. Seabrook, What Went Wrong? Working People and the Ideals of the Labour Movement (London: Victor Gollancz, 1978).

2. R. Greenslade (ed.), Goodbye to the Working Class (London: Marion Boyars, 1976); see also, R. Goldman (ed.), Breakthrough: Autobiographical Accounts of the Education

of some Socially Disadvantaged Children (Routledge and Kegan Paul, 1968).

3. K. Worpole, 'Educating the Labour Movement', Socialism and Education, Vol.9, No.3, 1982 p.11-13.

4. J. Lee, This Great Journey: A Volume of Autobiography 1904-45 (London: MacGibbon and McKee, 1963); H. Pollitt, Serving My Time: An Apprenticeship in Politics (London: Lawrence and Wishart, 1940); and R. Roberts, A Ragged Schooling: Growing Up in the Classic Slum (London: Fontana, 1976).

5. R. Tressell, The Ragged Trousered Philanthropists (St Albans, Granada, 1965); p.27.

6. J.F.C. Harrison, Learning and Living, 1760-1960 (London: Routledge and Kegan Paul, 1961), p.297.

7. P. Freire, Cultural Action for Freedom (Harmondsworth: Penguin, 1972).

8. T. Blackwell and J. Seabrook, 'Looking for the Working Class', New Society, 9 September 1982, p.411.

9. B. Simon, The Two Nations and the Educational Structure 1780-1870 (London: Lawrence and Wishart, 1974); Education and the Labour Movement 1870-1920 (London: Lawrence and Wishart, 1965).

10. R.W. Johnson, 'Notes on the schooling of the English working class 1750-1850', in R. Dale, G. Esland and M. MacDonald (eds), Schooling and Capitalism: A Sociological Reader (London: Routledge and Kegan Paul, 1976), pp.44-54; '"Really useful knowledge": radical education and working-class culture, 1790-1848' in J. Clarke, C. Critcher and R. Johnson (eds), Working-Class Culture (London: Hutchinson, 1979); reprinted in R. Dale, G. Esland, R. Fergusson and M. MacDonald (eds), Education and the State. Politics Vol. III, Patriarchy and Practice (Lewes: Falmer Press, 1981), pp.3-19.

11. Ibid., p.5.

12. See S. Shapin and B. Barnes, 'Science, nature and control: interpreting Mechanics' Institutes', in R. Dale, G. Esland and M. MacDonald (eds), Schooling and Capitalism: A Sociological reader (London: Routledge and Kegan Paul, 1976), pp.55-65.

13. Quoted by Worpole, 'Educating the Labour Movement', p.11.

14. The Times, Editorial, 2 September 1851, p.4.

15. Simon, The Two Nations and the Educational Structure 1780-1870, p.277.

16. Ibid., pp.281-99.

17. D. Reeder (ed.), Educating Our Masters (Leicester: Leicester University Press, 1980), p.15.

18. Ibid.

19. E. and C. Paul, Proletcult (London: Leonard Parsons, 1921), p.42.

20. Ibid., p.45.

21. Ibid., p.46.

22. Ibid., p.39.

23. J.F.C. Harrison, A History of the London Working Men's College 1854-1954 (London: Routledge and Kegan Pual, 1954).

24. The material for this paragraph was derived from the Working Men's College publicity booklet, 'Evening Classes for Men and Women, 1985-86', p.3.

25. Harrison, A History of the London Working Men's College, p.70.

26. E. and C. Paul, Proletcult, pp.38-9.

27. See, inter alia, N.A. Jepson, The Beginnings of English University Adult Education (London: Michael Joseph, 1973); and B. Jennings, New Lamps for Old? University Adult Education in Retrospect and Prospect (Hull: University of Hull, 1976).

28. R.D. Roberts, University Extension: Its Past and Future (Cambridge: Cambridge University Press, 1893), pp.3-4.

29. R.G. Moulton, The University Extension Movement (London, 1890), pp. 10-11.

30. This point is made in various places, including R. Taylor, K. Rockhill and R. Fieldhouse, University Adult Education in England and the USA (Beckenham: Croom Helm, 1985), p.4; J.F. and W. Horrabin, Working-Class Education (London: The Labour Publishing Company, 1924), p.30; and Simon, Education and the Labour Movement, op.cit., p.304.

31. Ibid., p.311.

32. Jennings, New Lamps for Old?, p.13.

33. R. Williams, Politics and Letters (London: Pluto Press, 1979), p.79.

34. Simon, Education and the Labour Movement, p.311.

35. See, for example, B. Jennings, 'Revolting Students - The Ruskin College Dsipute 1908-9', in Studies in Adult Education, Vol.9, No.1, April 1977, pp.1-16.

36. Blackwell and Seabrook, 'Looking for the Working Class', p.411.

37. E. and C. Paul, Proletcult, p.12.

38. National Council of Labour Colleges, Education for Emancipation: The Work of the National Council of Labour Colleges (Edinburgh: NCLC, 1926), p.31.

39. G.D.H. Cole, in The Highway, Winter 1923, quoted by G. Brown, 'Independence and Incorporation: the Labour College Movement and the Workers' Educational Association before the second world war', in J. Thompson (ed.), Adult Education for a Change (London: Hutchinson, 1980), p.123.

40. J.F. and W. Horrabin, Working-Class Education, p.40.

41. Brown, 'Independence and Incorporation', p.124.

42. Ibid.

43. The Plebs, Vol.1, No.7 (1909) p.136.

44. Simon, Education and the Labour Movement, p.326.

45. See J. Atkins, Neither Crumbs Nor Condescension: The Central Labour College, 1909-1915 (Aberdeen: Aberdeen People's Press/Workers' Educational Association, 1981); J.P.M.. Millar, The Labour College Movement (London: NCLC Publishing Society, 1979); and Simon, Education and the Labour Movement, pp.318-26.

46. Taylor, Rockhill and Fieldhouse, University Adult Education in England and the USA, p.5.

47. W. Mellor, quoted by Brown, 'Independence and Incorporation', p.113.

48. Ibid., p.114.

49. Ibid., p.115.

50. R. Fieldhouse, 'The WEA's Liberal Parameters', WEA News, new series, No.24, Spring 1983, Special Supplement, p.3.

51. WEA News, new series, No. 24, Spring 1983, Special Supplement, p.1.

52. Quoted by Jennings, Knowledge is Power, p.32.

53. W.W. Craik, The Central Labour College: 1909-1929 (London: Lawrence and Wishart, 1964).

54. Johnson, '"Really Useful Knowledge": Radical Education and Working Class Culture, 1790-1854', pp.3-4.

55. I have argued this elsewhere; see P.F. Armstrong, 'The myth of meeting needs in adult education and community development', in Critical Social Policy, Vol.2, No.2 (Autumn 1982), pp.24-37, and 'The "needs-meeting" ideology of liberal adult education', in International Journal of Lifelong Education, Vol.1, No.4 (1982) pp.293-321.

3

Domesticity and its Discontents: Feminism and Adult Education in Past Time (1870-1920)*

Sallie Westwood

INTRODUCTION

The current interest in women's education in all its diverse forms generates a terrain in which practices, forms and definitions are areas of competition and struggle, but we should not imagine that these struggles are necessarily novel. Debates over the form and content of women's education, the place of personal experience and expert knowledge, the role of teacher and learner, the curricula to be used and created, are part of an ongoing debate with a long history and this paper is part of the excavation of that debate. Crucial to any understanding of discussions surrounding women's education is an examination of the category 'women' and the way in which the social construction of 'woman' is located with specific ideologies.

Reconstructions of the past are highly problematic, but from the available literature it is possible to draw an outline across the historical material and to consider the issues raised by adult education in relation to the ideologies surrounding home and family in nineteenth century Britain. These ideologies placed women in relation to domesticity and motherhood in specific ways and the task of this paper will be to elaborate the ways in which feminism struggled with and around these ideologies while adult education, in its broadest sense, was the shifting ground on which the ideology of femininity and the social construction of woman as homemaker was both contested and reproduced at the same time. The way in which adult education was further articulated with the growing interventionist role of the state at a time when citizenship and suffrage were the main demands of the feminist movement forms the latter part of the account.

The paper is an exploration of the historical dimension as it is conventionally understood, as serial and bounded by temporality. But, there is another history generated by the interplay of knowledge and power which speaks through these contextual elements and which allows us to construct a series of interconnected discourses. It is important to acknowledge here that in drawing upon the work of Foucault we are not offered a method with which to work.[1] Instead, by his own work he has illuminated an alternative way of understanding which I have found useful in my attempts to unravel the contradictions of adult education in the nineteenth century. However, what follows is by no means a fully developed discourse analysis. Indeed, I share with the writers of Unpopular Education a certain disquiet about the current enthusiasm for discourse analysis as offering a definitive reading of social phenomena and support the view that: 'We do have to attend closely to the internal logic of public knowledge but we also have to move it away from the centre of the stage to consider agencies and determinations which it does not describe.'[2] Consequently, my account is an attempt to weave together the complex articulation between those ideologies and practices we have come to know as feminist, accepting that they are not a simple unity. Changes in the organisation of capitalist production, the response from the working classes through the developing labour movement to this, and changes in the role of the state and the way in which struggles related to the state became central in the latter part of the nineteenth century. The role of adult education must be seen in relation to these changes.[3] Adult education was part of the early popular movements in education but, by the turn of the century and the arrival of the '1919' Report, it had been given a role by the state in the reconstrcution of post-war Britain.

Jane Rendell reminds us of the difficulties of understanding the world of women in the nineteenth century in relation to feminism, a term not in use during the period of her study (1790-1860).[4] Using the work of Gerda Lerner she distinguishes between the demands made for women's rights and the wider view of 'women's emancipation' which incorporated, 'freedom from oppressive restrictions imposed by sex, self-determination, autonomy'.[5] It is this latter view that incorporates the essentials of feminism. Olive Banks' historical account views feminism as a combination of elements drawn from three major strands originating in the eighteenth century; evangelical Christianity (which at one and the same time had a major role to play in the development of the ideology of domesticity); the Enlightment philosophers and the socialism of the early socialists in a pre-Marxist period.[6] It was, in fact, the Utopian Socialist, Fourier, who coined the word <u>feminisme</u> which he alone used at the time. These three strands provide a useful starting point for our analysis when treated as discourses available in the nineteenth century with an impact throughout the social formation. Discourses are one area of discussion, but, as Sheila Rowbotham reminds us: 'Women started to campaign for particular reforms in the nineteenth century not because they saw themselves as feminists, but because circumstances in their own lives forced them to protest.'[7]

FEMINISM, CITIZENSHIP AND ADULT EDUCATION

In the lull that followed the agitational years of the 1830s and 1840s labour organised against the growing power of capital and a new power bloc; the industrialists, the new urban bourgeois, the landowners and urban gentry. Against this labour was increasingly organised around its differentiated sectors, the division between skilled and unskilled which cut across gender divisions, urban/rural differences and regional specificities. It was the craft-workers who came together to form unions and to protect their position as a labour aristocracy. This involved particular emphases within the ideological sphere; 'Working-class independence' could thus be obtained by self-improvement, within the existing framework of society. This is in striking contract to working-class consciousness in the Chartist period when its concern with injustice and inequality had articulated a conception of society reconstructed along democratic and egalitarian lines. The economics of working-class differentiation created, therefore, a mechanism for transmitting a negotiated version of the dominant ideology to a priveleged elite of labour during the third quarter of the nineteenth century.[8] This comment is part of Burgess's account of the accommodation between labour and capital worked through during the middle of the nineteenth century and he ties this not only to economic demands, but issues surrounding the franchise:

> The demand for household suffrage was conceived
> of and 'posed' as a test of respectability, a proof of
> the moral standing of the individual deserving the

61

vote. ... It appealed to respectable elements in the
working class but was not revolutionary in
threatening the power and authority of the
industrial bourgeoisie.[9]

By 1870 women were still not citizens with educational
rights, voting rights, property rights or union rights.[10] The
world was divided not only by class and culture, but by
gender; the patriarchal hegemony was secure but not
unchallenged.

As the century moved into the last quarter a new era in
British capitalism opened up[11] and a profound political,
economic and social restructuring began through the
development of the interventionist state.[12] The old view of
the state as referee was giving way to the new - the state as
regulator. As Hall and Schwarz comment:

> The identifications forged in this system between
> the free individual in civil society, the free
> market, private property and the patriarchal
> domestic household formed one of the most
> powerful and durable popular conceptions of state
> and society.[13]

This was a period of ferment in which recession and
poverty stood side by side with growth in union membership,
increased militant action and the development of socialist
ideas into organised political groups. At the same time the
development of the aristocracy of labour continued and with
this the further development of 'respectability':

> Central to the emergence of a more settled and
> respectable working-class way of life was the
> construction of the home as an arena of physical
> comfort and emotional support ... the fulfilment of
> the domestic ideal required the full-time labour of
> housewives. Better off workers in most parts of the
> country preferred their wives to stay at home. The
> notion of the 'family wage' - that a man's earnings
> should be sufficient to keep his wife and young
> children out of the labour market - was an
> important element in late nineteenth century
> working-class respectability, and it militated
> against any serious consideration of the case for
> equal work opportunities for women.[14]

Education was a crucial moment in the politics of the time, especially the world of adult education where the contradiction between the hegemonic world of liberalism and patriarchy were in collision with the counter-hegemonic forces of socialist ideas, but not necessarily those that brought feminist and socialist ideas together. For example, in his book, Proletarian Philosophies, Ree asserts the importance of the working-class autodidact in socialist history, but he enters a caveat: 'the man - it was unlikely to be a woman'.[15] Historical and literary accounts support this overall, either because female autodidacts were thin on the ground or, because they were more securely tied to the private world of the home, they were hidden. It is clear that Hannah Mitchell had a great desire for knowledge and education but that it was not so easily satisfied, nor taken so seriously, as it would have been had she been male. She did not have the model of Hardy's Jude held out to her.[16] Working-class men who wanted some part of university culture and knowledge were addressed by the universities' limited attempts to connect with the developing working class. The early Working Men's College (1854) was followed by University Extension which sent Oxford and Cambridge dons into the provinces in the 1870's and then the Settlement Movement that developed out of Toynbee Hall in 1884. Ree notes: 'To be excluded from the University was to be debarred from full citizenship...'[17] The extensionists had a mission, to imbue the working classes with a vision of a shared state and community in which citizenship was paramount.[18] The citizenship, of course, refers to men, but the aims to develop a unity among men in one nation were also frustrated:

> University Extension ... was taken over by a new
> class - the suburban 'lower middle-class', and
> mostly, as Carpenter (a university extension
> lecturer in astronomy) wearily noted, the 'young
> lady' class; it did not serve the urban proletariats
> for whom it had been wishfully designed.[19]

The 'young lady' class was precisely the world of Vera Brittain so carefully portrayed in her own writings and in which the extension lectures are an oasis in a desert of provincialism.[20] She, like other women of her time and class, declared herself for knowledge and higher education and she did receive assistance from a male lecturer in her efforts to go on to Oxford.

There are many interesting contradictions to be explored in relation to the development of University Adult Education. The work of Taylor, Rockhill and Fieldhouse in examining the liberal tradition emphasises the importance of the individualistic thrust of adult education; its commitment to the education of the individual, the widening of horizons, ideally, within an atmosphere where discussion and dissent are encouraged.[21] This setting provides the context for the autodidacts of Ree's study but it sits uneasily with notions of the collective subject although it did extend itself into areas of social concern, most especially 'education for citizenship'.[22] In the British context this has generated a discourse on the education of the working-class which continues to be a major area of discussion:

> This has been partly on grounds of social justice ... but also because of a deeply held belief that only through education could the working-class become equipped intellectually and politically to play its full role in a democratic society.[23]

There are many issues raised by this particular stance but what concerns us here is that the evident paternalism was exercised by men towards men - the male working-class in its respectable, skilled, organised form. It comes as no surprise, therefore, to see that the culmination of the university extension movement found in the divine inspiration of Albert Mansbridge (another autodidact) a movement which was initially designated: An Association to Promote the Higher Education of Working Men, and consisted initially of Albert and Francis Mansbridge. As Stocks points out: 'For an organisation which started its existence with a 50 per cent female membership, its name was lacking in descriptive accuracy and redolent of masculine arrogance.' And she continues: 'This defect was wholly unintentional ...'[24]

This comment speaks volumes. Mansbridge did not intentionally exclude women, exclusion requires a recognition of what, or who, is to be excluded, and there was none, because men as real material persons and men as socially constructed and defined were at issue, not men versus women. Adult education, despite the presence of women in the university extension movement and the support that they gave to the renamed Workers' Educational Association (1905) made women invisible. Workers were and are men, makers of culture, producers of wealth and involved in the struggle for power and knowledge. Women were domesticated, a passive element against which men measured their power, wealth and productivity. Women were not intentionally excluded by the naming of an organisation but its founding within an already constituted discourse which made women invisible insisted that they remain so. The WEA reproduced the labour movement's inability to see women as workers in an EQUAL STRUGGLE WITH MEN. Mansbridge had a vision but not one that could transcend the intersection of the variety of discourses within which adult education was itself formed.

One of the main opponents of Mansbridge in the early years was Mrs Bridges Adams, who was strongly suspicious of a working-class educational movement that was tied to the universities. It could only mean collusion and deradicalisation of the working class. Mansbridge was seen by her as an official subversive paid by, and in the hands of, the university authorities. She was clearly an adept and well-organised woman who managed to disrupt meetings and cause Mansbridge some discomfort. Her conspiratorial views need to be set within the context of an educational project born of the liberal tradition and Mansbridge's own commitment to university education. From the account by Mansbridge and Stocks the issue of class is pre-eminent, but Mrs Bridges Adams reappears to raise the issue of working women and their role in relation to knowledge and power.[25] Hers was not a lone voice, as Stocks notes, John Scurr and George Lansbury, among others, raised again the issue of working-class education tied to the largesse of institutions of the upper classes.[26]

The distrust for anything other than an independent working-class education erupted at Ruskin (the college founded in 1899 for working-class students), starting with the students' strike which culminated in the break away of the Plebs League as a forerunner to the development of the National Labour College Movement. The WEA launched Highway in 1908 and moved onwards towards the tutorial class movement. What is also interesting is the other development within the WEA which coincided with the development of the militant Plebs league. The WEA decided to devote its attention to women. Was this due to pressure from within the movement, or from without, or was it a sense that women were a ready source to be tapped and one, most importantly, that would not seek to challenge the claims of the WEA to represent working-class educational aspirations?

> In 1909 it [the WEA] launched out in a new direction. In the majority of classes it was noted that males constituted the overwhelming majority. Where were the women? It was a natural deduction that most of them were at home, 'sitting in' while their husbands, brothers, fathers, as the case might be, pursued the higher learning elsewhere.[27]

Stocks' comments show very clearly that the discourse which brought the WEA into being and sustained it was a structure in which women were invisible. That women should constitute a 'new direction' means that they had to be brought into this discourse; they had to be 'thought' in order to be the subject of this new direction. Similarly, the conception of women as domestic subjects is reiterated. Thus, they become visible in relation to their domesticity and more, in terms of kinship. Stocks continues:

> And as politically minded beings the women were certainly backward. It was nobody's business to see that they were not: for in these far-off days with which we are concerned it must be remembered that they had no votes. Political propagandists were not interested in them ... Women were ever the victims of rash and sweeping generalisations and statements about their backwardness may be both rash and sweeping. But the educational process was not made easy for them, either by their domestic circumstances or the attention paid to their needs.[28]

These statements again demonstrate the idea of the passive and culturally incompetent woman subject either to propaganda or education. But, the problems of educating women were seen to be many. Why? The answer lies in 'their domestic circumstances' not in the fact that they were engaged in domestic production and social production. Women were brought into the WEA as women whose lives were located in the home. Women were integrated into the WEA not as workers equal to men, but as a case of special need. Stocks, in fact, goes on to describe the special needs of women and reports that, following the Women's Advisory Committee, a full-time organiser was appointed.[29] The point here is not that women then, as now, need to be encouraged to participate in educational ventures, but that they should be considered as 'a problem'.

Women within the WEA in those early years fought battles on behalf of their sisters, battles that were not of their making. That they waged a struggle within a discourse that they could not alter was a measure of their status and power as women. Some, like Maude Royden, carried their struggle into the suffrage campaign, but the notion of the 'backward women' was to stay with the field of adult education and to re-emerge in subsequent struggles.

The idea of working-class uplift through encounters with higher education was challenged by a more political account of independent working-class education which introduced a discourse from Marxism and had a material effect in the founding of the National Council of Labour Colleges. Debates surrounding the NCLC took as their starting point an unread assumption about the relationship between men, knowledge and power. Thus, we search in vain for a discussion of women in the movement even though it is clear that the Women's Labour League advocated a Women's Labour College. In the two major accounts of the work of the Central Labour College and the NCLC by Craik and Millar, the issue of women students or workers is given little attention, but when it is the familiar definitions hold.[30] Craik's account notes the attempts of one, Mrs Bridges Adams (who proved such an irritant to Mansbridge) to found a Labour College for Working Women. He suggests that the idea for a women's college received no support from the trade union movement nor the Pankhurst suffragettes, but that it did have the support of Annie Kenney and the two students initially enrolled were Lancashire weavers. These women were integrated into the Labour College as non-resident members. A 'Women's League' of the college was founded which had among its functions, fund-raising for scholarships for men and women and 'helping in the social work of the college'. Craik's account of the helping function of women introduces the notion of 'this monstrous regiment of women' who, he believed, aided the college in achieving a 'more balanced way of living and working'.[31] In Craik's appendix he details former students, but no women are named here.[32]

Millar's account of the Labour College Movement praises the work done by Christine Millar and the contribution made by Winifred Horrabin, who became honorary secretary of the Plebs League. However, when Christine Millar did become a salaried employee, amid some opposition, this was after two years of arduous work as a volunteer. Christine Millar is to be found in the pages of the book organising the clerical work, administering the postal courses, putting together displays, attending conferences. There is no doubt that her time and energy contributed enormously to the success of the NCLC. Millar notes that 'about one in twenty of those who attended classes were women' and 'from time to time the question was raised of strengthening the role played by women in NCLC affairs ...'[33] But, somehow the right time or enough money was never available for this. Instead, the standard view of women as wives living lives defined by domesticity and the home was reproduced.

Despite the lack of attention to women's educational aspirations from the WEA or the NCLC, women organised in different ways to secure their rights. The Women's Labour League (1906) called on members to, 'educate themselves on political and social questions, work in social work, promote full citizenship rights for men and women. They will waken the interests of working women in their own neighbourhood, and strive, where possible, to improve their social and industrial conditions.'[34]

Ferguson's account of the work of the Women's Labour League in relation to social services provides a clear picture of socially concerned and well-organised women promoting the interests of women and children, the poor and the needy: school meals, baby clinics, pit-head baths all had a direct impact on the lives of working-class women.[35] At the same time, women like Eleanor Rathbone fought for benefits from the state to the poor.[36] Margherita Rendel, writing on the contribution of the League to the Suffrage campaign, notes that they appealed to women to come forward to serve on town councils, but in ways that insisted upon a woman's sphere: 'Women are badly needed for our MUNICIPAL HOUSEKEEPING. Let us use our WOMEN'S BRAINS AND HEARTS to guide the Labour policy.'[37]

The WLL consistently debated and raised the issue of women's suffrage and each conference brought new resolutions and different views on which tactic to adopt. (It was not until 1912 that the Labour Party adopted a much stronger resolution calling on the Labour Party to oppose any Government Bill for electoral reform unless it contained a clause enfranchising women.)[38] The WLL fought consistently for the vote for all women; they were not interested in pressing the claim for votes for women of property. But, as Rendell comments: 'Much of the material published by the WLL stressed the need for the vote in order to safeguard woman's role as wife and mother.'

> Our ideals of the good housewife, the ideal mother, are changing fast. We are coming to see that it is only possible for the woman whose chief work lies in her home, to fulfil efficiently her mission, thereby uniting with other women under the same conditions and with the same claims. Like the men members of her household she must think and work COLLECTIVELY in order to help herself and those dependent on her INDIVIDUALLY.[39]

Alongside the Labour-based women's organisations like WLL, the Fabian women and the militant WSPU was the women's section of the Cooperative Movement. The early co-ops inspired communities with a new vision of the world, and men's and women's lives within it, as well as emphasising the education of all, but this was later superseded by a form in which the cash nexus was paramount. The decision to pay dividends and turn the emphasis away from production and towards distribution has marked the Cooperative Movement ever since. This emphasis, upon the sphere of consumption, had important implications for the way in which women were made visible and the way in which the language of cooperation changed.

Harrison notes that the Cooperative Movement 'displayed some ambiguity towards educational enterprise' and this was mirrored by the cooperators: 'We want no eddication [sic] give us a bonus' (Leeds, 1872).[40]

No profits were allocated to education and the Yorkshire co-ops were credited with holding the view that formal education was no part of the Co-op movement. Many viewed the movement itself as an educational experience. There is an important truth in this and it is especially relevant to the lives of women cooperators.

Women were certainly encouraged to become co-op members and part of the reason for this was that they had a special role as consumers. The emphasis upon women as providers, through consumption, of nurture for their menfolk and children was consistent with the prevailing ideology of women's roles in the home, and it was this ideology which operated as a context for the work of the Cooperative Women's Guild.[41] But the Guild also developed a critique of the social construction of woman simply as a consumer and the lack of power this implied for women in the cooperative movement. However, the women of the Guild saw the need for an organisation of women which addressed the issues faced by women, but even this met with opposition. Jean Gaffin notes that the Guild enabled working-class women to play a larger part in the running of the Cooperative Movement itself. The social construction of woman as consumer remained and was reiterated in the title of Catherine Webb's history of the Guild, Woman with the Basket, and in the case made by the Guild in 1904 for full adult suffrage.[42] They claimed that as women were wages SPENDERS they were subject to government legislation and should, therefore, have a vote in electing the government. There was, however, another and very different strand to their argument: that the unpaid labour of women in the home was as important as waged labour in social production.

This is, of course, a forerunner to more recent feminist debates about the role of domestic labour in the capitalist economy. The Guild was, therefore, marked by contradictions. It campaigned for higher wages for women workers in the co-ops, but not for equal pay. In addition, partly in response to the leadership of Margaret Llewellyn Davies, the Guild took on wider issues and concerned itself with welfare benefits and divorce reform.[43] The National Insurance Act 1911 did not include the one major and radical suggestion made by the Guild, that maternity benefit should be paid to women and that provision should be made for sick pay to be paid to wage-earning women before and after the birth of the child. The Guild campaigned for a national system of maternity care at a time when there was concern over the health of the nation and the falling birth rate (to which I shall return). Consulted on the matter of divorce reform they advocated divorce by mutual consent after two years separation (it took until 1969 to achieve this). For this radical position the English Women's Guild was punished. Their grant from the Central Board of the Cooperative Union was withheld until, they were told, they ceased to agitate upon divorce reform, and further, until they agreed to concentrate on issues directly relevant to the Cooperative Movement and those the Board approved. The Guild, undeterred, entered into a bitter dispute on their autonomy and raised their own funds.

What is interesting about this dispute and the severity with which the Central Board dealt with it, is that the Guild was seen to be undermining family life by their interest in women's rights and divorce reform. Thus, the Guild would be excluded, made invisible by lack of funds because it dared to challenge the social construction of woman upon which it was based. The Guild fought their battles in the Cooperative Movement and the original rift was finally papered over, but the Guild did not stop, and in 1934 the Conference passed a resolution in favour of legalising abortion. The Guild women were brave, they asserted their autonomy against the power of the Cooperative Union and plotted a path beyond the members' conceptions of issues for women. They were ridiculed and faced hostility from male cooperators and husbands because they worked to shift the ground upon which they were defined. They saw the issues in the lives of their members - evidenced in the accounts of maternity collected by the Guild that remain as a testament to the privations and the strength of women in this period.[44] The Guild kept alive the feminist spirit in relation to a socialist purpose by its attention to the material conditions of women's lives and the collective spirit of campaigning that marked its work.[45] It also gave women the opportunity to come together in a space they called their own where they could share their expertise and their experiences. And in this it is marked by a continuity with what had gone before and what re-emerged as feminist practice in the latter half of the twentieth century. For, despite the fact that most of the members were the wives of artisans (the respectable working class), the women, prompted by Margaret Llewellyn Davies, took a radical stance defined by their commitment to improve the quality of women's lives in ways that would allow women more autonomy. Issues of power in the family, between wives and husbands, were crucial alongside reproductive rights at a time when motherhood was being recast by the Eugenicists. The impact of the Guild is summed up in the following: 'It is impossible for me to say how much I owe the Guild, it gave me education and recreation. ... From a shy nervous women, the Guild made a fighter.'[46]

WAR, THE STATE AND SOCIAL RECONSTRUCTION

The turn of the century brought an end to the Boer War (1902), the consequences of which reverberated throughout the country. In the lead-up to the First World War there was a new wave of militancy. Trade union membership doubled in the period 1910-14 and there was action in the mines which culminated in the first national strike in 1912. It was against this background that the Plebs League and the newly founded Labour College developed.

Women, at this time, continued to press for the vote but the relations between feminist practices and the developing socialist movement remained relatively unexplored:

> Feminism in this period was diffuse, inchoate and contradictory. It was not a clearly worked out ideology, but was rather a rebellion against the norms of bourgeois Victoria femininity. [However] It extended into every area of cultural life and it had an international impact.[47]

Many of the socialists of the period were committed to a class perspective which saw feminist politics as diversionary at a time when many men did not have the vote. Too often they characterised the suffrage campaign as a middle-class phenomenon, and feminist demands as located with this class. They were aware that only two-thirds of the adult male population qualified for the vote and it has been estimated that before 1918 no more than 95 of the 670 MPs were elected by working-class constituencies.[48] It would appear that only the left of the ILP had a sympathetic ear for feminist demands.

In the attempt to generate new discourses within which to situate demands, build a new culture and make over their lives, both socialists and feminists drew on ideas of the day, from Edward Carpenter's Love's Coming of Age and Morris's works to the ideas of the Eugenicists which were fuelled by the Boer War. Feminists saw in the eugenic arguments a new vision of womanhood, one tied to reproduction but for a larger aim, a motherhood with purpose and which conferred status on women rather than the feeble hysteria of the earlier period. Lorna Duffin, in charting the major concerns of the Eugenicists, points to the importance of education for motherhood and the role of the state in generating the conditions necessary to foster a eugenicist view:

> Eugenic feminism, the ideal of motherhood had nothing to do with feminism. Indeed it was the ultimate denial of woman's role and identity as an individual. She was to be sacrificed to the future.[49]

It was, on the contrary, the birth control advocates like Margaret Sanger and Stella Brown, who represented the emancipation of women through their emphasis upon 'voluntary motherhood' which presupposed that women would exercise control over their own reproduction.[50] The Eugenicists offered women the possibility of the biological production and nurturing of future citizens, but no citizenship rights for women themselves.

It is clear that motherhood was reconstructed at the turn of the century and that, although it drew on the nineteenth-century ideology of femininity, it also represented a break with this. The new motherhood emerged not simply from concern over the falling birth rate but from the importance of Empire and the power of the white 'race' in relation to the subject populations. Motherhood entered into the calculation at a public level and with that it became subjected to the power of the state and the importance of discourses on national efficiency. But, it was quite clear that if motherhood was to be so important, women would need to be prepared for it: 'Motherhood was to be given new dignity; it was the duty and destiny of women to be the "mothers of the race", but also their great reward.'[51]

Adult education was invoked in the service of the new motherhood and the education of the new mothers was much discussed, but it did not prove easy to implement the new classes because few girls were involved in further education and few in the extant girls clubs. It seemed important therefore, to insert mothercraft more specifically into the school agenda. Meanwhile the adult education variant, 'Schools for Mothers', came into being. Davin details the work of one of these schools, the St Pancras School for Mothers, where teaching was carried on through informal conversations and discussions and examples of good practice were demonstrated. Some 'Schools for Mothers' provided classes in domestic subjects which received subsidies.[52] The primary purpose was educational and related to mothercraft, but organisations like the Cooperative Women's Guild insisted on focusing on the health and well-being of mothers and publishing the privations and injuries incurred by working women, evidenced in their accounts of maternity. The 'Schools for Mothers' were essentially for working-class young women, an extension of the domestic skills on offer in the evening schools, and yet the emphasis in St Pancras on discussion and informality borrows from the work of the Guild.

The cult of motherhood was not just about the Empire, it was also about the changing nature of capitalist production which required a different type of workforce from the casual labour of before. But this was coupled with the introduction of marriage bars which maintained the position of male labour and kept women out of the labour market except in areas specifically defined as relevant to women; the new and growing state sector in education, health and welfare which was viewed as an extension both of women's roles as philanthropists and as an extension of their role in the family.[53] Women were to be not simply producers of the race and Empire builders, but Empire conservers. The state in its new and expanded interventionist guise was crucial to the realisation of the new motherhood and important to the way in which it was socially constructed to cut across class specificities. No account was taken of the material conditions of working-class life for women. Rather, the home was viewed as 'the cradle of the race ... Empire's first line of defence'.[54] The discourse operating around motherhood were suffused with notions of Empire and white supremacy tied to virility and masculinity produced by a nation of women anchored to their roles in the family and the home. The notion of the individual and sometimes failing mother who was so important later in the century was starting to emerge as a reworking of the earlier discourse on the feckless, 'sickening' working-class woman. As Davin concludes:

> In the context then of racism and imperialism at one level and of class exploitation and sex prejudice at another, we come back to the mothers. The mothers' role in the creation of a healthier workforce, as of a virile army and navy, was crucial. In the fixing of the workforce, the development of a new kind of family, with head and housewife and pride in possessions, bound to

one place and one job by a new level of emotional and financial investment in an increasingly substantial 'home' was also to play a central part.[55]

The implications of this within the sphere of adult education were worked out in relation to the development of the 'Women's Interest' curriculum which developed in the twentieth century in relation to the notion of the home as an arena for women's aesthetic senses not just their manual skills. So, while unions organised, socialists debated and women struggled to insert feminist ideas into the agenda, motherhood was remade and offered to all white women as their true destiny. The virility and manhood, so much a part of the discourse, was now to march towards a new war. The First World War crashed around the ears of the nation and changed it irrevocably. The suffrage campaign called a truce, although other women's organisations were much less inclined to support the war effort, and young men went to fight and die in France while women went into paid employment in unprecedented numbers - only to be ejected from this work at the end of the war.[56] Feminists campaigned against the marriage bar but public opinion ran with the men returned from the battlefields. Clearly, for many women paid employment did not begin and end with the war, they stayed in the jobs they had traditionally done, but for some it marked the final break with domestic service which declined as the century progressed.[57]

The end of the war marked the period hailed as one of reconstrcution when women were still required in the factories and the developing offices which would service capitalist expansion, but it was still the case that by 1921 women were going back into domestic service due to lack of paid work in other areas and the numbers of women in domestic service in 1921-31 increased by 200,000.[58]

The Russian Revolution fuelled the socialist imagination and fired the feminists to keep alive the radical work of the pre-war years. The syndicalists, unionists and radicals in the Labour Party saw the increased power of the state in relation to the economy and with this the politicisation of the economic relations between labour and the state. The relationship between schooling, class and the gender division of labour was further elaborated during this period when the differences in curricula for boys and girls became entrenched and the eugenicist arguments promoted education for motherhood and notions that too much intellectual stimulation was bad for female fertility. The educational struggles of this period reflect these contradictory demands upon schools and teachers. In adult education the power of the state was being invoked to set new directions for the field in relation to the post-war reconstruction evidenced in the '1919' Report.[59] I want to conclude my discussion by drawing out some of the main themes of the '1919' Report.

Adult education I have argued, like feminism, is a contradictory phenomenon with a creative tension manifest in the interplay of diverse discourses and this is nowhere more apparent than in the '1919' Report. The pages of the report abound with reformist zeal and missionary enthusiasm for the work of adult education. The members of the committee included Mansbridge as well as Tawney and 'the Master of Balliol'. The terms of reference of the report were, 'To consider the provision for, and possibilities of, Adult Education (other than technical and vocational) in Great Britain, and to make reconstructions'.[60]

The first part of the report was concerned with industrial and social conditions and its recommendations were radical and far-reaching: shorter working hours, paid holidays, special provision for heavy work, shorter shifts, limitations of night work. In relation to housing, the report stated that housing schemes should be brought into effect and that 'adequate washing facilities' should be provided in places of employment where it was essential. The report linked the lives of women especially to the home, noting, 'Housing is essentially a woman's question. Bad as may be the effects of present housing conditions for the man they are worse for the woman, since she has to endure them the whole day long.'[61] The vision of woman as homemaker and housewife is clearly apparent, but the report makes clear that the home is a workplace for domestic labourers. 'It is often overlooked that the housewife engaged in domestic duties is in some ways one of the worst sufferers from long hours of work, and is consequently largely debarred from participation in educational and social amenities.'[62] In fact, the report makes a clear connection between the needs of women for more knowledge in their new roles as citizens and the constraints of poor housing which demands all their time. They recommend that women are included in all committees dealing with housing and public health issues. The point about the recommendations of the interim report is that they are given 'on educational grounds' and this speaks of a concern far outside the classroom and, more directly, with the conditions of existence of people in Britain after the Great War. The report takes off from the tradition of socially concerned government enquiries and the work of the social statisticians considering it legitimate to comment on poor working conditions and workers' lack of control over production process. The interim report concludes with the following paragraph:

> We cannot stand still. We cannot return to the old ways, the old abuses, the old stupidities. We have been made conscious that we are heirs [sic] to a majestic inheritance, and that we have correspond-ing obligations. We have awakened to the splendid qualities that were latent in our people, the rank and file of the common people who before this war were often adjudged to be decadent, to have lost their patriotism, their religious faith, and their response to leadership; we were even told they were physically degenerate. Now we see what potentialities lie in this people, and what a charge lies upon us to give to these powers free-play. There is stirring through the whole country a sense of the duty we owe to our children ... to save them not only from the repetition of such a world-war and from the burdens of a crushing militarism, but to save them also from the obvious peril of civil dissension at home.[63]

This report demonstrates the world of reconstruction, the sense that changes had to be made to secure the national consensus and the state, in its collectivist and inter-ventionist role, was crucial to this. So too, was adult education in building a world after the war.

It is not possible to provide a detailed analysis of the report here but it is a fascinating document which brings together the liberal tradition with notions of 'social service', personal development with 'new standards of citizenship'.[64] The latter part of the report presents information from a survey of adult education and it includes details of projects involving women. Thus, in 1918-19, 57 Women's Institutes in London provided a programme of craft classes in housewifery, laundry, homecraft and in the arts.[65] Set against this familial curriculum, a continuation and amplification of the domesticity and cult of motherhood that marked the time, was the London College of Working Women which had 233 students in 1916/17. In its discussion of women and adult education the final report notes: '... women have far less opportunity than men for continuing their education, owing to the unceasing round of household duties and care of children.'[66]

As an antidote to this the report favours, 'increased educational facilities adapted to the peculiar difficulties and special circumstances of women' which will allow women 'to advance abreast with men along the educational highway'.[67] Conscious of the constraints upon women, both economically and in terms of childcare, the report suggests childcare facilities should be attached to classes.

The report is especially interesting in the section where it discusses the interest shown in education by women who are working outside the home. The interest, the report suggests, has been aroused in a number of ways, 'by propagandist or political organisations', such as the Women's Labour League and the National Union of Women Workers.[68] Thus, women who work outside the home are not ignored in the report, nor are they made invisible by a definition of woman that is only tied to domesticity. In fact, the report elaborated a more complex view distinguishing different types of women.

The first type of woman is one who seeks education in relation to personal development; the second type is spurred by her husband and children, keeping pace with the latter and possibly her husband's involvement in trade union or public affairs. The third type of woman is the woman who has been galvanised by a political or propagandist society, who, 'has come to feel more and more her own lack of intellectual equipment'.[69] Although the now familiar notion that women want education to keep pace with husbands and children is present and represents a view articulated by activist working men, the other suggestion is that women, independent of men or children, have defined a situation in which they wish to pursue educational goals. Woman, in this account, is not bounded by family and the private sphere. She operates in the public world of citizenship and politics and is credited with both intellectual curiosity and political motives. The differentations here are noteworthy given the cult of motherhood and the domestic ideologies operating at the time. The fact that the simple unity of 'woman' had been fractured is, in part, a consequence of the way in which feminist discourses had become part of the agenda of reconstruction. However, we return to more familiar themes when later in the same section it is suggested that women should be encouraged towards a 'sense of form and colour' and this is juxtaposed to an emphasis upon home-based pursuits.[70] Thus, the '1919' Report demonstrates the complexities of the diverse elements that have informed an understanding of the relationship between adult education and the social formation. The contradictions tended to be lost in the years that followed when a state-based local authority adult education produced a curriculum for women that emphasised again their home base and domestic pursuits ignoring the account of adult education offered in 1919 which characterised adult education as a 'movement':

> The adult educational movement is inextricably interwoven with the whole of the organised life of the community. Whilst on the one hand it originates in a desire among individuals for adequate opportunities for self-expression and the cultivation of personal powers and interests, it is, on the other hand, rooted in the social aspirations of the democratic movements of the country. In other words, it rests upon the twin principles of personal development and social service. It aims at satisfying the needs of the individual and at the attainment of new standards of citizenship and a better social order. In some cases the personal motive predominates. In perhaps the great majority of cases the dynamic character of adult education is due to its social motive.[71]

The ideas of one nation, the uplifting and ennobling qualities of adult education are central to the report, but adult education is to be tied to its social service element in the task of reconstruction. Given the ferment of the time and the way in which it developed in the post-war period, it is not surprising that adult education should be constructed as a means whereby citizenship could be more effectively learned and used. On this reading the effect of the report overall is to contribute to the making of the new consensus in post-war society in which management by the state of areas of social life not previously within its purview was crucial. The role of adult education was to engage in educational work as part of the new configuration between state and civil society as Britain moved into the 1920s.

CONCLUSION

Adult education found itself in two camps at once, committed to personal development and the liberal tradition while being conscious of its social responsibilities in times of change. The 1919 Report brings together the contradictions and speaks to them in ways that few other adult education documents do. But, the tensions here were more usually played out in relation to men and the male working class. On the whole, adult education took over from both the liberal hegemony and the concerns of the organised working class a version of woman that defined her as domesticated and home-based until women leapt into the public sphere in new ways that forced adult education to take note. The alternative was to start with the home and move out onto a larger stage in the manner that the Guild and Women's Labour League sought to do. It was quite clear that when women came together in a self-defined educational venture that the issues of women's emancipation were central. Emancipation was not only about votes, it was about freedom from hunger, from unwanted pregnancies, poverty and domesticity. The domesticated woman was never totally accepted by working-class or middle-class women, there was always another woman fighting to get out and for a time it seemed as though education offered a way forward, but it was not a feminist education or even a women's education; it was a patriarchal education which further reinforced the domestic ideology contributing to the hegemonic processes in the social formation. The contradictions of this time resonate with those of our own, the issues surrounding the generation and sustenance of an emancipatory education for women are the central concerns of current debate. An emancipatory education for women was only dreamed of and realised in small pockets through the energy of working-class and middle-class women. Ultimately, adult education worked with a notion of the incompetent woman in need of upgrading through adult education. For all its contradictions feminism was in direct opposition to this. The woman of feminist discourse was competent, active and struggling in and against the state, and the discourses that defined her personal and public world. Those struggles are ongoing.

* This paper is part of a larger project aimed at excavating the gender sub-text in adult education (forthcoming Open University Press). I am grateful to Ali Rattansi for comments on an earlier draft of this paper and to Maureen Cottrell for her technical skills.

REFERENCES

1. The work of Michel Foucault is contained in a number of volumes that analyse the development of the asylum, the hospital, the prison and discourses on sexuality: See for example, Madness and Civilization: A History of Insanity in the Age of Reason (London: Tavistock, 1977); Discipline and Punish: The Birth of the Prison (London: Penguin, 1979); Power/Knowledge. Selected Interviews and Other Writings 1972-1977, C. Gordon (ed.) (Brighton: Harvester Press, 1980).

2. CCCS, Unpopular Education: Schooling and Social Democracy in England since 1944 (London: Hutchinson, 1981), p.16.

3. Cf. Rachel Harrison and Frank Mort, 'Patriarchal Aspects of Nineteenth-Century State Formation: Property Relations, Marriage and Divorce and Sexuality', in P. Corrigan (ed.), Capitalism, State Formation and Marxist Theory (London: Quartet, 1980), pp.79-109.

4. Jane Rendell, The Origins of Modern Feminism: Women in Britain, France and the United States, 1780-1860 (New York: Schoken Books, 1984), pp.3-5.

5. Ibid., p.1.

6. Olive Banks, Faces of Feminism: A Study of Feminism as a Social Movement (Oxford: Martin Robertson, 1981).

7. Sheila Rowbotham, Hidden from History: Three Hundred Years of Women's Oppression and the Fight Against It (London: Pluto Press, 1973), p.49.

8. Keith Burgess, The Challenge of Labour: Shaping British Society 1850-1930 (London: Croom Helm, 1980), p.21. For an author who wishes to use Gramscian analysis there is little here about the deeply contradictory nature of the artisan sector of the working class. See, Hinton below for an alternative analysis.

9. Ibid., pp.36-7.

10. But see Annmarie Turnbull, 'So Extremely Like Parliament: the work of the women members of the London

School Board, 1870-1904', in London Feminist History Group (eds), The Sexual Dynamics of History: Men's Power, Women's Resistance (Pluto Press, 1983), pp.120-33.

11. James Hinton, Labour and Socialism: A History of the British Labour Movement 1867-1974 (Brighton: Wheatsheaf, 1983); E.J. Hobsbawm, The Age of Capital (London: Abacus, 1977); E.J. Hobsbawm, Industry and Empire (London: Penguin, 1969).

12. See Stuart Hall and Bill Schwarz, 'State and Society, 1880-1930', in M. Langan and B. Schwartz (eds), Crises in the British State 1880-1930 (London: Hutchinson, 1985), pp.7-32. And S. Hall, 'The Rise of the representative/interventionist State 1880-1920s', in G. McLennan et al. (eds), State and Society in Contemporary Britain: A Critical Introduction (Cambridge: Polity Press, 1984), pp.7-49.

13. Ibid., p.10.

14. Hinton, Labour and Socialism, p.32.

15. Jonathan Ree, Proletarian Philosophies: Problems in Socialist Culture in Britain, 1900-1940 (Oxford: OUP, 1984), p.6.

16. Hannah Mitchell, The Hard Way Up (Virago, 1977).

17. Ree, Proletarian Philosophies, p.17.

18. Ibid. See also Sheila Rowbotham, 'Travellers in a Strange Country: Responses of Working-Class Students to the University Extension Movement 1873-1910', History Workshop Journal (Autumn 1981), pp.63-95.

19. Ree, Proletarian Philosophies p.18.

20. Vera Brittain, Testament of Youth: An Autobiographical Study of the Years 1900-1925 (London: Virago, 1977). First published 1933.

21. R. Taylor, K. Rockhill and R. Fieldhouse, University Adult Education in England and the USA: A Reappraisal of the Liberal Tradition (London: Croom Helm, 1985).

22. Ibid., p.19.

23. Ibid., p.20.

24. Mary Stocks, The Workers' Educational Association: The First Fifty Years (London: Allen & Unwin, 1953) p.27. See in relation to 'divine inspiration', A. Mansbridge, The Kingdom of the Mind (Dent, 1944).

25. Stocks, The WEA, pp.48-9; and A. Mansbridge, The Trodden Road, p.63.

26. Stocks, The WEA, p.52-3.

27. Ibid.

28. Ibid.

29. Ibid.

30. W.W. Craik, The Central Labour College 1909-29 (Lawrence & Wishart, 1964); J.P.M. Millar, The Labour College Movement (London: NCLC, 1979).

31. Craik, The Central Labour Colleges, p.103.

32. Ibid., pp.172-86.

33. Millar, The Labour College Movement, p.108.

34. Sheila Ferguson, 'Labour Women and the Social Services', in Lucy Middleton (ed.), Women in the Labour Movement (London: Croom Helm, 1977), pp.38-56, p.40; Margherita Rendell, 'The Contribution of the Women's Labour League to the winning of the franchise', in Women in the Labour Movement.

35. Ibid.

36. See Mary Stocks, Eleanor Rathbone (London: Gollancz, 1984).

37. Rendell, The Origins of Modern Feminism, p.58.

38. Ibid., p.69.

39. Ibid., p.74.

40. J.F.C. Harrison, Learning and Living 1790-1960 (London: Routledge, 1961), p.105.

41. Jean Gaffin, 'Women and Co-operation', in Middleton (ed.), Women in the Labour Movement, pp.113-42. See also, Margaret Llewellyn Davies (ed.), Life As We Have Known It: by Co-operative Working Women (Virago, 1977; first published 1931). Jean Gaffin and David Thomas, Caring and Sharing: The Centenary History of the Co-operative Women's Guild (Manchester: Co-operative Union, 1983).

42. Gaffin, Women and Co-operation, p.117.

43. Ibid., p.118-19.

44. Women's Co-operative Guild, Maternity, Letters from Working Women (London: Bell, 1915).

45. Clearly evidenced in M.L. Davies, Life As We Have Known It.

46. Ibid., p.141.

47. Rowbotham, Hidden from History, p.90.

48. Hinton, Labour and Socialism, p.77.

49. Duffin, The Conspicuous Consumptive, p.88.

50. See, for example, S. Rowbotham, A New World for Women: Stella Browne, Socialist Feminist (London: Pluto Press, 1977).

51. Anna Davin, 'Imperialism and Motherhood', History Workshop Journal, 5 (Spring 1978), pp.9-65, p.13.

52. Ibid., p.42. Davin notes that, in 1913, 150 received grants and by 1918, 290. See also, Jane Lewis, 'The Working-Class Wife and Mother and State Intervention 1870-1918' in

idem., Labour and Love: Women's Experiences of Home and Family 1850-1940 (Oxford: Basil Blackwell, 1986), pp.100-20.

53. See, Davin, Imperialism and Motherhood, p.57.

54. Ibid., p.53.

55. Ibid., p.56.

56. Jane Lewis, Women in England 1870-1950: Sexual Divisions and Social Change (Brighton: Wheatsheaf, 1984), p.151.

57. Rowbotham, Hidden from History, notes p.110. In 1911 there were about 1,400,000 women in private domestic service. During the war about 400,000 of these women left to do other work. Between 1914-1918 a total of 792,000 entered industry. See also Roberts, A Woman's Place.

58. Elizabeth Roberts, A Woman's Place: An Oral History of Working Class Women 1890-1940 (Oxford: Blackwell, 1984).

59. The 1919 Report, the Final and Interim Reports of the Adult Education Committee of the Ministry of Reconstruction 1918-1919 (HMSO, 1919). Republished by Nottingham University, 1980.

60. Ibid., p.53.

61. Ibid., p.82.

62. Ibid.

63. Ibid., p.92.

64. Ibid., p.168.

65. Ibid., p.190.

66. Ibid., p.255.

67. Ibid.

68. Ibid.

69. Ibid., p.261.

70. Ibid., p.262.

71. Ibid., p.168.

4

Gramsci, Freire and Illich:
Their Contributions to Education for Socialism

Paula Allman*

INTRODUCTION

Whether considering education as a preparation for
socialism or as a means of sustaining socialism the most
central feature must be the role of human agency. E.P.
Thompson claims that the main lesson of historical
materialism is 'the crucial ambivalence of our human
presence in our own history, part subjects, part objects, the
voluntary agents of our own involuntary determinants'.[1]
However, as Perry Anderson has argued, while making a
case for the human agent in history as opposed to a
structurally determined object, Thompson's concept of
agency doesn't go far enough 'what's missing ... is any due
complementary emphasis on the cognitive dimensions of
agency'.[2] Anderson's point is of crucial importance if we are
to establish a concept of agency in which critical and
systematic thought is interwoven with action in the creation
and continuous recreation of our social and material
conditions.

However Anderson is only reminding us of the
centrality of the cognitive dimension in human agency. Marx
was always explicit about the interrelationship of critical
thought and action. He explained that we must come to a
critical understanding of how ideas, the ideology of the
dominant classes, deceive us by blinding us to our real
interests. However that understanding was only a beginning;
it could not eliminate the deceptions. We can only remove
them by acting, by changing the social relations which
support them.[3] It is within this Marxist concept of human
agency that the contributions of Gramsci, Freire and Illich
to education for socialism will be evaluated in this chapter.

QUESTIONS AND BACKGROUND

To determine whether these contributions inform our work

for a realisation of 'conscious human agency', I shall ask the following questions:

1. To what extent do they offer us an understanding of ideology and how dominant ideologies function?
2. Do they help us to understand whether our task is a) to develop a form of thinking which supersedes ideological thought; or whether it is b) to develop a more just and ethical (i.e. a more expansive) ideology, which reflects the interests of all human beings rather than just those of the dominant classes?[4]
3. Do they offer an approach to education aimed at the critical investigation of thinking and experience and aimed at enabling people to consciously transform ideas and social relations?
4. To what extent do they offer us ideas which are not vulnerable to incorporation or misinterpretation?

The last two questions need little explanation but to explain why the first two are critical gauges of whether radical intent results in radical effect, I must digress briefly into the hard but important lessons my own experience has taught. Four years ago I was given the opportunity to reorganise the major part of a diploma course for adult and community educators. Instead of the traditional discipline or subject focus, that part of the course was organised around the problems and issues which confronted the learning group in their own educational work with adults. Though the approach entailed a great deal more than just a change of focus, the important point is that it was based on Freire's writings and was intended as a radical initiative. The approach failed to create a radical effect because I failed to confront the issue of ideology.

The importance of ideology emerged as we became involved in an exploration of the first problem identified by the group. Overwhelmingly their central concern was how to increase the participation of working-class people in the programmes and courses they had on offer. The types of explanation that prevailed as the group discussed this problem focused on either working-class 'apathy' or their own professional incompetence in advertising and publicity. Whether current provision served the interests of working-class people or whether it simply was a replay of the same antagonistic messages communicated by 'schooling' were questions voiced by only a few group members. Very quickly, however, it became clear that the competing explanations derived from very different and competing conceptions of 'class'. Therefore we decided to explore these conceptions of class through academic theory and through testing them with reference to real or material conditions. It was that exploration which first led me to recognise the degree to which liberal democratic ideology is embedded in both the form and content of education.

It is important to mention that this diploma course is located in an institution which champions the 'liberal tradition' of education. What was revealing, however, was how deeply engrained that tradition was in each of us. One of the most essential features of the liberal tradition is the notion of 'balance'. As a colleague recently described it, 'it's the tradition that makes full use of the fact that most humans have two hands, i.e. the rhetoric of ... on the one hand this, and on the other hand that'.[5] The two hands were present in our initial discussion of working-class participation and continued to influence us in our study of class. We traced the post-war circumstances which led to sociological and commonsense concepts of class as something defined according to purchasing power and living standards. We also looked at Marx's concept of class as a relation to the means as well as the ownership, planning and control of production. Our discussions continued to be couched within the liberal rhetoric of 'on the one hand this, and on the other hand that'.

The concept of class which continued to influence the thinking of most colleagues in our group was the one which located class, and so defined it, in terms of the sphere of consumption and exchange. It also became increasingly apparent that starting from that definition makes the working class a problem, a disadvantaged target group, and just as inevitably the educational response focuses on ways of increasing access to current provision as a means to social and economic mobility. Some of us tried to pose this as a problem. Though it was not clear then what we were confronting was not only the content of liberal-democratic ideology but the thought processes which sustain it. We were not dealing with what could have been accurately termed a misconception because the preferred concept did not have a basis in the real relations and experiences of group members. But, as I have learned since, this conjuncture of the dominant ideology with some fragment or partial aspect of real life is one of the very powerful ways in which this ideology works.

That first topic or issue and all the questions it raised eventually led me to Gramsci's[6] work. More recently, as I shall discuss in detail later, my search for a deeper understanding of ideology has led to the writings of Althusser,[7] Poulantzas,[8] Hall,[9] Larrain[10] and back to Marx[11] himself. That search has convinced me that understanding ideology and how it functions is crucial to the creation of education for socialism. To ignore it, as I did at first, is to risk consequences which are far from radical. The worst of these is that our challenge, whether at the level of ideas or at the level of relating, communicating and acting, remains framed and therefore trapped within the dominant ideological discourse rather than aimed at disarticulating that frame and rearticulating our own transformed socialist frame.[12]

The second question, stated previously, has to do with whether our task is to create a counter-, more expansive, ideology or a type of thinking and understanding which is capable of critically breaking through ideology and therefore superseding it. The question began to germinate during our work on 'class' but derived especially from our attempts to understand the nature of dialectic thought. At the level of ideas, dominant ideologies produce an explanation of what is real and natural by the way in which certain social ideas are linked together forming a specific discourse. They also produce meaning by the way in which they focus or locate ideas. These processes, however, are actually forms of dislocation or displacement that are supported by formal logic or what is commonly referred to as 'rational' thought. Dialectic logic/thinking, the conceptual tool fully developed by Marx in his mature writings, also seeks to produce an explanation, but its processes differ in many fundamental ways from those utilised in our traditional mode of logic. It is important to examine a few of these differences in order to see how explanations structured within and deriving from these contrasting modes of logic would differ.

Dialectic thinking starts from the concept that our material world is formed out of contradictory elements and tendencies. These contradictions create a material world which is constantly moving and changing. By focusing on the contradictions, in their movement, we can understand how the 'internal relations', (i.e. the interaction of the contradictions), regulate the development of things, people and societies.[13] However, dialectic thought also involves simultaneously focusing on another type of movement. What we experience as real or natural has been removed from its historical and economic antecedents; therefore dialectic thinking also must trace back a current result or appearance to its contradictory source, its essence, be it historic, economic or both.

Formal logic or rational thought begins from a concept of the 'real' world as given or natural and conforming to universal laws. It follows that if human beings can discover these laws, they can control reality. According to this mode of logic, contradiction is an error in thinking; therefore the aim is to eliminate it. Eliminating contradiction is normally accomplished by the process of abstraction in which the object of thought is removed from the movement and total context of our material conditions. Once it has been displaced in this manner the object can be relocated in a specific or partial aspect of the total context. For example, we tend to think about a concept such as equality in terms of the abstract legal rhetoric that we are all equal before the eyes of the law. However when we consider the material and social 'inequalities' that exist in the real conditons of our lives the illusions shatter; they shatter because the contradictions reappear. Formal logic is a conceptual tool which is only useful for understanding things which are static and abstract, or more cynically, for rendering them as such. However, if our thinking is not dehistoricised and decontextualised, we know that human beings exist in complex and changing conditions. Therefore the only understanding of these things which we can cull from formal logic is a distorted one.

One question which needs our urgent attention is whether the explanations and understandings produced by dialectic thought, though more accurate, are still ideological. And that question ties in with deciding whether our primary aim is to produce a counter-system of ideas about social reality or a counter-system of thinking about, understanding and explaining it.

Of the contributors, the only one who does not tackle these questions is Ivan Illich. I shall begin this critique with his work.

IVAN ILLICH: HIS CONTRIBUTION

Illich's critique of schooling sounds similar in many ways to Freire's, but Illich locates the cause of the problem within institutions and the professionals who service them rather than within the socio-economic structures and relations of western societies. As a consequence, he focuses on symptoms or appearances and ignores the fact that these are the historical results of the economic organisation of society. Therefore both his critique and his strategies for change neglect any consideration of the existence and consequences of ideology. Since he fails to recognise the contradictory nature of material conditons as well as its ideological masking, his strategy is to eliminate the symptoms leaving the actual causes intact and, I would argue, even more capable of creating social divisions and inequalities.

However, there is no doubt that Illich fully intended his critique and his remedies to be radical. The real problem has to do with how Illich thinks about the problems of schooling and other institutional forms. His thinking provides a good example of how radical critique frequently becomes trapped along a one-dimensional or dichotomous continuum on which the poles are defined by the dominant ideology and culture. This leads Illich to the conclusion that since schooling is predominantly a negative experience with negative consequences for human nature we must 'de-school' or in other words eliminate the contradiction. Unfortunately, dichotomised analysis of a problem is easy to grasp and therefore holds great appeal. It appeals because change vis-à-vis elimination sounds easier than a strategy of transformation and the critical understanding and struggle that it implies. What remains after the dissolution of any sympton or appearance are the social relations which produced it in the first place and which will continue to produce symptoms until the relations are transformed. This is further complicated in Illich's writings because the major focus of his critique has to do with the organisation and location of education. He fails critically to consider traditional concepts of learning, thinking and knowledge and how these concepts legitimise and reinforce the social relations of schooling. As a consequence, it is difficult to see how 'schooling' in the coffee bar would constitute a fundamentally different and more enriching learning experience than it does in its present location. Knowledge, for example, remains a commodity that one person possesses and another wishes to consume.

Conversely some of Illich's suggestions, such as networks or learning webs, might be utilised effectively within an established socialist society. However to propose them for the 'developing' countries or any society constrained by national or multinational capitalism and the ideologies that help sustain these forms of economic organisation is to suggest piecemeal tactics which can lead only to securing further privilege for the dominant groups in these societies.

For all these reasons, Illich's ideas have become extremely vulnerable to incorporation within liberal as well as conservative frameworks. In the British context of the 1980s, we can see clearly where the following Illich conclusion regarding institutions takes us:

> Only by channelling dollars away from the institutions which now treat health, education and welfare can the further improvishment resulting from their disabling side effects be stopped.[14]

A Conservative government would like nothing better than to see us channel our money into insurance for private medicine or into private schools and charities. However, Illich's form of criticism hits a true note in terms of people's experiences with the institutions of our British welfare state. Health care at its very best should be that which conceives care as other than a commodity to be purchased directly by individuals or indirectly via government financing. It would be a service which actually sought to increase our perceived health-care needs and the same would apply to education and other aspects of social welfare. Our present institutions have developed in an alienating manner because they were conceived as a means of distributing, more fairly, services already realised as commodities rather than being constituted so as to challenge and transform these concepts. However to locate the problem within some sort of mystical quality of institutions per se is to disguise the actual source of the problem.

There is a great deal of merit, however, in Illich's identification of the problems and effects of institutions, professionalism and the intrusion of the USA, in particular, into the affairs of other nations. When his writings first

91

appeared in the 1960s, he succeeded in raising the consciousness of many people who felt genuine dissatisfaction. However, over the past twenty years, that 'feeling' of dissatisfaction and the response to it has clearly separated those people who want real social and economic transformation from those who either will settle for reform or those who simply wish to confront authority for the sake of libertarian values. During that period, those desiring real change have either offered or been informed by much more complex critiques of institutions and professionalism. Therefore, to continue in the 1980s to seek inspiration and understanding from Illich is to risk incorporation not just within reformist policy but equally and increasingly within the lair of neo-conservatism.

FREIRE AND GRAMSCI: SUBSTANTIVE CONTRIBUTIONS TO EDUCATION FOR SOCIALISM

When conceptualised together, the ideas of Freire and Gramsci offer a socialist approach to education which locates politics in education and education in politics. This is primarily because their ideas are informed by their practice; and because these are ideas grounded in specific forms of radical practice they should be assessed with reference to those locations. Freire's practice is specifically educational whereas Gramsci's was political activity and organisation. This, of course, affects the focus of their analyses as well as the nature of their contributions. Where they relate most clearly is in Freire's consideration of the political nature of education and in Gramsci's consideration of the educational nature of politics; it is within these areas that we find their important contribution to education for socialism.

Freire has moved from discussing oppression in a manner which led to the simplistic interpretation that it was something which we should become aware of and denounce[15] to a more explicit analysis of how oppression is the result of specific conditions that cannot be removed simply by either awareness or verbal denunciations.

> ... human beings do not get beyond the concrete situation, the conditions in which they find themselves, only by their consciousness or their intentions - however good those intentions may be.

... praxis is not blind action, deprived of intention and finality. It is action and reflection. ... In this sense, subjectivism - throwing itself into a simple verbal denunciation of social injustice ... while leaving intact the structure of society is just as negative as mistrusting a rigorous and permanent scientific analysis of objective reality ...[16]

Elsewhere in this article and others written since 1973, Freire has increasingly equated oppression with the class structure and class relations of capitalist societies. However, throughout his writings he adheres to a vision of socialism created and continuously recreated by conscious human agency rather than a socialism created and administered by elites; it is they he is referring to as 'mistrusting' in the passage above.

Freire's most basic tenet about education for socialism is that 'all true education investigates thinking'.[17] This is the only way to enable people to critically undermine their own collusion with oppression.

Manipulated by the ruling classes' myths, the dominated classes reflect a consciousness which is not properly their own. Hence their reformist tendencies. Permeated by the ruling class ideology, their aspirations to a large degree, do not correspond to their authentic being. These aspirations are superimposed by the most diversified means of social manipulation.[18]

Later in that article he expands on a variety of practices which the dominant classes employ in order to prevent the dominated classes from seeing themselves as dominated. One such practice is an ideological process by which one type of oppression is played off against another and people consequently are led to focus on their own specific form of oppression rather than understanding how one form links with another to constitute a structure of oppression. Recognition of this structure of oppression is an essential aspect of what Freire refers to as 'conscientisation'. Ironically, however, that concept has frequently been equated with specifically focused 'consciousness raising', i.e. precisely the limited and fragmented focus against which he cautions us and which, when confined to a particular type of oppression, leads to action that is inadequate with reference to the total historical situation.[19]

Readers who come to Freire's writings with an understanding of ideology, can readily interpret the idea of education investigating thinking as a process of ideology critique.[20] With that grounding much of what Freire writes can be seen as advocating a critical investigation of the way in which ideology is embedded in common sense, magical consciousness (what Gramsci terms folklore) and sometimes even revolutionary consciousness and practice. In fact, as far back as 1973, he uses ideology in the sense I am using it in this essay.

> I believe that one of the most difficult problems confronting a revolutionary party in the preparation of its militant cadres consists in rising above the canyon between the revolutionary option formulated verbally by the militants and the practice which is not always really revolutionary. The petit bourgeois [liberal-democractic] ideology that has permeated them in their class conditions interferes with what should be their revolutionary practice. ... It's in this sense that methodological errors are always an expression of an ideological vision. ... In so doing all they do is reproduce the dichotomy - typical of a class society - between teaching and learning. ... They refuse to learn with the people. ... Because of all this I'm convinced that the effort to clarify the process of ideologizing must make up one of the necessary introductory points in every seminar for preparing militants ...[21]

However, Freire's analyses of ideology and what we can take to be its opposite (viz. permanent scientific analysis, see note 14) are not comprehensive enough to do more than point us in the right direction.

A number of radical educators have argued that this sort of vagueness in Freire's writings lends itself to misappropriation by liberal-humanist, progressive educators who relentlessly reduce everything to methods, techniques or process. I agree that Freire's ideas have been and can be used in ways which are anything but radical. However this is a problem which lies at the point of reception not with the ideas, themselves. I also seriously doubt that further clarification or depth of analysis, on Freire's part, would make any difference to the way in which readers who are unaware of the sources and structure of oppression interpret his writings. Radical educators can undertake these clarification and analytical tasks themselves, indeed, they will have to do so once they become engaged in an approach to learning aimed at transforming the social relations of education.

Freire's educational approach is concerned with these transformations. It is an approach which enables us to challenge dominant ideologies as expressed and embedded in our thinking, feelings and actions. In the current context of western society and the exploited countries of the world, this approach should be conceived as a preparation for socialism, i.e. pre-figurative work.[22] However, in a post-revolutionary context, it is, in my opinion, the means by which conscious human agency would be constantly sustained.

Some misinterpretations of Freire's ideas have resulted from the failure of adult and community educators to distinguish between a philosophical approach to education and educational methods. Freire stresses that methods must be worked out specifically in accord with the cultural and historical context in which they are to be used.[23] Futhermore, simply to apply the methods which Freire utilised in literacy campaigns without fully comprehending the philosophical approach leads to gross misapplications of his ideas. Freire's approach is underpinned by two interrelated assumptions which are made explicit through a transformed type of communication which he calls dialogue. One assumption deals with what it means to be fully human and the other deals with the nature of education. Every aspect of the approach derives from these assumptions; therefore to use the approach in the radical way Freire intends it to be used one must share these assumptions.

For Freire the meaning of being 'fully human' entails the type of critically conscious agency, referred to earlier in this chapter, a human agency which is capable of planning and executing the transformation of society at all levels. However when Freire discusses his meaning of humanness he is referring to a potential, a possibility, rather than some lost human essence. According to Freire, people are conditioned in thought and behaviour to serve the interests of their oppressors, but they have the potential to overcome that conditioning.[24] As a corollary education can serve

95

either to maintain that conditioning or to enable people to become critically aware of it and critically engaged in transforming the relations which sustain it.

Therefore the most fundamental feature of Freire's approach is the transformation of relations. 'Banking education', i.e. education which domesticates and conditions people, is structured around a set of interlocking relations all of which are characterised by domination/subordination. Teachers are dominant over learners; a few learners, through competition, attain dominance over all the others; academic, legitimated, already existing knowledge not only dominates but excludes the possibility of creating new knowledge and theory or abstract thought dominates concrete thought and action which are usually deemed to be secondary or even inappropriate. To transform these relations entails overcoming the domination/subordination rather than eliminating either of the relating elements. Teachers initiate the transformation process by first recognising the oppressive and anti-educational nature of these relations, and then by challenging themselves and the learners to struggle together to create an entirely different set of interlocking relations. However, experience has taught me that the most crucial, the lynchpin, of all these relations is the one between all learners, and this includes teachers, and knowledge.

> While in education for domestication one cannot speak of a knowable object but only of knowledge which is complete, which the educator possesses and transfers to the educatee, in education for liberation there is no complete knowledge possessed by the educator, but a knowable object which mediates educator and educatee as subjects in the knowing process. Dialogue is established as the seal of the epistemological relationship between subjects in the knowing process.[25]

Knowledge is no longer seen as fixed but as a critical process of understanding a material reality which is moving and changing. Furthermore, the acquisition of knowledge ceases to be the ultimate objective of education. Instead the focus is relocated within the themes, issues or problems, viz. the 'knowable objects' of the learners' reality. Knowledge remains, of course, but becomes a tool for understanding, and as such its validity must be continuously subjected to testing against the movement of material conditions.

Knowing, when seen as a process rather than a commodity, necessitates interdependence and collaboration between learners and between learners and teachers rather than competition in the first relation and deference in the second. Teachers and learners work together to co-investigate their reality, to test the validity of existing knowledge and to create new knowledge in the process. This reveals the structure of oppression and its causes and develops an intolerance of it. Most importantly, the process develops the critical consciousness through which people can transform these conditons. But even before this reunion of critical thought with radical action, learners are prepared to relate and to live in a radically different way through the transformed communicative relations of dialogue.

Dialogue is an active and critical form of group communication in which people work collaboratively to create a more complex way of understanding some object or theme of their reality. It entails a conscious challenge to and tranformation of the relations and rituals of our normal form of group communication, discussion, wherein, though socially gathered, people operate as separate individuals verbally expressing, sometimes exchanging, what they already know. Dialogue is also the means by which people make explicit the assumptions about humanness and education, discussed previously, as well as the means through which they express the transformed relations.

When Freire proposes that education for liberation involves creating new knowledge and describes how this can be accomplished through dialogue, he comes quite close to defining what he means by 'a permanent scientific analysis'. It seems to me that what he is referring to is synonymous with the description I gave earlier of dialectic thinking. Consequently it would appear that Freire is advocating a way of thinking which is capable of superseding ideological thought, but since he does not offer us a comprehensive analysis of ideological thought or ideology, it is not clear where he stands on this crucial issue.

Nevertheless Freire's approach to education does offer a framework within which people can work together to understand ideology as well as to counter it. As mentioned previously, Marx made it quite clear that ideological deception, i.e. how it functions, can be understood but will remain until we change the social relations that produce it.

97

Within traditional approaches to education we can, of course, transfer to learners our knowledge about ideology and how it works. However even if we could guarantee that they had received or understood this knowledge, we would all continue to exist within what Marx referred to as the 'veil of deception' until the essential social relations were transformed. Obviously educational relations are not the most essential ones, but until educators challenge, and together with learners, transform the oppressive relations of 'banking education' they can hardly pretend to be preparing themselves or others to undertake the larger-scale and more essential changes that are necessary.

Pedagogy of the Oppressed which contains the most complete expression of Freire's approach, became available in Britain at a time when radical adult and community educators already had begun to disagree over the issue of whether process or content should be the central focus of radical practice. Regardless of which side one took in the ensuing debate, the response was framed within the ideology of the liberal tradition. The interpretations of Freire's ideas were influenced by liberal concerns and assumptions which went unexamined and consequently unchallenged. 'Process radicals' missed the fundamental concept of transforming relations but embraced Freire's concern for the oppressed as support for student-centred methods, negotiated curricula, active and experiential learning, as well as the rejection of objective or academic knowledge. The feminist movement added further fuel to that rejection and at one point began unwittingly to constitute a new form of 'positivism' which located 'truth' in subjectivity rather than objectivity; consequently ignoring the way in which ideology can be embedded also in feeling or emotion.[26]

'Content radicals' also missed the crucial concept of transformation and tended to dismiss Freire because they could see no space for the insertion of radical content or explanation. The important factor in both cases, however, is not the misinterpretation but that in the absence of an understanding of ideology misinterpretation is bound to occur. Until we begin to understand ideology and the way in which it is embedded in our thinking and lived relations, we shall continue to interpret, to think and to act with an ideology which is not appropriate for socialist education.

Over the past fifteen years a great deal has happened which makes possible a radical rereading of Freire. Socialist educators have accumulated a variety of experiences in attempting radical initiatives within the dominant liberal-democratic framework. The experiences, alone, might have taught only frustration, but they have been complemented by increasingly sophisticated anlayses of liberal education, social-democratic politics and ideology. The publication of Gramsci's work in English has been one of the most important influences in preparing us for the rereading and radical use of Freire's ideas.

Gramsci's most important contribution to socialism, in general, is his reformulation of revolutionary strategy, a strategy which is essentially 'education for socialism'. Prior to Gramsci, revolutionary strategy was focused primarily on seizing the political apparatuses of the state. Gramsci did not dismiss this strategy but argued that in western capitalist societies a great deal of pre-figurative work must be accomplished first. This argument is based on his analysis of the difference between how power was exercised in western as opposed to eastern societies, such as Russia. Under advanced western capitalism, civil society as an instrument of power is well developed. Civil society is made up of private organisations (e.g. trade unions, churches, political parties, cultural associations, the family) i.e. all those forms of social organisation which are distinct from the organisation of production and the political apparatuses of the state.[27] Power is exercised and maintained through ethical and political leadership, or what Gramsci calls hegemony. Hegemony elicits consent from people rather than coercing them to act, relate and think in certain ways. Of course, if this hegemony begins to break down, then the coercive apparatuses of political society will be utilised to maintain order and wield power; and this is why revolution must entail also the seizing of these apparatuses.[28] The first stage of socialist revolution, which infuses into and must endure after a seizure of the state, is to transform the hegemony in civil society in order to create a broad-based collective will for socialist revolution. Though he does not use the term, it is quite clear that Gramsci's concept of socialism, and even more so communism, is one which entails conscious human agency.[29]

Hegemony is cemented together by ideology. However Gramsci makes it quite clear that the meaning of ideology has undergone an erroneous change. Therefore he distinguishes between using the term to mean 'the science of ideas' and the 'analysis of the origin of ideas', the original meaning, and using the term to refer to a 'system of ideas', the error.[30] He was also the first Marxist in this century to expand the concept of ideology by locating its expression not just in ideas and thought but also in the material relations, practices and fabric of society, some of which but not all of which could be directly traced to the current social relations of production.[31] Gramsci's analysis also offers important distinctions between the hegemony of the bourgeois class, in Italy what was referred to as 'transformism', and the hegemony which would be necessary within a revolutionary strategy. And because ideology is the cement of hegemony, these distinctions add further to our understanding of what our task is with reference to ideology.

To rule by consent, i.e. to establish hegemony, a class must articulate the interests of other classes and groups to its own interests. Bourgeois hegemony takes advantage of people's commonsense conceptions of the world. These conceptions contain the uncritical and unsystematic, the disorganised fragments or substrata of various ideologies, i.e. of 'systems of ideas'. The hegemony of the capitalists is achieved by either the absorption or the neutralisation of both allied and antagonistic groups.[32] Leadership, therefore, is exercised through ideological domination. Gramsci stresses that every hegemonic relation is an educative one;[33] however his analysis of bourgeois hegemony (specifically transformism) reveals that the educative relation is one of domination/subordination, the type of relation Freire identifies as characteristic of class-divided societies. This type of hegemony is fragile for two reasons. The activity of antagonistic groups with reference to their material conditions leads to the expression of a counter-ideology in practice and of which people can become consciously aware. It is also fragile because while the capitalist can make certain concessions to other groups, they can not go so far as to threaten their own class interests. Therefore the ethical and moral bases of their leadership will be shown up in times of economic crisis.[34] Gramsci's analysis of 'transformism' relates to a specific historical condition. On the other hand, his discussion of working-class hegemony, though informed by his previous political activity, suggests a strategy to be realised, a strategy of intellectual and moral reform.

He conceives working-class hegemony as more expansive, better able to articulate the interests of all groups in society, because the interests of the working class are not based on exploitation. Therefore they can make genuine and lasting concessions to other groups and it is in their human interests to do so.[35] There is also the implication, whenever Gramsci refers to this revolutionary strategy, that the educative relation within working-class hegemony must be entirely transformed. This implication becomes clearer when we consider other points raised by Gramsci in his Notebooks.

In a section entitled, 'What is Man?', he posits the notion of human beings as process, as becoming. At any one point in history, they are the ensemble of the social relations entered into, the existing relations and the history of these relations. It follows then, that people are rich in possibilities, they can become more by first recognising how existing relations constrain possibilities and then by transforming those relations. The essence of human nature has the possibility of becoming the result of conscious human agency.[36]

Even Gramsci's concept of people within existing social relations is positive in the sense that he argues that all people are intellectuals, i.e. they think and hold conceptions of the world.[37] This is positive because it rules out the notion of intellectual and moral reform instituted from above, the replacement of one system of ideas by another, and necessitates an educative relation in which people are helped to render an already existing activity, viz. thinking, critical and systematic. The working class must develop its own intellectuals who will be capable of introducing a critical class consciousness into sites of economic, political and social practice. And that introduction must be located within a new type of educative relation.

> ... the relationship between teacher and pupil is active and reciprocal so that every teacher is always a pupil and every pupil a teacher. But the educational relationship should not be restricted to the field of the strictly 'scholastic' ... This form of relationship exists throughout society as a whole and for every individual relative to other individuals ... Every relationship of 'hegemony' is necessarily an educative relationship ...[38]

Earlier in the Notebooks he makes quite clear his conception of what the new educative relationship should lead to when he asks:

... is it better to think, without critical awareness, in a disjointed and episodic way? ... to take part in a conception of the world mechanically imposed ... by one of the many social groups in which everyone is automatically involved ... Or, on the other hand, is it better to work out consciously and critically one's own conception of the world and thus, in connection with the labours of one's own brain, choose one's sphere of activity, take an active part in the creation of the history of the world, be one's own guide, refusing to accept passively and supinely from outside the molding of one's personality?[39]

However, to understand more precisely what Gramsci means by 'working out consciously and critically', it is necessary to draw upon various points he makes about 'the philosophy of praxis', i.e. Marxism. The vast majority of his references to 'the philosophy of praxis' in both his Notebooks and letters indicate that he recognised that Marxism is a mode of thinking capable of breaking through existing ideology and of eventually superseding ideological thought.[40] His awareness of Marx's dialectic method is also evidenced in his application of the method in his analyses of his own concrete historical situation. Another clear indication can be found in a letter written to Tania, on 30 May 1932. In that letter he excitedly postulates that Marx's method not only developed from Hegel but Ricardo's 'whole way of thinking', and he urges Tania to find out if anyone has written anything about this.[41] I shall be returning to the significance of this connection later, but here it is important to note that while others had linked Marx's economic concepts to Ricardo's, no one before Gramsci, except Marx, himself, had established the link between their conceptual methods.

Lynne Lawner, in her introduction to Letters from Prison, is unequivocal in stating what Gramsci's notion of Marxism is:

The point of departure for a Marxist thinker is always culture as a whole not, as many people argue abstractly, a presumed set of Marxist doctrines torn from their original context. Indeed, Marxism demands constant confrontations with a historically determined culture, together with the effort to supersede it - that is, to make the culture scientific by removing every trace of ideology.[42]

However, his concept of Marxism has not always been interpreted in the way Lawner and I are suggesting. If there is some ambiguity, it could be because Gramsci does not offer a comprehensive theory of ideology.[43] However, he does point us in the right direction. His analysis of the ideology which cements bourgeois hegemony indicates that it offers distorted and partial explanations.[44] On the other hand, when he discusses working-class hegemony, he refers to ideology as ideology in the 'highest sense', viz. a system of analysis;[45] but as indicated earlier, that meaning only becomes clear through a careful consideration of what he says about 'the philosophy of praxis'.

With reference to the questions cited earlier in this chapter, Gramsci takes us a long way forward in understanding the dominant ideology of our own society and how this ideology works. He also gives us a clear directive that our task is to replace ideology with a more advanced or developed method of thinking. However, during the struggle to establish hegemony within civil society we are also faced with the task of expressing socialist ideology, a conception of the world and human beings, through transformed social relationships. This solution to the question regarding our task also reveals that the way I orginally posed the question was flawed by dichotomised thinking. Once Gramsci established the materiality of ideology the answer regarding strategy became more complicated, but he clearly suggests how we must deal with that complexity, i.e. to conceive of it and deal with it as a twofold task. One aspect of the task is the development of a mode of thinking and the other aspect involves countering the expression of ideology in our material relations and practices by transforming those relations and practices.

This twofold task or strategy is also Gramsci's major contribution to an educational approach. It was not his intent to formulate an educational approach, but his discussion of the educative relationship is entirely compatible with Freire's emphasis on transforming relations. Freire takes us much further in understanding which relations need to be transformed and in understanding what these transformations would entail. However Gramsci's analysis of the material expressions of ideology enables us to understand more fully what the purpose of Freirean dialogue is and how it relates to an overall struggle for socialist hegemony. Dialogue, according to Freire, is the seal of a transformed epistemological relationship but is also the seal of the educative relationship appropriate for socialist hegemony.

Freire offers the principles which establish a process of dialogue; however it is Gramsci who provides example after example of dialogue in practice. Because of his circumstances these examples are not of dialogue with groups of people but of attempts, in isolation, to dialogue with Marxist and other intellectuals. There are also examples of how dialogue can be applied to one's own concrete historical situation as well as to other periods of history. Whether engaging with ideas on material conditions, in all these examples of dialogue, Gramsci begins with the dialectical concepts of contradiction and movement and then proceeds to criticise the problems but equally to draw out the 'good sense' and 'good tendencies'.[46] This is exactly the way in which each participant in a group dialogue must engage with each other's thinking, and the rigour he brings to these encounters provides a good example of how the mental labour of thinking and learning must be equally as arduous as manual labour.

Finally we must consider whether Gramsci's ideas are vulnerable to incorporation or misinterpretation either because of some problem located in the ideas or because of the way they have been interpreted. There is no question that Gramsci's ideas, especially those which deal with education, have been misinterpreted.[47] This is due in part to the style of the Prison Notebooks which demands the sort of serious reading and study one would undertake if trying to interpret history from primary source documents. His ideas about education cannot be comprehended without careful analysis of how he developed other concepts and without posing fundamental questions regarding the nature of ideology and the dialectic method. Misinterpretations have also occurred when Gramsci's persistence in using the dialectic method has been ignored. For example, Laclau and Mouffe have argued that Gramsci's concept of hegemony needs to be democratised because '... moral and intellectual leadership [hegemony] could still be understood as the ideological inculcation by a hegemonic class of a whole range of subordinate sectors'.[48]

Their fear has been fuelled, of course, by the way in which some people have interpreted Gramsci, but the problem is firmly with those interpretations rather than the ideas. The fear is grounded in a static conception of the economic base and the class composition arising from it; however Gramsci's conceptions are never static. Throughout his prison writings there is an insistence that political strategy must derive from a critical analysis of the material conditions present at the time of anlaysis, i.e. an insistence on conceptualising the dialectic movement of material and social forces.

When considered together, Gramsci and Freire's contributions go a long way towards providing a strategy for education for socialism. Gramsci, of course, takes us far beyond the specific concerns of organised education yet enables us to understand the need for an educative relationship in every aspect of political practice. Freire offers us a specific approach by which we can seek to establish an appropriate set of socialist educative relationships. The only question towards which neither Freire or Gramsci takes us quite far enough is the one which pertains to our understanding of ideology. If we are to achieve a radical effect in specifically education or broadly the whole of civil society, we must seek a more comprehensive understanding of ideology. We can move someway forward towards that understanding by considering other contributions that help us to distinguish between science and ideology.

SCIENCE AND IDEOLOGY

Marx himself contributed a great deal to our understanding of ideology but much of what he said seems to have been forgotten, ignored or misinterpreted. Part of that tendency can be attributed to the confusion over the relation between science and ideology. This confusion may have been unavoidable because even in Marx's time the term science had acquired the dominant meaning of knowledge, truth or a fixed body of content. At times Marx uses this meaning but he also uses science to indicate a conceptual method. Taking into consideration the context wherein he uses the term, the distinction between these two meanings is clear in Marx's writings, but perhaps only when one reads Marx with the understanding that advances in science have never been solely about the accumulation of knowledge. They also entail the development of new conceptual tools capable of deriving from a quantity of evidence a new quality of understanding. In fact, Marx predicted what would happen within Marxism in his analysis of what had happened to Ricardo's economics, viz. that those who followed Ricardo would focus on the knowledge generated by his method rather than the method, therefore as the material conditions which gave rise to the knowledge changed, the knowledge would become ideological dogma.[49]

According to Marx three conditions must pertain for an idea or set of ideas (and if we draw on Gramsci, a set of material relations or practices) to be considered ideology. These ideas, practices or relations must conceal contradiction; they also conceal the way in which they serve the interests of dominant classes, and they conceal that the appearance we observe is an historical result - they dehistoricise.[50] Marx uses these conditions to reveal what happened to Ricardo's economic theory. Marx considered Ricardo's theory, though erroneous, to be scientific because his method involved the study of contradictions. The errors in the concepts generated by the method were made because the study took place when the contradictions were just emerging, i.e. between the transition from one historical epoch to another. In Marx's time, these contradictions had become fully manifest; therefore he considered that classical economics had become ideology because it was based on the congealed concepts generated by Ricardo's method rather than the application of the method within the existing material conditions.

> Knowledge has to be judged not only in relation to the social contradictions present at the moment of the production of such knowledge, but also in relation to the contradictions present at the moment of passing judgement. A piece of knowledge be it correct or erroneous, but not at first ideological, can perfectly become ideological if certain new contradictions come into existence and are consequently objectively concealed by that knowledge.[51]

Another essential point which Marx makes about ideology is the one referred to much earlier in this chapter, viz. that science does not eliminate ideology.[52]

Although science has discovered its real essence,

this appearance, Marx argues, remains for the producers as real and final as the fact that the atmosphere remains unaltered after the scientific discovery of its component gases. One may dispel the deceptive appearances only by practically changing the social relations which support them.[53]

In the past a great deal of Marxist theorising seems to have been confused regarding the distinction between the two meanings of science in Marx's writing and their relation to ideology. However there have been important break-throughs. Gramsci's Prison Notebooks should be seen as one of the most comprehensive attempts to counteract this confusion in Marxist thought. Certainly Lukacs' admonition that the method of natural science is ideological because it 'rejects the idea of contradiction and antagonism in its subject matter'[54] derives from a consideration of these distinctions as do the following comments from Althusser.

... Marx's Dialectics would have been very relevant to us today, since it would have been the theory of Marx's theoretical practice ... today we so miss the Dialectics ... even though we know perfectly well that we have it and where it is: in Marx's theoretical works, in Capital, etc. - yes, and of course we can find it there, but not in the theoretical state![55]

According to Althusser, not even Lenin's recognition of the importance of Marx's method resulted in the clear theoretical or methodological formulation we needed.[56] The implication inherent in all these writings is that we can gain greater clarity about ideology be developing our under-standing of Marx's method, his science, and the reverse holds true as well.

With reference to the reverse, Hall[57] and Poulantzas[58] have added to our understanding of Marxism the method through their analyses of how the dominant liberal-democratic ideology works. In an earlier section I drew briefly on their ideas in discussing the process of dislocation or displacement. It is important now to return to those ideas and to consider them more fully. Regardless of whether they focus their analyses on a set of ideas, a discourse, or some aspect of materiality, Hall and Poulantzas expose a process of displacement which serves to mask or conceal reality. This process involves four interrelated components, viz. three displacements and one concealment. First, there is the displacement of emphasis or focus from the sphere of production, wherein the real relations of power are constituted, to the sphere of exchange and consumption - what Marx referred to as the 'noisy sphere'. Second, there is a displacement from the concrete or actual to the abstract or formal. Also there is a displacement from the total to the partial. If we consider the set of ideas, 'freedom of the press', we can see the displacement components at work. We can talk about such a freedom only so long as we focus on our freedom to consume the 'news' of our choice. If, also, we focus on our freedom to express our views or to own the means by which we could produce or disseminate news, we can understand that the notion 'freedom of the press' only .works in an abstract and partial sense which emphasises our freedom to consume. The moment we return the abstract notion to concrete reality and apply it to the concrete totality of all people, classes and groups, rather than to the partial category of people who are the owners of capital, we can understand how ideology does not need to falsify in the strict sense because the masking function of the displacement process achieves the same ends.

However the reason why the displacement process is able to mask reality is because the meaning we make of a concept such as freedom is determined within the dominant region of ideology and then that determination becomes neutralised and so concealed. According to Poulantzas, under the capitalist formation this dominant region is the judicial-political, but the fact that this is the dominant region is masked. Therefore the level of real determination, the economic, is concealed, but so too is the level which plays the dominant role in the masking process.[59]

From such an analysis it might also be argued that any method of thinking, such as formal logic, which seeks to eliminate contradiction or to abstract concepts out of their historical movement, supports the production of ideology and distracts us from a complex understanding of our reality.[60] Unfortunately, our epistemological concepts and the social relations within which knowledge is produced and disseminated are so embedded with ideology that it is difficult to envision alternative ways of thinking and relating. Throughout human history the concept of truth has been linked to a quest for some finite object. Riddled with that meaning it becomes extremely difficult to reconceptualise the quest as an infinite struggle to understand that which is moving and which only ceases to move by a deception or conjuring trick of the human mind.

Nevertheless the democratised form of socialism implied by conscious human agency and the type of hegemony needed to create it and vigilantly sustain it, must involve dialectic rather than ideological thought. If our vision is of a society created by the voluntary agents of our own (voluntary) determinants, then we must infuse agency with a new form of cognition. Dialectic thinking makes it possible for us to not only believe but to understand that each individual's interest is inextricably linked with the interests of humankind as well as all other species and the environment.

It is urgent for socialists to work together to explicate more fully the dialectic method. However, we need equally to learn to work together and relate in ways which will support this form of thinking. I have tried to argue that Illich's contributions lie outside these tasks. However Freire offers us an educational approach which strikes at the heart of the relations which sustain ideology. Of course, our task is much larger. Gramsci offers us a strategy by which we can begin the conscious struggle to create the ethical political leadership that will lead to a will and a collective understanding of the need for socialist revolution. However, lest we forget, it was Marx who first offered us the vision of the future for which we should be striving, a future wherein human beings, freed from necessity, will be free to think, and through that thinking and their own agency, create a socialist future, but one which will be always in the 'making' and never 'made'.

* This chapter is dedicated to and results from the learner colleagues with whom I have worked from 1983 to 1986.

REFERENCES

1. E.P. Thompson, The Poverty of Theory and Other Essays (London: Penguin, 1978), p.280.

2. P. Anderson, Arguments Within English Marxism (London; Verso, 1980), p.23.

3. K. Marx, Capital: A Critique of Political Economy, Vol. 1, trans. B. Fowkes (London: Penguin, 1974), pp.163-77, 270-82. However Marx's mature concept of ideology figures in many parts of Capital. As a guide see J. Mepham, 'The Theory of Ideology in Capital', in Cultural Studies 6 (Birmingham: Centre for Contemporary Cultural Studies, Autumn, 1974), pp.98-123.

4. Here I am not referring to the social-democratic proclamation of 'an end to ideology' by means of reformist politics. That proclamation is based on a concept of ideology which equates it with extremist - right and left - political theory. The concept of ideology will be developed throughout this chapter, but a preliminary definition is that it is a set of ideas which offers an explanation of social reality. Also, throughout this chapter I shall refer to dominant classes or groups, rather than the singular class or group, in recognition of the competing interests within the capitalist class as a whole and in recognition of how the ideologies of patriarchy and race cross-cut and interact with liberal-democratic ideology.

5. P. Armstrong, 'The History of Adult Education'. A lecture given to the Diploma in Adult Education group (Nottingham, October 1986).

6. A. Gramsci, Selections from the Prison Notebooks of Antonio Gramsci, Q. Hoare and G.N. Smith (eds & trans.) (London: Lawrence and Wishart, 1971) and Letters from Prison, L. Lawner (intro. & trans.) (London: Quartet, 1979).

7. L. Althusser, For Marx, trans. B. Brewster (Harmondsworth: Penguin, 1966). In my opinion Althusser's most important statements regarding ideology and Marx's dialectic method.

8. N. Poulantzas, Political Power and Social Classes, trans. T. O'Hagan (London: Verso, 1978).

9. S. Hall, 'The Hinderland of Science: Ideology and The Sociology of Knowledge', in On Ideology, Centre for Contemporary Cultural Studies (London: Hutchinson, 1978). This is but one contribution of many by Hall to this topic. For an excellent introduction to ideology, see Unit 21 by Hall, in The Open University Social Science Foundation Course D102-Block 5.

10. J. Larrain, The Concept of Ideology (London: Hutchinson, 1979).

11. K. Marx, as in note 3, but also 1875 Introduction to the Grundrisse trans. M. Nicolaus (London: Pelican, 1973).

12. C. Mouffe, 'Hegemony and Ideology in Gramsci', in

T. Bennett, et al. (eds), Culture, Ideology and Social Practice (London: Batsford in association with The Open University, 1981), pp.219-34. Also Poulantzas, Political Power and Social Classes; see note 8, p.223.

13. I would like to elaborate on how an internal relation differs from an external relation and how that difference affects our conceptual focus as well as the resulting analysis, but I shall need a visual aid to explain this:

External Relations

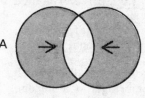

Internal Relations

The focus is on how the existing properties of A and B interact to create something - the familiar notion of thesis/antithesis/synthesis.

The focus begins with the interaction of relation and the analysis involves understanding how this regulates the development of A and B, i.e. the contradictory opposite tendencies.

14. I. Illich, Deschooling Society (London: Calder & Boyars, 1971), p.4. This is the text I have drawn on for most of this discussion; however, also see Tools for Conviviality (London: Calder & Boyars, 1973).

15. P. Freire, 'An Invitation to Conscientization and Deschooling', in The Politics of Education trans. D. Macedo (London: Macmillan, 1985), pp.167-73. Freire makes this point himself in this article originally published by the World Council of Churches in 1975. He is referring to his stance in Educacao Como Practica da Liberdade published in 1967 and translated into English under the title Education for Critical Consciousness (London: Steed and Ward, 1974), and later republished as Education: The Practice of Freedom (London: Writers and Readers Publishing Cooperative, 1976).

16. P. Freire, Conscientization and Liberation (Geneva: Institute of Cultural Action), IDAC Document no. 1 (1973), p.3; or see The Politics of Education for a reprint, pp.154-5.

17. P. Freire, Pedagogy of the Oppressed (Harmondsworth: Penguin, 1972), p.81.

18. P. Freire, Conscientization and Liberation, p. 8; or The Politics of Education, p.159.

19. Ibid., p.10, or The Politics of Education, p.161.

20. H. Giroux, Ideology Culure and the Process of Schooling (London: Falmer, 1981).

21. P. Freire, Conscientization and Liberation, p.13; or The Politics of Education, p.163.

22. CCCS Education Group, Unpopular Education (London: Hutchinson, 1981).

23. P. Freire, The Politics of Education, p.172. The idea is also quite clear in Pedagogy of the Oppressed.

24. Ibid., p.69. But note this is a reprint of 'Cultural Action and Conscientization', Harvard Educational Review, Vol. 70, No. 3 (August 1970), pp.452-77.

25. P. Freire, 'Education: domestication or liberation?' in I. Lister (ed.), Deschooling (Cambridge: Cambridge University Press, 1974), pp.20-1.

26. R. Jacoby, Social Amnesia (London: Harvester, 1977).

27. Gramsci, SPN p.12; see note 6.

28. Ibid., pp.238, 268.

29. Ibid., pp.263, 323, 351-7. Also a comparison should be made between Gramsci's ideas about revolutionary strategy and what Freire terms cultural action and its relation to permanent cultural revolution. See P. Freire, 'Cultural Action and Conscientization', Harvard Educational Review Vol. 70, No. 3 (August 1970), pp.452-77. Also in The Politics of Education, Ch.7.

30. Ibid., pp.375-7.

31. Ibid., pp.241, 326, 349, 367.

32. Ibid., p.57-9 (but also for a clear discussion of these ideas see C. Mouffe, 'Hegemony and Ideology in Gramsci', note 12, p.223).

33. Ibid., p.350.

34. Ibid., pp.161, 60-61 (but also see C. Mouffe, Hegemony and Ideology in Gramsci, p.244).

35. Mouffe, Hegemony and Ideology in Gramsci, p.244.

36. Gramsci, SPN, p.360.

37. Ibid., p.9.

38. Ibid., p.350.

39. Ibid., p.323.

40. Ibid., for example pp.172, 370, 372, 376, 406-7, 412, 427, 435.

41. A. Gramsci, Letters from Prison see n.6, p.240.

42. Ibid., L. Lawner, Introduction, p.45.

43. S. Hall, B. Lumley and G. McLennan, 'Politics and Ideology: Gramsci', in On Ideology, see n.9, p.71.

44. A. Gramsci, SPN pp.59-60.

45. Ibid., pp.376, 407.

46. R. Simon, Gramsci's Political Thought: An Introduction (London; Lawrence and Wishart, 1982).

47. H. Entwistle, Antonio Gramsci: Conservative Schooling for Radical Politics (London: Routledge and Kegan Paul, 1979).

48. E. Laclau, and C. Mouffe, Hegemony and Socialist Strategy: Towards a Radical Democratic Politics (London: Verso, 1985), p.67.

49. J. Larrain, The Concept of Ideology, see n.10, pp.186-7.

50. Marx, Grundrisse, see n.11, p.164.

51. Larrain, The Concept of Ideology, p.187.

52. K. Marx, Capital Vol. 1, p.167.

53. Larrain, The Concept of Ideology, p.181.

54. G. Lukacs, History and Class Consciousness (London: Merlin, 1971) p.10.

55. Althusser, For Marx, see n.7, p.174.

56. Ibid., p.175.

57. Hall, Unit 21-D102, see n.9.

58. Poulantzas, Political Power and Social Class, see n.8, pp.201-24.

59. Ibid., p.211.

60. However I get a good deal of support for this argument from Marx, and from Poulantzas as well, who draws a great deal of his analysis of ideology from Marx.

5

Adult Education in Radical US Social and Ethnic Movements: From Case Studies to Typology to Explanation

Rolland G. Paulston and Richard J. Altenbaugh

INTRODUCTION

While most radical movements seeking fundamental change in values and society use adult education (defined here as structured, non-degree educational programmes for adults) in various degrees, the contributions of such pedagogical efforts have to date remained largely unexamined, if not simply ignored. Now with the emergence of critical studies of adult education using historical and social science perspectives, this lacuna is being addressed in promising ways.[1] Moreover, this attention promises to provide a more detailed and theoretical understanding of the adult education/social change nexus. With more conceptually-framed studies of the phenomena we should be better able to generalise about under what conditions 'radical adult education' (RAE) is created, practised, and how its contributions might be evaluated. This in turn should also facilitate policy efforts to plan and use RAE in future change undertakings. In this chapter we should like to join in this endeavour to advance our understanding of theory and practice in adult education.

To this end, the chapter is divided into three parts. The first section assesses the value of typology in a pre-theoretical field - such as the sociology of adult education - and seeks to illustrate utility with the creation of a typology that sorts out programmatic variations along two key variables, i.e. change goals and programme control. This allows for the identification of five different types of adult education, and enables us to define and juxtapose RAE in light of what it is and is not. In the second section, we present two illustrative historical cases of RAE in the United States: the first at Work Peoples' College in the radical labour movement and the second in the Black Panther Party, a radical branch of the Black Civil Rights Movement. Both examples are described, albeit briefly, with regard to their origins, pedagogical processes and contributions to individual and/or social change. In the concluding sections we present some tentative generalisations about key variables associated with the relative effectiveness of RAE programmes, and suggest what knowledge we believe is most needed to advance the field given findings to date.

ON THE UTILITY OF TYPOLOGY

If there is nothing more practical than a 'good' theory in pedagogical and social research, then taxonomy as prototheory must come to be viewed as a legitimate effort in attempts to make this work more analytical and theoretically grounded. Clearly, efforts in adult education and development to date have only rarely been guided by theory, or systematic causal explanation. If this situation is to be addressed, we shall have to pay closer attention to typological classification and the advantages and disadvantages of such methodology in qualitative analysis, in generalisation, and in theory construction and testing.

As a specific instance of the general logic of classification, any typological procedure requires that each and every member of a population chosen for study - such as types of adult education programmes - may be classified in only one of the major types or categories delineated. The overall typology must be comprehensive and each category must be mutually exclusive.

The dimensions which are differentiated into types must be clearly and explicitly stated, i.e. what indicators have been used and why? Dimensions chosen must be of central importance for the research task at hand and have obvious systemic import.[2]

Additional methodological criteria for a 'good' typological classification would include the criterion of fruitfulness, i.e. the typology may have heuristic significance in facilitating understanding of relations between types, and change of types under certain conditions. The parsimony criterion, i.e. the fewest meaningful or significant major types possible to cover the largest number of observations or phenomena, is also essential. As Tiryakian argues, the methodological functions and significance of typological classification are basically twofold: codification and prediction:

> ... A typology goes beyond sheer description by
> simplifying the ordering of the elements of a
> population, and the known relevant traits of that
> population, into distinct groupings; in this capacity
> a typological classification creates order out of the
> potential chaos of discrete, discontinuous, or
> heterogeneous observations. But in so codifying
> phenomena, it also permits the observer to seek
> and predict relationships between phenomena that
> do not seem to be connected in any obvious way.
> This is because a good typology is not a collection
> of undifferentiated entities but is composed of a
> cluster of traits which do in reality 'hang
> together'.[3]

Typology is a valuable method to type phenomena and
suggest causal relations. No matter how elegant and sophisticated it may be, typology must never be viewed as an end
in itself but, rather, as a link in efforts to achieve a more
scientific understanding of natural or social phenomena.[4]
A word of caution concerning the limitations of
typology in adult education is also very much in order. As
noted, typology at its best can provide a theoretical model
of adult education programmes by specifying conditions
under which change from one type to another occurs. Badly
done, typology can deform reality and serve teleological or
ideological ends. Typology in US pedagogical and social
sciences has been criticised in this regard as essentially
conservative, as the undemocratic assignment of individuals
into fixed groups, to a predetermined social status. From an
egalitarian outlook, typology serves the interests of hierarchy and is never able to eliminate the problem of how to
account for observable variations and gradations. But if the
typologist may be so over-concerned with the central
tendency of a population that he may disregard dispersion in
time and space, so also may the anti-typologist run the risk
of being so concerned with individual or type deviations that
he may lose sight of the central tendency that gives the
group its mean or aggregate characteristic.
Typology is often criticised as the creation of artificial
categories that have no counterpart in the empirical world.
The question of whether types are 'real' is best left to the
philosophers. For our purposes, types might be best viewed
as central tendencies of a population that give the group its
meaning or aggregate characteristics.

... What may be [concluded] here is that for the purposes of scientific research, types treated as central tendencies are no less necessary than variations from the type. Sophisticated users of typologies have fully realized that quantitative differences between individuals assigned to the same category may be, for another part of the investigation, as significant as qualitative differences between the categories themselves. In other words, differences in degree are as essential to a good typology as differences in kind. If this caveat is observed, and if one also remembers that, in our everyday life, we experience nature as a continuum (<u>Natura non facit saltus</u>), the social scientist may put typology classification to fruitful use and by-pass the ideological issues.[5]

But lacking theory on adult education or educational change, we should not expect too much from typological research. We have no macro- or even middle-range theory explaining how adult education systems evolve, work or interact with other social systems. We have no linked sets of propositions which clarify the pedagogical process of adult learning or how change occurs in the formal and non-formal structures in which adult education takes place. We even lack a well-defined technical language to help us describe and compare adult educational programmes and attempts to link them to economic and social development efforts.[6] What we do have, however, is a rather extensive body of historical research and a good deal of largely atheoretical empirical research - and perhaps some rudimentary and beginning insights via heuristic typology-building pertaining to the general topic of adult education and social change and the specific question, 'under what conditions?'[7]

In Figure 5.1, we present out typological view of the sociology of adult education programmes. Five distinct types are identified according to their characteristics or 'central tendencies' <u>vis-à-vis</u> their orientation to change and control.[8]

Type 1, 'Conventional' Adult Education programmes are, for example, low in their change goals and are located at the formal systems pole of the programme control continuum. This is where most traditional adult education takes place in formal educational systems, in business, in the military, and the like. It is training seeking to enhance individual and socio-economic efficiency and productivity. Simply put, it serves the status quo.[9]

In Type 2, 'Consumption' Adult Education programmes' change goals are also low or moderate, but control rests with individuals or groups seeking more private goals for self-realisation, creativity, growth, leisure and the like. Both Types 1 and 2 are essentially regulatory and seek incremental individual change within the status quo.[10]

In Type 3, 'Radical' Adult Education, both participant control and change orientation reach polar highs. Here groups opposing the status quo and seeking radical change use adult education as anti-structure, as another weapon in their struggle for what they view as social justice.[11] In this cell, we might note two somewhat different contexts for RAE, i.e. in movements seeking human liberation - as in radical religious movements, utopian communities, counter-culture movements and the like: and in radical movements seeking basic restructuring of social and economic systems - as in Marxist or Fascist revolutionary movements, radical populist movements etc.

In Type 4, 'Transformational' Adult Education, revolutionary movements have actually taken control and are using state power to transform social, economic and educational systems so as to achieve the ideological goals of the revolution.[12]

In Type 5, we propose something of a hybrid type: 'Reformist' Adult Education. Here collective change efforts largely outside of formal systems control use adult education in incremental change efforts seeking greater equity via civil rights movements, labour movements, peace and environmental movements.[13]

The value of this typology will be found in how well it meets the criteria previously stated, and in the extent to which it provokes critique and useful re-conceptualisation. It may also be assessed in how well it serves as a means to choose and compare cases illustrating the types identified, and how change on the two key dimensions, i.e. in programme goals and control, will lead to predictable shifts in programme type. Let us now turn to two examples of radical adult education as it took place at Work Peoples' College in the violent struggle for a socialist America, and in the Black Panther Movement seeking the revolutionary restructuring of American ethnic relations.

Figure 1: A typology of Adult Education Programmes

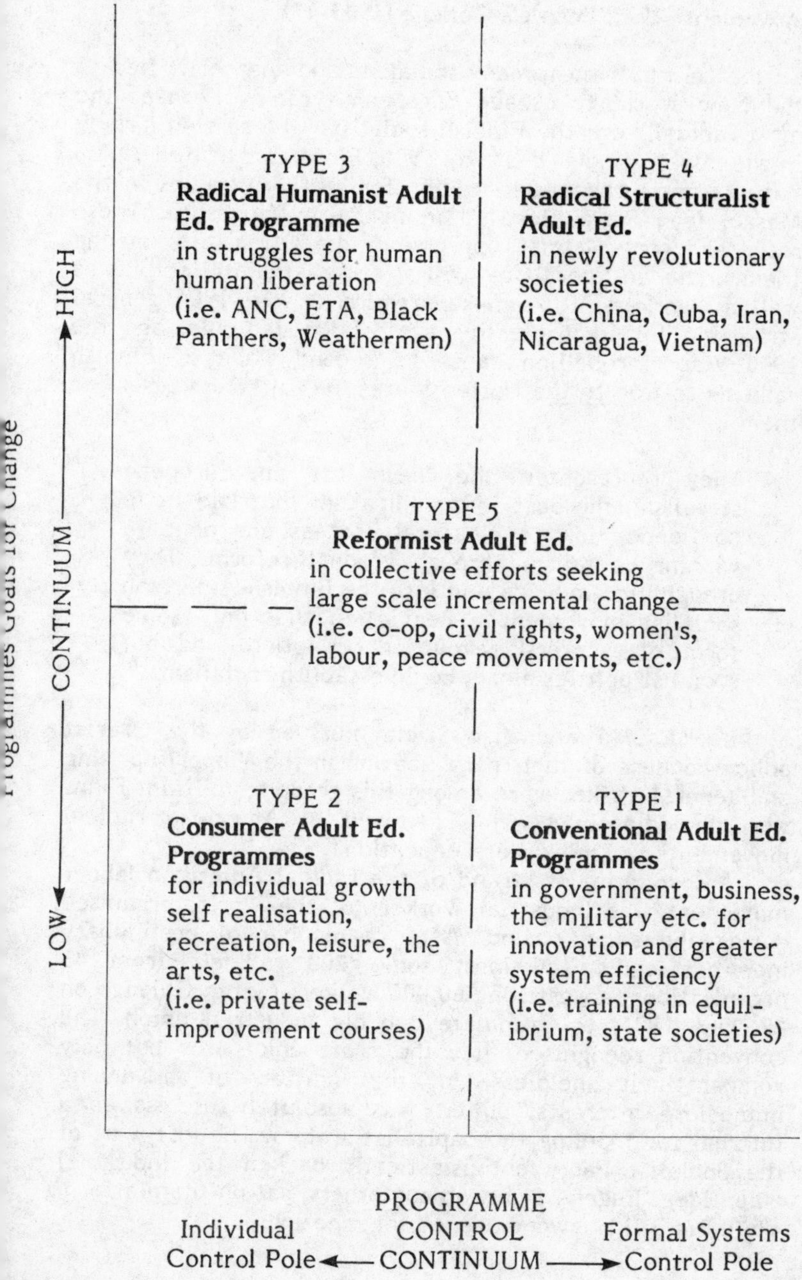

TYPE 3
Radical Humanist Adult Ed. Programme
in struggles for human
human liberation
(i.e. ANC, ETA, Black
Panthers, Weathermen)

TYPE 4
Radical Structuralist Adult Ed.
in newly revolutionary
societies
(i.e. China, Cuba, Iran,
Nicaragua, Vietnam)

TYPE 5
Reformist Adult Ed.
in collective efforts seeking
large scale incremental change
(i.e. co-op, civil rights, women's,
labour, peace movements, etc.)

TYPE 2
Consumer Adult Ed. Programmes
for individual growth
self realisation,
recreation, leisure, the
arts, etc.
(i.e. private self-
improvement courses)

TYPE 1
Conventional Adult Ed. Programmes
in government, business,
the military etc. for
innovation and greater
system efficiency
(i.e. training in equil-
ibrium, state societies)

Programmes Goals for Change

HIGH ← CONTINUUM → LOW

PROGRAMME
CONTROL
CONTINUUM

Individual
Control Pole ← → Formal Systems
Control Pole

Case 1: Radical adult education in the American labour movement: Work People's College (1903–41)

By the century's turn, many socialists and anarchists fled to the New World to escape European tyranny. Perhaps the most radical were the Finnish socialists who settled largely in the upper Middle West. By 1905, Finns constituted 39.8% - the largest proportion - of the foreign-born groups in the Mesabi Iron Range located in northern Minnesota. These refugees from Czarist oppression, draft resisters among them, included liberals as well as socialists, intellectuals as well as workers. Russian suppression of the 1905 general strike in Finland, protesting against Russian rule, and the 1906 Viapori rebellion caused a second wave of Finnish radicals to flee to the United States. As Carl Ross describes them:

> They represented the 'new left' in European socialism: the post-1905 radicalism that had little confidence in the electoral process and none in winning socialism through gradual reform. They brought to America and into the Finnish-American socialist movement a conviction that only some form of workers' revolutionary action, and not socialist politics alone, could establish socialism.[14]

Leo Laukki and Yrjo Sirola, pursued by the Czarist police because of their participation in the Viapori uprising and general strike, were among this group of militant Finns who immediately became involved in American radical movements and in workers' education.

A second major strand of the radical American labour movement, the Industrial Workers of the World, organised during the same period. After a number of preliminary meetings and discussions, some 200 radicals from 43 organisations representing 60,000 workers met in Chicago on 27 June 1905, to formulate one big industrial union. The convention recognised that the craft union was not only comparatively helpless in the matter of advancing immediate interests, but it was absolutely useless as a fulcrum for toppling the capitalist system. The left wing of the Socialist Party enthusiastically backed the industrial union idea. Eugene Debs, among others, sat on the platform while Big Bill Haywood opened the meeting:

Fellow workers ... This is the Continental Congress of the working class. We are here to confederate the workers of this country into a working-class movement that shall have for its purpose the emancipation of the working class from the slave bondage of capitalism. There is no organisation that has for its purpose the same object as that for which you are called together today. The aims and objects of this organisation should be to put the working class in possession of the economic power, the means of life, in control of the machinery of production and distribution, without regard to capitalist masters. The American Federation of Labor, which presumes to be the labour movement of this country, is not a working-class movement. It does not represent the working class. There are organisations that are ... loosely affiliated with the AF of L, which in their constitution and by-laws prohibit the initiation of or conferring of the obligation on a coloured man; that prohibit the conferring of the obligation on foreigners. What we want to establish ... is a labour organisation that will open wide its doors to every man that earns his livelihood either by his brain or his muscle ... there is a continuous struggle between the two classes, and this organisation will be formed, based and founded on the class struggle, and but one object and one purpose and that is to bring the workers of this country into the possession of the full value of the product of their toil.[15]

By calling for the dissolution of the existing economic system, the IWW adhered to far more radical goals than the AFL. The IWW also accepted any wage-earner, regardless of skill, race or sex, as a member. To facilitate this, enrolment fees averaged a dollar while monthly dues seldom exceeded 25 cents. Meanwhile, the Federation restricted its membership through high enrolment fees. As Foner summarises it:

... the IWW after 1908 operated chiefly among the workers whom the AF of L would not and did not reach - the migratory workers of the West and the unskilled industrial workers of the East - the most poorly paid and ill-treated.[16]

These two segments of the radical labour movement sought the common goal of a new social order and came together for a short period in a workers' college in Northern Minnesota. This adult education centre with its links to the radical Finns and the IWW offers perhaps the best example of Type 3 adult education in the US, until the re-emergence of social struggle in the 1960s.

On 15 September 1903, authorities of the Finnish Evangelical Lutheran National Church sponsored the opening of a residential adult folk high school in Minneapolis, Minnesota. The main purpose of the school would be to train ministers, but with only eight students enrolled, the school closed after twelve days. The clergymen decided to move the school to Duluth in late 1903 and incorporated it on 5 January 1904, as the Finnish People's College. They purchased a three-storey building by Spirit Lake and endeavoured to teach Finnish immigrants religion, Finnish culture and nationalism: clearly a Type 1 adult education programme. The school obtained financial support from Finns who purchased shares at a dollar apiece.

However, the school faced an uncertain future. A Board of Directors, consisting of lay members and church officials, controlled the secular aspects of the school while the church supervised the school's theological seminary. The clerics, who were anti-socialist and the socialists (lay members), who were anti-clerical, continually vied for control of the school. At the same time, the majority of the students came from Finnish socialist homes. In their late twenties, the students resented the religious restrictions and courses imposed upon them by the church, and, as a result, led a strike to protest the 'oppressive' nature of the school in the fall of 1904.

Finnish socialists ultimately gained complete control over the school in 1907 and changed its outlook and renamed it Work People's College. The Board of Directors hired K.L. Haataja, a socialist, as Director and as an instructor while Leo Laukki, and later Yrjo Sirola, joined the teaching staff. Reino Salo, a socialist from Cloquet, Minnesota, was elected secretary and business manager. Since a large percentage of the Finns had little or no formal education, the college's first goal concerned itself with providing basic educational skills, especially in the use of the English language. The Finnish socialist community also hoped to develop its own internal leadership, especially editors, teachers and agitators. The Finns relied upon their own non-degree adult educational programmes to accomplish this goal because the American education system trained children not to appreciate 'the enthusiasm and social aims of their socialistic parents'.[17]

The IWW formally acknowledged the Work People's College as its official school in 1921. However, several years before this, radical Finns sympathetic to the IWW, like their earlier socialist counterparts, secured a majority of the college's stock and voted to officially adopt the union's doctrine. Furthermore, under the tutelage of Laukki and Sirola, the school had continued its political drift leftward to industrial unionism. At times, Laukki suggested that sabotage was sometimes necessary in order to bring a successful industrial revolution. Sirola evoked a less militant position: 'While he accepted the industrial form of unionism in preference to craft unionism and even recognized the IWW ... as a pioneer for industrial unionism, he never accepted IWW's syndicalist theories or methods, destruction of property or the means of production, or any forms of sabotage.'[18]

The 'Announcement of Courses' for the 1923-24 school year set out the school's revolutionary orientation and adherence to IWW precepts:

> This school recognizes the existence of class struggle in society, and its courses of study have been prepared so that industrially organized workers, both men and women, dissatisfied with conditions under our capitalist system, can more efficiently carry on an organized class struggle for the attainment of industrial demands, and realistically of a new social order.[19]

The Work People's College sought to help prepare a revolutionary working class capable of generating social change, and to prepare individual workers to govern the new socialist order. Working-class education was viewed as an integral component of the necessary revolutionary change that was expected to take place in the control of the means of production and distribution of wealth. Therefore, the Work People's College did not educate workers to rise out of their social class, but rather trained them to become more powerful actors in the class struggle.

Here, the philosophy of the Work People's College rejected the capitalist hegemony propagated by the formal school system. By using adult education programmes to teach English to Finnish working-class immigrants and to imbue them with socialist and, later, IWW doctrine, the founders and proponents of the school hoped that its students, as activists, would contribute to the success of the radical labour movement.[20]

The College reached its apex before World War I, before most US labour colleges even existed. Student enrolment steadily increased from 130 in 1911-12 to 147 in 1913-14, and at the peak, the faculty consisted of eight members. After its transition from socialism to industrial unionism, the school's attendance dipped to 38 but increased to 65 students during the 1916-17 school year. Although Work People's College managed to attract some non-Finns, it never recaptured its pre-war following. Between 1920 and 1925, the average yearly enrolment was 70, then dropped to 48 between 1926 and 1930. By 1936, this had dwindled to 36 students.

The Work People's College closed in 1941. Because of its affiliation with the IWW, the school isolated itself within the Finnish radical community. By 1917 Work People's College had severed its connection with the Socialist Party and Finnish socialists. The school also played no part in the vital Finnish cooperative movement of the 1920s and 1930s, and rejected communism in the 1920s. Moreover, the IWW and the Work People's College refused to support the Congress of Industrial Organizations movement of the 1930s. The acculturation of the Finns also created problems for the College. Put simply, second-generation, English-speaking Finns, avoided Work People's College because they were often ashamed of their immigrant parents' radicalism. They chose, instead, to attend the public schools because attendance at the Work People's College was not calculated to give Finnish-American youth status in their own peer groups.[21] Also, the arrest of Leo Laukki, and his subsequent flight to the Soviet Union, eliminated the last Marxist theorist from Work People's College. Finally, unlike other labour colleges such as Brookwood and Commonwealth, Work People's College never cultivated a diverse base of support.

The Work People's College nevertheless died slowly. Although regular classes were suspended in September 1941, summer classes continued for a while. Because of a housing shortage during the Second World War, the United States government leased the remaining building in 1941 and converted it to a block of flats for war industry workers. The government terminated its lease in 1950 and the Board of Directors elected to sell the building for $14,000 in 1953. The Board of Directors continued to repurchase outstanding shares from stockholders and in 1963 dispersed the remaining college funds.

The founders of Work People's College formulated two basic goals for the school which reflected their view of the social and educational needs of the working class. First, the school endeavoured to train labour leaders and activists to organise and to lead workers in social change activity. Second, it was hoped that this activity would culminate in the realisation of a new social order controlled by workers and free from exploitation. In spite of external harassment and internal struggles, the college maintained these aspirations and trained many labour leaders and activists. During its existence, Work People's College supplied thousands of graduates who became active in the political, union and cooperative movements of the Finns as organisers, newspapermen, speakers and propagandists for the Finnish industrial union movement. Thus, Work People's College not only grew from the socialist inspiration and leadership which came from Finland, but it also supplemented it by developing new leaders in the United States.

It is equally clear, however, that neither the college nor the labour college movement achieved its larger goal of social reconstruction. A new social order as they envisaged it did not come into being. None the less, many labour college graduates successfully altered the structure of the labour movement. In spite of official IWW opposition, many individuals played leading roles in the development of the Congress of Industrial Organizations.

Case 2: The adult educational programmes of the Black Panther Party (1966–1971)

When Huey P. Newton and Bobby Seale started the Black Panther Party in 1966 and wrote the Ten-Point Platform and Programme, 'What We Want' and 'What We Believe', they were reacting to, and speaking about, that contradiction between the stated ideal and the real racist practices which separated and excluded blacks in US society from equal treatment and opportunity.

The Black Panther Party originated in the streets of

125

Oakland, California's black neighbourhoods. The philosophical basis for some of the ideology and even quotations in its Platform and Programme was the Declaration of Independence made by the American colonists to King George III. Other revolutionary heroes such as Stokely Carmichael, Frantz Fanon, veteran of the Algerian revolution, Malcolm X and Mao were quoted or used in what can only be viewed as a highly eclectic party ideology. Identification with the lumpenproletariat was important to the Black Panther ideology, as stressed by Eldridge Cleaver in the pamphlet, on the Ideology of the Black Panther Party (Part 1) (Oakland, Cal., 1969). He made distinctions between the Mother Country and the Black Colony and within both between the working class and the lumpenproletariat. Cleaver characterised the lumpen as having nowhere else to rebel but in the streets because 'the lumpen have been locked outside of the economy'.

Given this brief overview of Black Panther Party origins in 1966, we now need to examine the specific activities and adult educational programmes sponsored and directed in an effort to create a more egalitarian society, and what specific educational tools were used to convey ideology, raise individual consciousness, and secure commitment to the struggle for radically different social, political and economic relations with the dominant white majority.

First period: 1966-68

In the Black Panther Party's development as a social movement and political force, their programmes, activities, and public statements, primarily as expounded in their newspaper, incorporated three distinct emphases between 1966 and 1971. From its founding in 1966 until 1969 as the Black Panther Party for Self-Defence, the emphasis was on self-defence and military power, revolutionary nationalism and self-determination. During that period, carrying a gun was an important tenet of the party. Newton's statements in the Black Panther newspaper included epigrams of the Chinese Communist Party Chairman Mao Tse-Tung which reiterated the Panthers' own emphasis on guns.

Education by example, rather than structured classes in their educational programmes at that time, was the rule. Guerilla war training was undertaken in some chapters. These were the only tightly structured classes during that period. Members acquired guns, took classes in the care and use of weapons and even engaged in close order drills and marksmanship practice. The 16 November 1969 edition of The Black Panther carried an article on 'Grenades and Bombs: Anti-Property and Anti-Personnel'. This product of national headquarters gave detailed, step-by-step instructions for making small hand-grenades and fire-bombs.

In relation to experiential learning and education by example, the Minister of Defence of the Party, Huey P. Newton, started carrying out some of the policies outlined above by learning all the California laws relating to guns as well as the rights of persons carrying them, what types were legal and illegal, and the rights of persons when arrested. He and Bobby Seale put this knowledge into practice almost immediately as they carried guns legally. The rules of the Black Panther Party reflect the legal right to carry guns, which many Panthers did until it became illegal. This was, of course, extremely upsetting to the police of Oakland. They were not comfortable when people, particularly black people, confronted them with loaded guns.

Internationalism was strengthened as Panthers visited various foreign countries, in addition to going all over the United States to organise 'Free Huey' rallies. The purpose of the rallies held in support of that campaign was also utilised as way to educate people about the party's programmes and the conditions under which black people lived in the US.

Another facet of the Black Panther Party's programmes in 1969 were branches of what they called 'National Committees to Combat Fascism'. Not only the lumpen-proletariat but other parts of the working class and students were invited to work for such goals as decentralised police forces and increased community control. Mao Tse-tung was often quoted as many of the educational programmes instituted during this second period were based on his statements related to meeting the desires and needs of the people.

Second period: 1968-70

Major changes were effected in the organisational structure and political statements of the Party in 1969. Programmes were added specifically to carry out more directly Point Five of the Platform and Programme which pertains to education. The four programmes initiated over a period of time by many chapters were:

127

1. circulation in various cities of petitions to obtain a referendum vote on decentralisation of city police forces;
2. initiation of free breakfasts for school children of welfare recipients, to be served in neighbourhood churches;
3. institution of free health clinics in black communities;
4. the fourth 'key' programme called for the establishment of 'black liberation schools'. Later, more simply labelled 'liberation schools', they were suggested by national headquarters as a summertime placement for free breakfasts for school children with the addition of lunches. Black history reflecting the basic Panther outlook toward society was the proposed curriculum.[22]

The first programme listed was also the one first put into action. The petitions for decentralisation of police forces were circulated not only by the chapters of NCCF, as previously mentioned, but also as an activity of the Peace and Freedom Party. Eventually, they were successful in getting the issue on the ballot in Berkeley, California, in April 1971. The issue lost.

The second programme, Free Breakfasts for School-children, was initiated in many cities, as were the free health clinics. Liberation schools began in the summer of 1969. In addition, various types of adult education classes and courses were offered by the Panther chapters in Oakland and elsewhere.

The liberation schools and political education classes, the adult component, were opened in three places by the end of June 1969.

According to an article entitled 'Liberation Means Freedom', the liberation school is the 'second of many socialistic and educational programs that will be implemented by the Black Panther Party to meet the needs of the people. In addition to their plans to conduct schools for black children, the party also announced that 'Community Political Education classes will also be starting in the evening for adults'.

Throughout the summer months of 1969, various chapters reported on the progress of their particular 'Liberation School'. The following is an example of the curriculum set forth by several of the chapters.

Monday is Revolutionary History Day
Tuesday is Revolutionary Culture Day
Wednesday is Current Events Day
Thursday is Movie Day
Friday is Field Trip Day.[23]

Liberation schools encountered many difficulties which were even noted in the Panther newspaper. However, they did teach much about the Panther politics and included exercise, songs, etc. Political education classes for adults were slightly more successful. Such things as the history of the party, the class struggle, sayings of Mao were included in the curriculum. Many affiliate chapters started classes, but had trouble keeping them going for any appreciable length of time.

Thus it would seem that the period between 1968 and 1970 was a very productive one in terms of educational programmes of different types, from feeding people to teaching them about history and culture, and helping them take better care of their bodies through free clinics or health classes.

Third period: 1970-71

After Huey came out of jail in 1970 he changed the emphasis of the party philosophy to one of intercommunalism, although the educational programmes of the party that were being conducted continued. The following statement helps to explain what intercommunalism is and how he came to that position.

We found that in order to be Internationalists we had to be also Nationalists, or at least acknowledge nationhood. Internationalism, if I understand the word, means the interrelationship among a group of nations. But since no nation exists, and since the United States is in fact an empire, it is impossible for us to be Internationalists. These transformations and phenomena require us to call ourselves 'intercommunalists' because nations have been transformed into communities of the world. The Black Panther Party now disclaims inter-

129

nationalism and supports intercommunalism. This
would be the time when the people seize the means
of production and distribute the wealth and the
technology in an egalitarian way to the many
communities of the world.[24]

It would seem that there was an obvious growth process
taking place in the philosophy of the party as expounded by
Newton. From seeing themselves as a colony within another
country, they had come to see themselves as part of a larger
group of oppressed people, striving to obtain equal rights as
human beings.

During 1970, the Panther organisations added yet
another type of group to the roster of those already
connected with them. Community information centres held
classes and assisted people in many types of communities
across the country. They were also inter-racial, as were the
National Committees to Combat Fascism.

They were set up in some cities where a Panther
chapter also operated. In at least one case its
address was the same as Panther headquarters [as
in Seattle]; but more often they were at
completely different locations ... In [some] cities
... the party was represented solely by a
community information center, according to the
Panther paper ...

A statement from an Oakland centre in The Black
Panther of 31 May 1970 explained:

The purpose of opening the community information
centers is that we realize that in order to be close
to the people in the community it is necessary that
we locate ourselves among the masses. The centers
will be able to reach more people and bring the
Black Panther Party closer to the people.
    The community centers are set up primarily as
a base in the community for the people to identify
with, work, and claim as their own.[25]

Two of the major efforts and educational tools of the
Black Panther Party in 1970 were the Planning and Plenary
Sessions for the Revolutionary People's Constitutional Con-
vention held respectively in Philadelphia and Washington,

DC, at which the emphasis was on planning to write a new Constitution. That may sound strange in light of their philosophical focus on intercommunalism, but they believed that it was necessary to have a Constitution which would guarantee wealth and technology to all people.

> WE THEREFORE, CALL FOR A REVOLUTION-ARY PEOPLE'S CONSTITUTIONAL CONVENTION, TO BE CONVENED BY THE AMERICAN PEOPLE, TO WRITE A NEW CONSTITUTION THAT WILL GUARANTEEE AND DELIVER TO EVERY AMERICAN CITIZEN THE INVIOLABLE HUMAN RIGHT TO LIFE, LIBERTY, AND THE PURSUIT OF HAPPINESS.
>
> We call upon the American people to rise up, repudiate, and restrain the forces of fascism that are now rampant between us and a rational resolution of the national crisis.
>
> We believe that black people are not the only group within America that stands in need of a new Constitution. Other oppressed ethnic groups, the youth of America, women, young men who are slaughtered as cannon fodder in mad, avaricious wars of aggression, our neglected elderly people all have an interest in a new Constitution that will guarantee us a society in which Human Rights are supreme and justice is assured to every man, woman, and child within its jurisdiction. For it is only through this means that America, as a nation, can live together in peace with our brothers and sisters the world over. Only through this means can the present character of America, the purveyor of exploitation, misery, death and wanton destruction all over the planet earth, be changed.[26]

Many groups were invited and attended, from Gay Liberationists to Peace/Anti-War Movements. Thus it seems the Panthers might have been trying to appeal to, and gain support from, even greater numbers of people. Rewriting the Constitution probably appealed to many persons and groups who believed they had been denied their human rights under the present Constitution. It is difficult to say with any authority what the real outcomes of the Planning and Plenary Sessions were as there is not much information available about them. Neither affair was successful, however: the actual convention never took place.

The Black Panther, a tabloid newspaper, was the major educational tool of the party across all three periods. This section will assess the newspaper briefly and discuss the artwork, growth and finances connected with the newspaper. The first issue was sold in Oakland, California, on 15 May 1967. Its editor was the Minister of Information, Eldridge Cleaver. The major tool for identifying the three periodic emphases of the Black Panther Party discussed earlier was the newspaper, as reported by US House of Representatives Committee reports. Many statements by its leaders given to other media were often reproduced in the pages of the newspaper. In addition, articles by, or letters from, members of chapters across the country were included, often related to specific problems experienced in a particular city or about some national party focus. Thus there was great diversity of style and content in each issue.

During the period of self-defence, revolutionary nationalism and self-determination, many articles were featured on guerilla warfare tactics, materials related to firearms, bombs etc., and the necessity for self-defence. Articles related to the police and problems with them all over the country were featured in almost every issue of the paper after 1968. When internationalism and socialism became the main ideological thrust of the Party and its political stance Marxist-Leninist statements were quoted often in the articles as were quotes of Mao Tse-tung, Stalin, etc. Fulfilling the needs and desires of the people was stressed as the aim of the Party rather than the need for self-defence. The many educational and community programmes initiated during that time were often cited as ways in which the needs of the people were being met.

Clearly, those who directed the party's activities realised the importance of different kinds of activities to appeal to different types of people. Newspapers, for example, presented revolutionary cartoons, poetry, and articles about black people around the country and the world. Articles covered black history, culture, health and legal aid classes and courses, to the free breakfasts programme for children and efforts to rewrite the Constitution. The Black Panthers' educational activities ran the gamut from self-defence to fulfilling the physical and mental needs of the people, directly and indirectly. Leaders changed the party ideology and activities as their awareness grew, and thus the Party was able to develop through the process of struggle and reflection.

As part of the radical wing of the US civil rights movement, the Black Panther Party enjoyed much early success in securing members and in publicising their views, primarily through their own newspaper. The Panthers' efforts to mobilise what they chose to designate as the lumpenproletariat were to a fair degree successful. Thousands of youth and young adults joined the Party. Many thousands of other black people in the US also supported Panther goals, as evidenced by polls taken and reported in the mass media. A Harris Poll for Time magazine published in the 30 March 1970 issue revealed that:

> two million black Americans, count themselves as 'revolutionaries', ... while 75 per cent of blacks admired the NAACP 'a great deal', 25 per cent had this view of the Black Panthers.

That achievement for an organisation less than five years old is little short of amazing in light of the fact that most of the mass media reporting the Panthers was distorted, or worse. In fact, the Panther programme and the ideas of Panther leaders were conveyed to the public literally in spite of the establishment mass media.

The Panthers, nevertheless, like other radical groups before them, suffered a number of serious shortcomings. Probably the most debilitating was lack of a thorough radical analysis coupled with a strong, organised set of strategies and programmes. Too much publicity and concern with image-making may have clouded their own ideas of what they wanted to do. But, even with frequent policy shifts and lack of feedback to guide them they did amazingly well in such a short period of time, given the few resources they were able to command. Many of the Black Panther programmes and their platform may not be truly revolutionary - but they were well chosen given the critical needs of urban black communities. And, in the case of community health, education, and other social services, they served as valuable prototypes for later reforms by local, state and federal governments.

CONCLUSIONS

In this chapter we have presented a typology of adult

education programmes that enables us to describe some of the defining characteristics of what we call 'radical adult education'. These characteristics include inter alia the incorporation of RAE in collective change efforts seeking to mobilise popular power to secure radical changes in individuals and/or social structures; and the creation of pedagogical efforts built around a critical assessment of the status quo and the need for people to understand what can be done, and the role of education in preparing people to work effectively for the changes sought.

How well do the cases serve to illustrate this type? Clearly, in both, the movement leadership articulated goals for fundamental change in, for example, economic and ethnic relations. When these goals linked-up with people's experiences, recruitment and commitment was possible. Where a new generation sought different goals, or where established authorities used overwhelming repression, few would risk opposition.

Radical adult education is perhaps best understood as radical because of its service to radical movements. As we can see, a large part of such programmes is concerned with teaching rather basic skills such as literacy or running a co-op or a health centre, or a union, and only to a limited extent with ideological indoctrination. When the tolerance parameters in a society open - as in the 1930s in the USA when labour unions became legal with the Wagner Act, or when racial segregation was outlawed by the US Civil Rights Act - radical movements along with their adult education programmes collapse, or undergo goal transformation, and conventional and consumer adult education programmes come to the fore by popular choice.

On the basis of the very tentative beginning offered by this paper to type and juxtapose adult education programmes in socio-political context, what knowledge needs might future research address? Our choice would be to focus inquiry on the following questions:

1. How does commitment to radical change vary among movement leaders and followers, teachers and students? How significant is variation in explaining learning outcomes and application?
2. What pedagogical activities are most effective, i.e., correlate most strongly in achieving radical adult education's goals seeking to raise critical consciousness and commitment to struggle?

3. How do radical movements and their adult education programmes shift within types or across types as the tolerance parameters for protest, or oppressive conditions within the larger socio-economic and political context change?

Obviously these are only three areas where scholarly work offers promise to advance our understanding of the origins, activities, and contributions of radical adult education. Others might well select quite different questions. No matter, the field of adult education stands to gain much from such attempts to define, type, and advance explanation. And, as future research begins to show how the types identified share paradigmatic characteristics of common world-view, epistemology, appropriate puzzles to be solved and the like, the field will have moved in the direction of post-industrial scholarship.

REFERENCES

1. J. Cassell, A Group Called Woman: Sisterhood and Symbolism in the Feminist Movement (New York: David McKay, 1977); and W.E. Styler, Adult Education and Political Systems (University of Nottingham, Dept. of Adult Education, 1984).

2. J.C. McKinney, Construct Typology and Social Theory (New York: Appleton, 1966) and 'The Polar Variables of Type Construction', Social Forces, 35 (1957), pp. 300-6.

3. E.A. Tiryakian, 'Typologies' in the Encyclopedia of the Social Sciences (New York: Macmillan, 1979), p.235.

4. C.G. Hemphill, 'Typological Methods in the Social Sciences', in M.A. Natanson (ed.), Philosophy of the Social Sciences (New York: Random House, 1963), pp. 210-30.

15. Tiryakian, 'Typologies', p.237.

6. A.N. Charters et al., Comparing Adult Education Worldwide (London: Jossey-Bass, 1981) and R.E. Peterson et al., Adult Education and Training in Industrialised Countries (New York: Praeger, 1982).

7. R. Paulston, Other Dreams, Other Schools: Folk Colleges in Social and Ethnic Movements (Pittsburgh: University of Pittsburgh Centre for International Studies, 1980).

8. Styler, Adult Education and Political Systems.

9. R. Barnhardt, 'Administrative Influences in Alaskan

Native Education', in Cross-Cultural Issues in Alaskan Education (Fairbanks: University of Alaska Centre for Northern Educational Research, 1977), pp. 57-64; J.F, Concercoa, 'Government Programmes in Adult Education', in International Encyclopedia of Higher Education, Vol. II (London: Jossey-Bass, 1979); M.S. Knowles, The Adult Education Movement in the United States (New York: Holt, Rinehart and Winston, 1963).

10. R.G. Paulston and G. LeRoy, 'Non-Formal Education and Change from Below', in P. Altbach et al., (eds), Comparative Education (New York: Macmillan, 1982), pp. 336-62.

11. R.J. Altenbaugh and R. Paulston, 'Work Peoples' College: A Finnish Folk High School in the American Labour Movement', in Paedagogica Historica, International Journal of the History of Education, 18, 2 (1978), pp. 237-56; V.N. Turner, The Ritual Process: Structure and Antistructure (Chicago: Aldine, 1969).

12. R.R. Fagan, Cuba: The Political Content of Adult Education, Hoover Institution Studies No. 4 (Stanford; Stanford University, 1964); T. Hsi-en-Chen, The Maoist Educational Revolution (New York: Praeger, 1974); T.J. Labella, Non-Formal Education and the Poor in Latin America (New York: Praeger, 1986).

13. F. Adams, Unearthing Seeds of Fire; the Idea of Highlander (Winston-Salem, N.C: J.F. Blair, 1975); R.J. Altenbaugh, 'Forming the Structure of a New Society within the Shell of the Old: A Study of Three Labour Colleges and their Contributions to the American Labour Movement', PhD Dissertation, University of Pittsburgh 1980; M. Coady, Master of their own Destiny (Nova Scotia: Formal Publishing, 1980); B.L. Hall and J.R. Kidd, Adult Learning: A Design for Action (Oxford: Pergamon Press, 1978).

14. C. Ross, The Finn Factor in American Labour (New York Mills, M.N.: Parta Printers, 1977), p.49.

15. W.D. Haywood, The Autobiography of Big Bill Haywood (New York: International Publishers, 1974), p.63 (Original work published in 1929).

16. P.S. Foner, History of the Labour Movement in the United States: the Industrial Workers of the World, 1905-1917, Vol. 4 (New York: International Publishers, 1973), p.104.

17. M.G. Karni et al., For the Common Good: Finnish Immigrants and the Radical Response to Industrial America (Superior, W1: Tyomies Society, 1977), p.88. See also P.

Kivisto, Immigrant Socialists in the United States: The Case of the Finns and the Left (Cranbury, N.J.: Associated University Press, 1984).

18. Karni, p.105.

19. Work People's College Announcement of Courses (Dulworth, M N: The College, 1923), p.2.

20. R.J. Altenbaugh, 'Proletarian Drama: An Educational Tool of the American Labour College Movement', in Theatre Journal, 34, 2; 1978, pp. 197–210.

21. Karni, For the Common Good: Finnish Immigrants and the Radical Response to Industrial America.

22. M.A. Mason, The Educational Programmes and Activities of the Black Panther Party, 1966-1971: An Analysis and Assessment (International and Development Education Programme, University of Pittsburgh, 1976), p.25.

23. Ibid., p.27.

24. Ibid., p.28.

25. Ibid., p.29.

26. Ibid., p.30.

PART II

CONTEMPORARY INITIATIVES

6

Community Education and Community Action

Tom Lovett

Richard Johnson in his essay on the early nineteenth-century radical educators emphasised the relationship between the activities of the latter and the tremendous social, economic and political changes brought about by the industrial revolution. He rightly stressed the resonances between that period and the issues and problems facing educators and activists today and the fact that the historical investigation of the former is usually impelled by the concerns of the latter. Many adult educators would agree that the reason for their interest in the past is because of the apparent similarities between past and present. Community educators in particular would argue that we are faced with a crisis of a similar magnitude - a crisis in social, economic and political structures and a 'cultural' upheaval like the one in the early nineteenth century outlined by Johnson.

The tremendous economic and technological changes of the last two decades have affected every aspect of life, from the intimate details of personal and family relationships to the wider world of social, institutional, economic and political structures. As with every crisis of this magnitude there are opportunities for advancement or retrenchment; for liberating the human spirit, and removing gross inequalities, or for the reinforcement of injustices and an extension of inequalities.

It will not be possible in the space available to detail these changes but I would like to briefly mention some. For instance, in the cultural and moral area the most marked changes have occured in family life; in the role of, and relationship between, the sexes; in the position of women; in the attitude to established morality and tradition and in attitudes to authority generally. Traditional roles and relationships have fragmented, producing a demand for more democratic relations in daily life: between men and women, between parents and children; indeed in all spheres where people come together by necessity or choice. But the reality is that, whilst such liberation has had its positive effects, many people, particularly in working-class communities, do not have the opportunity, do not have access to either money or education, to make positive use of such a philosophy of personal liberation except in very restricted terms. As Jeremy Seabrook so vividly illustrates in his many books,[1] working-class areas have instead become the victims of a process of mindless violence, the community turning in on itself in the search for thrills, kicks, money.

Liberation has turned sour producing anomie and alienation, severely undermining any sense of collective responsibility or response. It is a bleak picture. Many would argue that he paints a very romantic image of working-class communities in the past and exaggerates the collective 'breakdown' of the present. However for many who live and/or work in such communities the picture he paints is recognisable. It does express some of the deeper discontents and anxieties of the contemporary working class, particularly a real sense of loss, which is not nostalgic but a genuine understanding of the cost of 'progress' in terms of any sense of community or collective responsibility.

In the social sphere the chages are as great. For many in the working-class the role of state and its agencies in the provision of housing, education, health and welfare services was initially seen as a move towards greater equality. However even before it came under attack from conservative administrations it had failed on two counts. First, it failed because it did not benefit the poor as much as it did the middle classes. Second, it failed because of its bureaucratic and institutional nature. It became an impersonal, distant, uncaring, social and welfare service. Thus, despite the movement towards a welfare state it is obvious that in the details of people's lives, in the new housing estates and tower blocks, people have been relieved of the worst of their miseries, encouraged to think rich and live poor, to become in effect the permanent prisoners of someone else's conception of their happiness.

Finally the economic and technological changes of the last decade, with mass unemployment, the growth of widespread poverty and the attacks on the remaining aspects of the welfare state have made such problems even worse. Behind the optimistic rhetoric of a new definition of work and increased opportunities for leisure is the spectre of enforced idleness, wasted resources and the squandering of a whole generation of human potential. New attitudes to work and leisure require radically new social and economic policies which few politicians, of the left or right, are prepared to contemplate.

The tensions and contradictions in this scenario have produced a response, not from politicians, but from a small but growing section of the population involved in various forms of social and community action. The growth of such organisations - community groups, tenants' associations, welfare rights groups, women's groups, community employment groups, popular planning associations, unemployed centres, alternative technology groups, co-operatives - bear witness to a general discontent with existing social and political structures. Those involved are attempting to come to grips with the injustices, the inequalities and the prejudices of a political system in which the practice of representative democracy appears to have little relevance to their plight as they battle against the social and economic problems briefly outlined above.

They are concerned to find new ways and means whereby individuals can be freed from existing constraints and afforded the possibility of individual growth and development through collective action. Theirs is an essentially optimistic view of human nature, one which stresses co-operation, fraternity, egalitarianism. It is basically a call for people, oppressed people, to have more control over their own lives, to shape their world and to use modern resources and technology to do so. It emphasises the need for participation rather than representation; a call in short for social and political structures which offer people the possibility of control of the resources of modern society to care for each other in an active, convivial manner. It presupposes that it is possible, in modern circumstances, using modern tools and resources, to find a way whereby men and women can become more fully integrated into their social environment and find in it something deeply expressive of their own personality and aspirations.

Such a new sense of community requires a common culture, a cultural democracy. However, as Tawney pointed out, a common culture cannot be created merely by desiring it. It rests upon economic foundations. It involves, in short, a large measure of economic equality. It also requires political action.

If the great mass of the people are to make a cultural democracy for themselves a prime

> objective must be the development of political awareness and action so that they can achieve command of their own culture and control of the socio-economic forces which affect it, surmounting the crises of a world of crises. Political competence, social commitment and community participation are among the essential characteristics of a man of culture.[2]

This is the major challenge facing adult educators today, the extent to which they can actively assist this process. This is what Freire means when he states:

> The starting point for organising the programme content of education or political action must be the present existential concrete situation reflecting the aspirations of the people. Utilising certain basic contradictions we must pose this essential situation to the people as a problem which challenges them and requires a response, not just at the intellectual level, but at the level of action.[3]

This is what he means by 'cultural action for freedom'.

In the following chapters in this book there are many illustrations of how adult educators have attempted to take up this challenge working with women, peace groups, the unemployed, ecology groups, trade unions, cooperatives, people in the Third World. In this chapter I want to concentrate on the response of community educators, particularly their reaction to the problems and issues facing the working class. I then want to conclude with an outline of my own personal experiences in this field here in Northern Ireland.

THE RESPONSE OF COMMUNITY EDUCATION

The role of community education in the process of social change has aroused a great deal of discussion and action by socially committed adult educators over the last two decades. It has also generated considerable disagreement. On the one hand are those adult educators who see in it exciting possibilities to extend the concept of adult learning, making it more relevant to the issues and problems facing 'disadvantaged' groups, helping them to participate more effectively in society, gaining more recognition and resources, removing gross inequalities and injustices. On the other hand are those who feel that adult educators should be wary when they are offered the resplendent new garments of 'community educators' intended to transform their perception of themselves and their role in society, particularly vis-à-vis the working class. They believe that the role of the community educator is much more limited than the rhetoric often implies.

This gap, between rhetoric and practice, this expanded view of community educators as major actors and agents in the arena of social change, versus a more limited, cautious role is, in some respects, though not all, a division between those concerned with access and those concerned with content in community education: between those concerned with 'merely useful knowledge' and those interested in 'really useful knowledge'.

This division has its roots in developments which took place in the late 1960s and 1970s, particularly in Great Britain. Then the question of social purpose once again became a relevant and important theme for adult educators. There was increased pressure on organisations like the Workers' Education Association to concentrate on the needs of the working class. There was also a great deal of debate about: the need to popularise knowledge, utilising aspects of working-class and popular culture in adult education; the problem of linking adult education more effectively to social and economic issues in local communities; the necessity for greater informality and flexibility in the provision of adult education; the importance of community-based adult education initiatives; the challenge of creating new educational 'networks' to provide a comprehensive community education service linking a range of education providers, formal and non-formal, to the needs and interests of working-class communities.

Important theoretical influences at the time were the writings of Bernstein, Illich and Freire. Berstein reinforced the belief that language and culture were major barriers in attracting working-class adults to education.[4] Consequently, more attention was paid to working-class and popular culture. Freire confirmed this approach with his concept of cultural invasion and the importance of using everyday life and experience as cultural material in an educational dialogue about concrete issues and problems, linking reflection and action in a continuing praxis.[5] Illich stressed the need to de-institutionalise education, to think instead of creative and dynamic 'learning networks' utilising a variety of educaional resources, formal and informal, including the skills and talents of people themselves.[6]

At a more practical level adult educators, like their counterparts in social work and education, were influenced by the initiatives taken by the federal agencies in the United States of America to resolve the problem of poverty and deprivation in inner city areas. The concept of the community school and community development were important influences here.

As far as the former is concerned, adult educators saw the emphasis on home/school links and parental involvement in schools as an opportunity for involving working-class parents in relevant education meeting a real need, i.e. their children's education. The concept of the 'community' school was regarded as a means of widening the role of the latter, making it a 'community resource' with a special stress on the provision of adult education and resources for community development - an educational powerhouse in each community.[7]

Community development, with its stress on community involvement in the search for solutions to local problems, was seen as an informal 'learning through doing' process which would benefit from the involvement of adult educators and vice versa. Many adult educators also regarded its concern for 'effective service delivery', i.e. coordinating all the relevant social, health, environmental, housing agencies and concentrating their expertise and resources on particular disadvantaged communities, linking them more effectively to local needs, as a total 'community learning network'.[8] They saw adult education as an important primary resource for all those local people and professionals involved in the search for solutions to local community problems.

This view of community education and development is well summed up in the first Gulbenkian Report on Community Work.

> Community work is essentially concerned with affecting the course of social change through the two processes of analysing social situations and forming relationships with different groups to bring about some desirable change. It has three main

aims: the first is the democratic process of involving people in thinking, dealing, planning and playing an active part in the development and operation of services that affect their daily lives: the second relates to the value for personal fulfilment of belonging to a community: the third is concerned with the need in community planning to think of actual people in their relation to other people and the satisfaction of their needs as persons rather than to focus attention upon a series of separate needs and problems.[9]

The end-result of these developments in the 1970s was a great variety of educational initiatives in working-class communities under the general umbrella of community education and action, e.g. neighbourhood learning centres, community arts and media centres, community learning exchanges, participatory research units, trade union and community resource centres, community schools, community development projects.

Even as far away as Australia commentators talked about a quiet revolution in the way Australians and their communities were responding to the types of learning challenges being presented to them by the changing social conditions of the 1970s and early 1980s.

One cannot but be struck by the extent to which traditional adult and community providers such as universities, colleges of advanced education, technical and further education colleges, workers' education associations and the plethora of service based organizations such as YMCAs and CWAS and so on, are being by-passed as people link up with, or fashion, their own community based continuing education capabilities. Such community based and genuinely continuing education orientated phenomena would form a major challenge to the power, prestige and relevance of large, established and more traditionally structured adult education providers.[10]

That sentiment, and the optimism expressed in such statements, farily accurately reflected the views of those involved in similar activities with working-class and oppressed groups in Great Britain and the United States of

America in the 1970s and early 1980s.

Thus, while Richard Johnson refers to the counter-education challenge to traditional education by the student movement, and the women's movement in the early 1970s, it is often forgotten that another site of opposition was in community-based education and action in working-class communities. It was, and is, in community-based education programmes that the problems of resources, space, control, content and method, mentioned by Johnson as the key issues in radical education, have been debated and explored. It is here that efforts have been made to open up resources to working-class communities and/or to provide access into educational institutions. Many of the lessons of this experience have been utilised by those involved in work with women, the unemployed and other oppressed minorities.

Yet community education in working-class communities has not grown to offer a radical alternative to traditional adult education provision. What went wrong? Some have suggested that the response was too wide and varied, like a catherine wheel - plenty of sparks and action but little sense of direction and inclined to chase its own tail. This back-handed compliment is, in fact, a tribute to the imagination and commitment of community educators. It also underlines one of the main reasons why community education did not become a radical movement for social change. Not the lack of direction but the fact that the various initiatives were going in different directions! The common concern with access and resources often disguised quite different assumptions about the nature of the problems facing the working class and the means to resolve them. However, this was not simply a conflict between radical process and radical content.

Like the situation in the nineteenth and early twentieth centuries, it was a struggle to resolve some basic contradictions, i.e. a desire to involve the working class in the control of their own education and a concern to link that education to a process of social and community action. It soon became clear however that the former was easier than the latter. Local community-based education projects, even when organised and controlled by local people, often mirrored the very education offered by traditional providers and rejected by a large section of the working class. A concern with personal growth and development was apparently in conflict with an emphasis on collective growth and development. Informal structures and local spaces for education with people 'doing it themselves' did not always produce a new definition of practical knowledge and/or a radical content.

Obviously, and understandably, working-class men and women took a very instrumental view of education and how it related to their needs and the opportunities available and open to them in society. They wanted education which offered some evidence of achievement, some possibility of widening their choices in life. Some adult educators felt that the 'alternative education' offered to such communities was not a real alternative. It was too informal, too concerned with non-directiveness and a limited concept of need and relevance, too immersed in 'learning through doing', particularly as far as community action was concerned. They decided to offer an alternative which, whilst concerned with collective efforts to improve social and economic conditions, would provide an education offering a real sense of achievement within an alternative curriculum linking local concerns with wider social and economic issues, hoping to provide an educational arm for the working class.

Two examples of these very different approaches, one concerned with community control of adult education the other with strengthening community and collective action, will, I hope, highlight some of the problems and difficulties, some of the tensions and contradictions in these efforts to reach the working-class with relevant education. One is from Scotland, the other from England.

The Strone and Maukinhill Informal Education Project

The problem of space and local control was an important element in the successful community education project in Greenock, Scotland. The Strone and Maukinhill Information Education Project was operated and controlled by local residents and financially supported by the local education authority.[11] It was situated in a post-war housing estate on the outskirts of Greenock and suffered from the same sort of social and economic problems found in the working class communities elsewhere. The project arose out of the work of a Community Action Project established in the area in 1972 and financed by the Rowntree Trust. This project worked with existing community groups in the area, helping to set up new groups and acting as a resource for community action. As a result of a request from the project to a local

College of Further Education for someone to provide an 'O' level class for mothers involved in a pre-school play-group, discussions took place about the possibility of setting up an educational project to complement and support the work of the community action project. In the summer of 1974 a public meeting was called and SMIEP (the Strone and Maukinhill Informal Education Project) was established. From the start it was controlled and directed by representatives from the community groups in the area, plus a representative from the college. The chair rotated annually and committee membership was limited to two successive years in order to avoid the dangers of elitism and institutionalisation. This particular initiative in community education, although building on a period of active community involvement, set out at an early stage to involve local residents in controlling the educational programme and establishing a structure for participation which, it was hoped, would avoid the sort of elitism which beset the WEA.

The classes offered by the project reflected an emphasis on instrumental and vocational education. Such classes appear to have formed the bulk of the programme and little was offered which could be seen as particularly relevant to community action or the problems of social change. Rather they were with practical home skills and formal qualifications. Thus in the autumn of 1974 classes were held in 'O' level English and Modern Studies and in Typing, Dressmaking, Car Care and Home Maintenance. This reflects the range of subjects found in other community education projects and confirms the view that community education can become, in many instances, more of the same, although taking place informally in local neighbourhood centres. In the SMIEP Project, classes were held in community halls and local homes and the resources were in the main provided by the James Watt College, illustrating once again that if an educational institution is prepared to venture out into the community, meet people on equal terms and offer its resources, then adult education can attract people who normally do not attend its classes or courses. The outreach approach has now been successfully attempted by many projects and institutions confirming the view of those who insist that educational institutions must be more open and outgoing if they are to provide a worthwhile community education service.

The Greenock Project summarised the lessons of its initiatives thus:

That, given co-operation and tact, there is a fund of goodwill in the bureaucracy, people with open minds who are prepared to try something new. That such projects should evolve, that the people involved should be allowed to feel their way gradually (they should be the doers) - mistakes in this game are really only important after they have been repeated. That a college like the James Watt should be prepared to play second fiddle, should never patronise but should be ready with sensible advice when asked for it. As community education begins to work through the community then the colleges (or any other resource of this nature) should recede even further.[12]

Although this particular initiative was successful in providing a community education service operated and controlled by local people, and subsidised by the local authority, it was very limited in scope. In fact, there was a contradiction at the heart of the project in terms of the aims and objectives of those involved in it. In discussing their views on community education they state that

> there is a serious side to community education and it is highly political in nature, that it should be directed towards equalising political power at local level, that communities should be learning skills to enable them to work with, and if necessary to confront local bureaucracy. If power is to be devolved to the people they must learn how to use power. This is just another way of describing community development and this you will not get without good solid, useful community education.[13]

Very radical indeed! Yet the actual educational work of the project was, as indicated above, very vocational and recreationally oriented (in the traditional sense) and confined to subjects such as 'O' levels, Typing, Dressmaking, Car Care, Home Maintenance, Conversational French. Hardly the stuff to enable local people to learn how to use power! In fact, experience would suggest that, when education is deinstitutionalised those with an interest in traditional subjects are likely to come forward first since they have already defined their interest but have been deterred by the formal procedure.

This is not to condemn such initiatives but to indicate the gap between their objectives and the actual work on the ground. It raises problems to do with the role and objectives of the professionals engaged in such work. Are they merely providers, acting as a resource for local communities, responding to needs and demands which are often based on past experience of education or have they a duty to seek ways and means of broadening the role of education into areas with which it is not normally associated such as changes in family and community life, the problems of poverty, inequality, and the general lack of local control over the formal decision-making process? This dilemma was referred to in a Council of Europe paper on Permanent Education.

> Whereas the aim of social advancement is to reduce individual inequalities but the social environment which produced them is left intact (on the assumption that these inequalities are due to inadequate education effort on the part of individuals, the state or to inequality of 'education gifts'), the aim of the collective advancement is to give individual education and, at the same time, influence the social context in which the individuals live: an effort is made to involve as many persons as possible in the education campaign. It will always be based on the concrete problems encountered by communities in real situations. Education will be a means of enabling them to develop; structural changes in the situation will make education easier and useful. Without collective advancement there can be no genuine individual advancement , but only uprooting.[14]

However, many community education projects have a social and political philosophy which sees community problems as the result of inadequate education effort on the part of institutions and the state, to be remedied by locally controlled community education networks. Acceptance of such a community philosophy ignores the fact:

(a) that many local community problems are in fact national, structural problems;
(b) that too much concentration on meeting articulated needs in an unimaginative and uncritical manner can

result in a community education programme which, whilst reaching a section of the population never catered for before, in fact assists individual advancement but does little to assist collective advancement towards solutions to the problems of poverty and inequality found in working-class communities.

This is not an easy dilemma to resolve and most community education projects have sought to provide both types of education based usually on a liberal, reformist view of education and social change. This latter ideology is in fact one which runs through most of the liberal adult education tradition in Britain. It is a tradition which emphasises a commitment to the working class as a section of society which should be the object of positive discrimination so that they can avail themselves of educational resources and opportunities. Community education can be seen as a means of ensuring the widening of such opportunities through a more effective delivery and coordination of education resources. It can cater more effectively than traditional methods for the wide range of individual needs and interests and also provide an educational back-up service for groups engaged in the process of community action. But those concerned seldom commit themselves to collective advancement on social and political issues, rarely setting themselves social and political as well as educational objectives. This creates the dilemma illustrated in the project discussed above, of appearing to meet local needs when in fact such actions do little about the real causes of social problems and may indeed aggravate them by uprooting local leaders. Other initiatives in community education have taken a more critical view of 'community development' and adopted a more radical approach.

The Liverpool Second Chance to Learn Project

This particular project began in Liverpool in 1976 and has established itself as a national model for radical working-class adult education. It has its roots in the work of Jackson, Yarnit and Ashcroft in Vauxhall, Liverpool in the early 1970's. They were involved in a great deal of supportive educational work with community groups and other working-class organisations in that area of the city.

However, the educational team took a more openly

153

critical view of the community development process and the philosophy underlying it.

> In our own project we have seen no alternative but to see local people as part of the working-class, exploited more than many of their fellows elsewhere by their social, economic and cultural environment in the centre of a large city, whose economy is shaky and uncertain in Britain's present stage of development. This determines the educational structures we must encourage emphasising wider contacts rather than local paro-chialism and the debate we think should take place around local social action. It is clear that this position creates difficulties when operating in the context of community development. Solidarity with working-class activists sits unhappily with non-directive help offered to autonomous community groups.[15]

The team thus took a much more radical, class, view of the problems facing residents in working-class communities and did not see themselves simply responding to any educational need or demand: '... the educationalist should be forced to recognise his responsibility to intervene positively and con-structively not just respond to any demand'.[16]

The team had an explicit position to debate with local residents and did not hide its philosophy and politics behind a bushel. It tried to define more clearly those occasions when it could make a positive and explicit contribution to solving the problems facing local activists rather than just becoming involved in learning-through-doing activities with the latter. This created problems which were not easily resolved since, given the team's philosophy, it was essential to operate in the context of 'solidarity with working-class activists'. However, they did make important contributions to the education of local residents involved in the problems of vandalism, lack of recreational facilities and housing.

Throughout the early reports there is a constant emphasis on the level and content of the work, in an obvious attempt to stress that adults in 'deprived' areas are capable of undertaking sustained, demanding education if it is seen to be relevant to their needs. As a result of this experience, and this emphasis on educational standards, it was decided in 1976 to establish a Second Chance to Learn course for local activists from various parts of the city. The course is run one day a week over 30 weeks for 60 students. It is organised and taught by tutors from the WEA and the Liverpool University Department of Adult Education.

When the course began in 1976 its tutors believed that content was more important than process. 'To put content before form is not to deny the importance of pedagogy, or to equate content with a perpetual diet of politics. It is merely to affirm that in the end if education is to grow deep roots in the working-class, they will be nourished more by what people learn than how they learn'.[17] However, since then the course has realised the importance of methodology and its value as one complementary to content.

A more fundamental change in the course over the years is the emphasis on individual development and growth within a radical perspective. There is now some questioning as to whether the stress on working-class adult education may in fact present a narrow version of the possibilities for social change which excludes other social movements and oppressed groups in society. It is also clear from a recent evaluation that, despite the fact that the course was originally concerned with recruiting activists and not concerned with qualifications, the activists are now in the minority and that the course has become for many a means of access into higher education.[18]

This is not surprising. It echoes the experience of Ruskin and other residential adult education colleges. It also echoes the experience of similar day-release courses for working-class adult students. However, if the original social and education objectives of the course have not been met it has nevertheless succeeded in tapping the hidden intellectual and educational potential of many working-class men and women. It is in terms of the latter and their involvement in, and influence on, movements for social change that the project will be judged radical or not. In some respects it is an initiative influenced by the experience of the Plebs League and the NCLC, discussed in previous chapters. It has sought to avoid the narrow dogmatism of the latter, combining a radical analysis with democratic participatory teaching methods. However this effort to resolve the problems of access and content within an institutional framework has apparently seriously weakened the earlier close ties with social and political movements in working-class communities in the city.

Another attempt to resolve this dilemma, to provide really useful knowledge, <u>outside</u> of institutions and in close cooperation with the working class and other oppressed groups, is to be found in N. Ireland, i.e. The Ulster Peoples' College. However before examining it I want to say something about the general response of community educators to the problems facing the working-class in N. Ireland.

COMMUNITY EDUCATION IN NORTHERN IRELAND – THE RESPONSE

Northern Ireland has been described as a society under siege, a society where there is a problem for every solution! The usual picture is one of violence and sectarianism. However it is, in fact, a society facing all the social and economic problems outlined at the beginning of this paper plus armed conflict and community division. It has one of the highest unemployment rates in the EEC. The situation is well summed up by a community worker in the Creggan area of Derry, a city profoundly affected by these changes.

When I think of all the social problems there are I mean Creggan has everything. It's got poor housing. It's got people on low incomes. Those that are employed are on low wages; the majority are unemployed. When you're talking in terms of Creggan - widows, pensioners, single parent families - you name it we've got it. We've got poor facilities medically; we've got poor facilities as far as shopping is concerned; no telephone, no place to post your letters. I sometimes think that if we were back in biblical days and John the Baptist was running around looking for a wilderness he wouldn't go to the desert he would come to Creggan! This is an estate of two and a half thousand homes and there is something like a population of 13,000 people. Perhaps the authorities are fortunate that the people up here have a certain amount of self respect for themselves. God knows how they manage to keep this about themselves with the situation as it is. But somehow, the people manage to keep themselves together. Maybe it's a pity that people haven't lost the head a bit; that they haven't gone berserk and showed up the authorities for what they are - I don't know, unfeeling, inhuman, unconcerned. That's the impression we get up here; nobody cares, nobody's interested.[19]

It is obvious from the above comments that many of the problems facing the working-class in Northern Ireland are similar to those found elsewhere. However, in Northern Ireland they are compounded by violence and sectarianism. Some commentators see it as a society suffering from a vast nervous breakdown at community level, with the social fabric slowly disintegrating. This is far from the truth. The people are brave, resilient, humorous, friendly in the face of great change and adversity. They have responded to their troubles and problems with imagination and initiative. They have been involved in various forms of community action designed to protect and regenerate community life and to tackle the social, economic and cultural problems common to both communities - Catholic and Protestant.

This process of community action has involved people from both communities, people with no politics, people with radical views, people with connections with paramilitary groups. It has resulted in the formation of numerous community associations, tenants' groups, community resource centres, welfare rights centres, women's groups, cooperatives, etc.

These developments provided, for a short period, a bridge between the two divided communities emphasising their common problems, their common culture. It even had some influence on paramilitary groups like the Protestant Ulster Defence Association. One of their spokesmen commented,

We are aware that socially and economically we have more in common with our opposite numbers in the Republican (Catholic) side than we have with loyalist (Protestant) big-wigs. But, how are we going to put this over? What formula are we going to find to get the ordinary people of Ulster to vote on real issues which concern them and not on the entrenched sectarian issues into which we are brainwashed.[20]

A Catholic community leader echoing the above sentiment said,

> No matter what happens to the National question
> in the final analysis the community struggle goes
> on, the struggle against the hopelessness and help-
> lessness of ordinary people to manage to cope in a
> very complex society. We cannot separate politics
> from community action, no matter what we try to
> do about it, no matter how idealistic we may be.[21]

This popular response in the 1970s presented community
educators with a real challenge. It indicated that community
education for peace and reconstruction offered a possible
alternative to violence and conflict by building a united
working-class movement based on local community action.
The response was, however, like the catherine wheel
analogy, wide and varied - community education workshops,
community education programmes and projects, social
studies groups, community work, education forums, women's
education projects, second chance projects.

Like similar developments in Europe, North America
and Australia, these initiatives reflected a wide range of
activities and corresponding educational, social and political
philosophies, sometimes openly stated, often not. The result
was a certain pragmatic consensus which glossed over their
ideological differences in favour of meeting local 'needs' and
an emphasis on process at the expense of content and
direction.

However, by the late 1970s these ideological divisions
surfaced in the debates between, and amongst, community
activists and community educators. The pragmatic
consensus weakened as people became more aware of the
tensions and contradictions between these different
approaches to community education and working-class
community action. It was obvious that the latter had
brought no great changes in the problems of poverty and
inequality facing the working class in Northern Ireland. In
fact their position had worsened considerably. There is no
evidence that people had any more influence on the policies
of major institutions. There are no programmes of participation in schools, social welfare agencies, planning departments, housing authorities, etc. Local community action
had in fact failed to make any important impact on the
larger social and economic political structures in Northern
Ireland. This is not to decry the small, but important,
changes and victories at local level. However, community
education does not present an alternative, radical analysis

and vision for those involved in this process. Instead, in the main, it has concentrated on access, second chance, and a limited concept of training for community activists. With some notable exceptions it assists the process of individual growth and development but does little for collective growth and development. One such exception was the Ulster People's College.

THE ULSTER PEOPLE'S COLLEGE

At the beginning of the 1980s a group of community activists, trade unionists, community educators, peace workers and feminists met and agreed that what was needed was a reappraisal of previous efforts in the field, a conscious effort to determine their own social and political position and to choose an educational model or approach which reflected the latter.

This group felt that the community movement of the 1970s had been too romantic, too naïve, too easily influenced by the popular educational theories and conventional wisdoms of the decade. They applauded the attempt to cross the sectarian divide to stress the problems common to members of the working-class in both communities. However, they felt that this did not grasp the nettle of community division and conflict between the two sections of the working class. They believed that it was necessary to combine the best in local community action and larger social concerns; to bring the fragments of social and community action together, e.g. community groups, trade unions, women's groups, etc. to work towards a vision of a new society based on a radical analysis of existing structures and the lessons and aspirations of the men and women attempting to create new structures at local level; to stress objectives and content in education as well as methods and process.

From previous experience it was obvious that, on the one hand, not all alternatives in adult education were necessarily radical. On the other hand, there were grave limitations in using existing adult education institutions for radical education and action. Their sense of social responsibility is to society at large. Work with the poor and the oppressed is a marginal activity. This is not to decry the useful, and often innovative, work done by such institutions. However, the concept of social responsibility and service is of limited use in developing a radical social movement.

The group decided to go back to other dreams, other schools like some of those discussed in the earlier chapters of this book. They were particularly struck by the work of the Highlander Centre in the USA[22] founded over fifty years ago by Myles Horton. Its maxim is, 'Learn from the people and start education where they are.' Highlander has worked closely with various social movements in the USA, e.g. trade unions, farmers, civil rights. It has sought to educate people away from the trap of individualism and to reinforce those instincts which lead to cooperation and collective solutions to problems. It has survived from the early 1930s because of its craggy independence, its non-institutional base, its ability to adapt to new social movements thrown up by the working-class and oppressed groups and, most important, its radical philosophy and perspective.

With this as a model and financial support from various trusts and charities, the Ulster People's College was established in 1982.[23] It is situated in Belfast and has short-term accommodation for 30 people. This central resource is used to complement and strengthen the work in the field; to extend the process of action and learning in local communities; to bring together people from both sides of the religious divide, and from different movements, to reflect on their common problem; to learn from their different experiences and to discuss their cultural and political differences.

The College is thus issue and problem-oriented. It is not concerned with access, second chance or certification. It is openly committed to radical social change and the concept of individual and collective growth and development. As well as providing space for workshops and conferences on various social, economic and political issues as they arise, the College is developing an alternative curriculum based on the issues and problems facing men, women and youth in working-class communities throughout Northern Ireland. It is also seeking to explore ways and means whereby men and women can play a larger part in the reconstruction of local working-class communities through the establishment of new forms of social and economic structures designed to meet local needs in a collective fashion.

What the Ulster People's College is about is developing an alternative vision of society. Until recently, educational initiatives concerned with such alternative views have been severely neglected in the discussion about community education and social change. Yet the evidence, as outlined in the earlier chapters of this book, is that, historically, such alternatives played an important role in encouraging, supporting and strengthening movements for social change. This is part of the hidden history of education.

As indicated in this chapter, many contemporary initiatives in community education are not really radical alternatives but various extensions of the prevailing liberal ideology in adult education. Yet never was the need greater to think in terms of real alternatives in adult education, helping people to dream <u>their</u> dreams, to construct their version of a better society out of their own experiences.

Such a search for educational alternatives can reach back to that radical historical tradition in adult education which drew no fine distinction between action and education. This is the challenge facing community educators: a challenge which requires them to engage in a process of reflection on their action: to clarify their views of the crisis facing the working class: to face up to certain contradictions in their practice: to sharpen their sense of social commitment. Only then will they have a clearer, more honest assessment of what exactly is their role in relation to social, economic and political inequalities and injustices. Only then will they be able to decide whether they see community education as something complementary to the formal adult education provision or an alternative system pursuing distinct and radical objectives.

In the Australian experience referred to earlier, those engaged in the study of alternative community-based educational initiatives stressed the former rather than the latter, 'The innovating organisation will only survive if it can show them (the statutory bodies and local power groups) that its power is complementary rather than invasive.'[24] Much community education is struggling to achieve that objective. However, radical community education is not concerned with complementing or invasion. It is concerned with <u>challenging</u> the way things are.

NOTES

1. Jeremy Seabrook, <u>What Went Wrong</u>? (London: Victor Gollancz, 1978). See also <u>Unemployment</u> (London: Granada, 1983).
2. J.A. Simpson, <u>Towards Cultural Democracy</u> (Council

for Cultural Cooperation, Council of Europe, Strasbourg, 1976), p.34.

3. Paulo Freire, Pedagogy of the Oppressed (Harmondsworth: Penguin, 1972), p.68.

4. B. Bernstein, Class, Codes and Control, Vol. I (London: Routledge and Kegan Paul, 1971).

5. P. Freire, Pedagogy of the Oppressed and Cultural Action for Freedom (Harmondsworth: Penguin, 1974).

6. I. Illich, Deschooling Society (London: Calder and Boyars, 1972).

7. Eric Midwinter, Priority Education (Harmondsworth: Penguin, 1972).

8. Keith Jackson 'Adult Education and Community Development', in Studies in Adult Education, November 1970.

9. Calouste Gulbenkian Foundation, Community Work and Social Change: A Report on Training (London: Longmans, 1968), p.4.

10. Michael Glostor, 'Non-Formal Education: Implications for the Recurrent Education of Teachers'. Paper presented to the Australian Adult Education Association (November 1980), p.1.

11. J. Jackson, 'The Strove and Maukinhall Informal Education Project - A Greenock Experiment', Scottish Journal of Education, Spring 1976.

12. Ibid., p.7.

13. Ibid., p.6.

14. Council of Europe, Permanent Education -Evaluation of Pilot Experiments, Interim Report (Strasbourg: Council for Cultural Cooperation Steering Group on Permanent Education, 1974), p.3.

15. K. Jackson, 'The Marginality of Community Development. Implications for Adult Education', International Review of Community Development, Summer 1973, p.38.

16. Ibid., p.26.

17. Judith Edwards, Working-Class Education in Liverpool: A Radical Approach, Manchester Monographs (Manchester: University of Manchester, Centre for Adult and Higher Education, 1986), p.7.

18. Ibid., p.4.

19. T. Lovett and P. McAteer, Working-Class Community in N. Ireland (Belfast: The Ulster People's College), forthcoming.

20. Ibid.

21. Quoted in, T. Lovett, C. Clarke and A. Kilmurray,

Adult Education and Community Action (London: Croom Helm, 1983), p.56.

22. F. Adams, Unearthing Seeds of Fire - The Story of Highlander (N. Carolina: J.F. Blair, 1975).

23. The Ulster People's College, A Discussion Document (Belfast: The Ulster People's College, 1982).

24. M. Glostor, 'Non-Formal Education', Appendix B, p.2.

7

Adult Education and the Peace Movement

Budd L. Hall
(Dedicated to the memory of Nabila Breir)

INTRODUCTION

As I sit here in the kitchen of my home trying to begin this paper I admit to having one of the symptoms of our times - a feeling of helplessness. It is my hope that by writing something for others, itself an act, I shall be able to see more clearly what some of the next steps should be.

Two weeks ago a very good friend was assassinated in Beirut. Her name was Nabila Breir. She was my age. She had a twelve-year-old daughter and a husband and brothers and friends. She played the piano and sang. One of her favourite songs was 'Besame Mucho' which she sang off-key and with great passion. She worked for UNICEF in the refugee camps of southern Lebanon as an adult educator.

She was on her way to the office in the morning by taxi. At one of the checkposts, she was taken from the taxi by three gunmen with machine guns. One gun was emptied into her head, another into her stomach. Now she is dead.

And I write this article for Tom Lovett, living and working in Northern Ireland where there have been so many Nabilas. Each death ripples through a circle of families and friends and crushes them.

Since 1945 and the signing of the peace agreements at the end of the Second World War, 20 million Nabilas have died in 150 wars of various sizes.

Is it enough yet? I guess not as there have been further deaths in Beirut since then and further deaths elsewhere. What of Iran and Iraq? How is it that arms continue to be sold to both of those countries by the same sources?

And I don't like it. And you don't like it. And the families of the dead don't like it.

And from my childhood a phrase, 'On and on and on it goes, where it stops nobody knows.'

Having started this in such a personal vein, I shall continue. You need to know my own limitations in writing an article about peace education if you are to be able to know how to use this.

Involvement in peace education in a formal sense began in 1980 when Helena Kekkonen, a friend from Finland, asked whether the International Council for Adult Education might consider giving support to a Peace Education network. We agreed to do so and I began to learn about peace education for adults.

Another person who has continued to be important to me in this regard has been Betty Reardon, an American peace educator who lives and works out of New York. She has helped me to understand the links between militarism and masculinity. Murray Thomson of Peacefund Canada has been the one who has taught me the most about organising for peace. His lifetime devotion to non-violence has been a critical element in my beginning to understand peace.

In addition to supporting the peace education network of the ICAE, I have taught a course on Peace Education and Mass Movements at the Ontario Institute for Studies in Education and have helped to start an organisation for the financial support of peace education in Canada and elsewhere called Peacefund Canada.

In the context of supporting others and trying in modest ways to make a personal contribution to the peace movement, I have learned several things about peace. In spite of the fact that almost everybody seems to be for peace, it remains at least in Canada a controversial subject. It is not an automatic part of the school curricula. My own children, one 16 the other 11, have not studied anything about peace yet, and it seems unlikely that they will have the chance. Attempts to introduce balanced discussions about living in a nuclear age into the city school system have been met with a combination of reluctant acceptance on the part of the majority of the school trustees and outright hostility on the part of some parents. So suspicion and fear accompany the concept of peace.

Another aspect that I have learned is that peace is a most complex concept. It is, not surprisingly, framed by the context we live in. For Europeans the thought of missiles whooshing overhead from both the US and USSR has led to a focus on the East-West conflict. In Northern Ireland, peace has a more immediate focus, the end to the years of killing. For Palestinians peace means having at last a homeland. For Nicaraguans peace means an end to US aggression. For most of the Third World peace means an end to structural violence as well as ending the direct oppression of despotic governments such as those in Chile and South Africa. The daily violence against women is appropriate content for peace education in Canada and elsewhere.

Perhaps the most common experience that I have encountered is that people feel disenfranchised about peace. Peace is not something that ordinary people can do anything about. What we can do will not make a difference. Peace is the subject of diplomats and generals. And the films depicting the horrors of nuclear war often do nothing more than freeze us still more. We are mentally numb from the staggering immensity of it all. We feel what all oppressed people feel, a sense of powerlessness.

You will note that I am not an historian of the peace movement. I am not an academic specialist in peace studies. I am an adult educator who shares with many others a profound concern that we should not kill each other to solve problems on a small or large scale. I am willing to contribute some ideas based on my personal experience which might lend support to you in your work for similar goals. My ideas are organised as follows:

1. Peace education: an historic role for adult education.
2. The role of peace education within the peace movement.
3. The content of peace education for adults.
4. A new legitimacy for peace education?
5. Action and empowerment.

The Most Dangerous

The most dangerous is not hate
No-one can hate for long
For it hurts

Apathy is more comfortable
But most dangerous
Because it has no feeling
Living in Apathy is excellent

We live it
Until we die.

Agneta Ara

PEACE EDUCATION: AN HISTORIC ROLE FOR ADULT EDUCATION

Adult educators have been preoccupied with issues of international understanding, solidarity and peace for many years, long before UNESCO or the International Council for Adult Education. As early as 1928, adult educators gathered in Cambridge, England, for the first world gathering under the banner of the World Association for Adult Education, with Albert Mansbridge as Secretary and Thomas Masaryk, President of Czechoslovakia as President. Although the World Association faded away, its hopes had been high and accurate regarding the determination of adult educators eventually to find ways of working together for international understanding and peace. Mansbridge himself said at the time,

> There can be no failure. The way may be difficult, long years may be spent upon it, but every step forward increases the multitude of the wise, the welfare of the world.[1]

Peace, and the role which adult education might play in achieving it, was a priority at the 1949 World Conference on Adult Education organised by UNESCO in Denmark. People from 40 countries came together to look at what might be done through education to rebuild a world split by the long violence of the Second World War.

Ned Corbett, the Secretary of the Canadian Adult Education Association, noted that, 'It gave the adult education movement throughout the world new impetus, a larger vision, and renewed hope for a world at peace.'[2]

In 1960, a second UNESCO meeting on adult education was held in Montreal. It was a time, much like our own, with high tension and mistrust between the United States and the Soviet Union. The U-2 spy plane incident had just happened and the official governmental delegations were expected to split over political differences.

What emerged from that conference was an eloquent statement on the priority for adult education. From the 'Montreal Declaration':

> Our first problem is to survive. It is not a question of the survival of the fittest: either we survive together or we perish together. Survival requires

that the countries of the world must learn to live
together in peace. 'Learn' is the operative word.
Mutual respect, understanding, sympathy are qualities that are destroyed by ignorance, and fostered
by knowledge. In the field of international
understanding, adult education in today's divided
world takes on a new importance.[3]

In 1976, UNESCO held its general conference in
Nairobi, Kenya. One of the actions taken there and adopted
by the 122 governments present was the Recommendation
on Adult Education.[4] This document was worked out in a
consultative manner over a period of several years. It is a
quite remarkable instrument which deserves reading by
activist adult educators.

In this document, four Aims for Adult Education are:

(a) promoting work for peace, international understanding
     and cooperation;
(b) developing a critical understanding of major contem-
     porary problems and social changes and the ability to
     play an active part in the progress of society;
(c) creating an understanding of, and respect for, the
     diversity of custom and cultures on both the national
     and international planes;
(d) promoting increasing awareness of, and giving effect to,
     various forms of community and solidarity at the family,
     local, national, regional and international levels.

In October of 1981, Helena Kekkonen, then secretary of
the Finnish Association of Adult Education organisations
was awarded the first UNESCO Peace Education Prize in
recognition of her many years of peace education. This act
was both a recognition of the importance of her work as
well as recognition of the importance of the contributions of
adult education to the peace movement in general.

In June 1982, all the nations of the United Nations met
for the Second Special Session on Disarmament in New York
City. About one million people took to the streets to lend
support to the governments in the hope that they would take
substantial action towards disarmament. Governments were
unable, however, to make progress on the critical issues on
the agenda. The one exception to this was the support given
for the creation of the World Disarmament Campaign. The
campaign was created, 'to inform, to educate, and to

generate public understanding and support' for the UN's disarmament efforts.

As one of the architects of the World Disarmament Campaign, Murray Thomson of Canada, has noted, 'The world's decision-makers had thereby admitted, wittingly or not, that without a large-scale, global educational movement, the normal political processes in which they were engaged would be ineffective.'[5]

In June 1983 at the meeting of the ICAE Peace Education Network and the annual 'Meeting in Finland' the assembled adult educators made an international call to action to all adult educators.

> We adult educators from twenty-one countries... aware that our profession is dedicated to life-long learning in a world which spends $650 billion a year on arms ($950 million in 1987) and in which 900 million adults are illiterate.
>
> And concerned that our efforts to seek, 'the full development of the human personality and the strengthening of respect for fundamental liberties' [UN Declaration of Human Rights] are increasingly threatened...
>
> Therefore call on all adult educators... to join with us in a global effort to help stop the arms race and to urge that substantial resources now spent on weapons to be used to:
>
> 1. promote adult literacy and learning for international understanding;
> 2. meet basic human need, such as primary health care and the elimination of poverty and unemployment;
> 3. create the conditions for guaranteeing and enforcing basic rights and freedoms in all countries;
> 4. help to create an awareness of existing unjust economic relations in the world and to support UN efforts for a New International Economic Order.[6]

From you I receive
To you I give
Together we share
From this we live
(Sufi song)

THE ROLE OF PEACE EDUCATION WITHIN THE PEACE MOVEMENT

There are several ways one can understand learning and the peace movement. In one sense the peace movement can as a whole be examined as an example of a mass learning campaign. The goal of the peace movement being to inform people and encourage them to take action towards specific political objectives. In this way of looking at learning and the peace movement, the decision to become involved in one aspect or another of the peace movement triggers further learning. The further learning can be conscious and deliberate such as the selection and reading of papers, reports and books about the nature of violence, the state of the arms race or the various options of weapons as sources of security. This often occurs with newcomers to the peace movement.

Learning still more often takes a more informal form. One may have agreed to work on the local peace committee as a special events organiser. The specific activities are working on a poster or leaflet for a public discussion which is coming up, finding someone to help with child-care during the session and collecting contributions from the participants for further work. In the course of doing this kind of organising one has to inform others about the event, talk with fellow-workers while doing the work, listen to the talk or information session or argue with one's friends or partners about why it is important to be involved in this kind of activity. The learning which takes place in these contexts is powerful and important.

The peace movement needs to be aware that such a learning process is going on all the time. In fact reflection on how this learning happens, how to strengthen it or how to extend it represents a powerful tool for strengthening the overall movement.

There is another way to think about the role of peace education within the peace movement. Peace education forms a conscious part of many broad-based peace movements. In a larger peace group, it is common to have a committee or working group with a specific task of peace education. There may be other committees on political action, fund-raising, research and liaison with other groups.

A third way to see peace education within the overall movement is to examine the functions of the different types of organisations which are making a contribution. There are some which concentrate on mobilisation and political action, those which do research and investigation and those which focus on education. I would submit that of the three functions outlined (mobilisation, research and education), the educational dimension is the weakest at present.

Betty Reardon in discussing the roles of peace education talks about the 'Three A's' of peace education - Awareness, Analysis and Action.

Awareness refers to a combination of identifying and providing accurate information and the fostering of situations in which women and men can begin to believe that change is possible. Good films have often been the beginning of becoming aware of the threat of nuclear holocaust for people living in the industrialised nations. The eloquent speakers of the peace movement have also played very strong roles in catching people's attention for the first time. Good books and television programmes have also been strong motivational tools in the peace movement. The key to whether something will work to create awareness is whether it can touch the person directly. Does it have the power to bring the deadly but abstract concept of nuclear horror to a personal level?

The provision of information in this work is very difficult. Information about violence, war, arms, peace and security is highly flavoured and shaped by the interests of those who own or control our societies. National and international security is one of the most central concerns of our governments and other groups. It is sometimes difficult to get information one feels is accurate or to know whose ideas stand behind the articles, booklets or television programmes that one sees.

There are however some kinds of data and information which can be proven and are effective. The Palme Commission, for example, was made up of prominent worlds figures including persons from the South as well as persons from the United States and the Soviet Union. They were able to agree on what was happening in 1982.

The World Disarmament Campaign of the United Nations also provides a broad set of materials on all aspects of arms control and security issues. These have the broad support of all the members of the United Nations and are therefore good sources of information.

Analysis, the second 'A', refers to the study, discussion and more in-depth reflection which follows an early raising of one's consciousness. It is important that we test the information we are hearing. What does it really mean? What is the specific case for our town, our country? What are the links between research in our universities and war industries? Why is so much money spent on arms? What else could such money be used for?

The questions are limitless. There are entire sets of concerns about security which could be explored. Are arms the only way to protect our national or regional interests? What are the alternative security measures that could be tried? What would international security really mean instead of national security? Clearly the techniques of adult education, the experience with small group methods and the many lessons in stimulating learning have a strong potential in this arena.

Action, the final 'A', again takes on a broad and varied form depending on the context. Action may take the form of direct communication with different levels of government authorities. It may be physical action as with the various attempts to halt the deployment of missiles in Europe. It may be symbolic as with the women of Greenham Common or the tying of a yellow ribbon around the Pentagon in Washington. It may be the organisation of a network, the writing of a book or even the writing of a chapter for a book! It comes from analysis and discussions of strategy as well as a sense of the political. It means doing what one can wherever one is. It means that all actions count.

Crazy Train

Crazy, but that's how it goes
Millions of people living as foes
Maybe it's not too late
To learn how to love
And forget how to hate

Mental wounds not healing
Life's a bitter shame
I'm going off the rails on a crazy train

(Words from a song by heavy-metal rocker, Ozzy Osborne)

THE CONTENT OF PEACE EDUCATION

I like one of the definitions of peace education which Helena Kekkonen uses. She says that peace education is a process which gives 'the possibility for people to grow in consciousness of the world's problems, as citizens who work actively on behalf of world-wide positive peace'.[7]

Our goals as peace educators should be to contribute to the creation of a culture of peace. We need to construct visions of a world without armed struggles. We must engender a reverence for life, a love for life. We must enable ourselves and others to understand and act on the fact that social justice and human equity should go before economic profit. And the fact of our interdependence and global sisterhood and brotherhood needs to be stressed and supported.

The 1974 Recommendation on Education for International Understanding, Co-operation and Peace Education adopted by UNESCO provides a broad base for peace education.

> Education... should bring every person to understand and assume his or her responsibility for the maintenance of peace. It should contribute to international understanding and strengthening of world peace and to the activities in the struggle against colonialism and neo-colonialism in all their forms and manifestations and against all forms and varieties of racism, fascism and apartheid.[8]

Many peace educators stress the importance of the concept of permeability. By this they mean that peace education needs to permeate all levels and forms of education. There is room for the basic goals of peace education in all subject matters. If, for example, our entire school system were structured with the creation of a culture of peace as a goal the need for special remedial peace education for adults would be different.

Helena Kekkonen refers to several sectors of peace education:[9]

1. <u>Cultural education.</u> This is educational work directed at the understanding of the different cultures of people in our own countries and in other countries. The creation of fear, suspicion and distortion of the 'enemy' is

critical to achieving on-going support for war, war expenditures and aggression. It is not enough simply to reduce this distortion, positive concepts and information must replace the distrust.

2. Environmental Education. The destruction of our physical environment is real. Deeper understanding of the laws of nature and harmonious ways of living with our natural world are part of our structures of peace. The human focus on hunger and disease as a result of environmental destruction are important to understand as contributors to tension.

3. Human rights education. Understanding of three aspects of human rights are needed; political and civic rights which western nations have particularly stressed, economic and social rights which socialist countries have stressed and social justice and development rights which Third World nations have stressed.

4. Disarmament education. Specific facts about the role, presence and need for reduction or elimination of arms as means of conflict resolution. The damage and the cost of these weapons is staggering and can be conveyed more often and in more effective ways.

5. Equality Education. Women are targets of aggression in our world. This should end. Women are also the safe-keepers of a core of values, attitudes and behaviour which seek survival. Qualities of compromise, negotiation, cooperation and tenderness, associated most often with women, need to be part of human qualities. Peace begins at home.

6. Development education. Two-thirds of the people of the world live in the nations of Latin America, Africa and Asia. The structures by which these people's poverty and dependence is prolonged need to be understood by more people. The rich history, literature and culture of these majority cultures and their contributions to a more peaceful world are key.

Feelings and the Culture of Peace

Music, poetry, literature, drawing, painting, sculpture and all the arts have a particularly important role to play. Effective education, effective life is based on feelings and emotions. Learning which has as its goal the construction of a culture of peace can make effective use of all the arts.

Music reaches a part of our minds which a lecture will not. Creating music together or writing songs together can reinforce at an emotional level concepts which have been difficult to understand simply through reading or discussion.

Our ability to imagine a different world is critical to our ability to change. The elements of new culture already exist in our present world, but in fragmented and scattered forms. Through aesthetic sharing we draw the pieces together and experience momentary glimpses of a new reality. In my own experience in seminars, conferences or workshops, the use of drama, music and art has been the most effective method for bringing the concepts of peace education together. From the setting of moods to prepare people for a relaxed seminar, to the use of collective drawing to help us visualise complex political and social relations, to the writing of plays about everyday experiences with peace, positive results have nearly always occurred.

A NEW LEGITIMACY FOR PEACE EDUCATION

One of my first reactions to being asked to write these notes for a collection on the radical tradition in adult education, was one of lament. Lament for the fact that peace, the central goal of humanity, should so often be the content of the programmes of the courageous minority of activists who dare to be unpopular and provocative. Lament as well for the fact that peace educators are the ones still operating cake sales, jumble sales and auctions for peace while the generals have the big budgets. How I long to see a cake sale organised by the generals to buy a new missile!

But then I think again about the new nature of the peace movement in Canada. In addition to the traditional groups working for peace such as the Quakers (Society of Friends), many socialists, communists, ageing ban-the-bombers, solidarity committees and other spiritually based groups such as Gandhians, there are new peace constituencies.

We have in Canada just now, Lawyers for Social Responsibility, Physicians for Social Responsibility, Educators for Social Responsibility, Cartoonists for Peace, Adult Educators for Peace, Parents for Peace, Seniors for Peace, the Peace Education Project, Artists for Peace, Business for Peace, Mothers for Peace, the Voice of Women, the Group of 78, Parlimentarians for Peace, even Generals and War Veterans for Peace! And there must be more groups which do not spring to mind while writing.

Within the adult education movement alone in Canada there are peace committees within the Institut Canadien d'éducation des Adultes, the Canadian Adult Education Association, the Canadian Association for the Study of Adult Education, the Ontario Institute for Adult Education (called 'A Place for Peace Study'), the Rural Learning Association and several of the provincial adult education associations.

Is peace aquiring a broader constituency? It is worth noting that, again in Canada, when the United States was putting considerable pressure on the Conservative government of Canada to join with them on the Star Wars initiative, a tremendous upswelling of public opinion against this prevented the Prime Minister from giving official government support. As it was the government still gave permission for private companies to participate.

Again in late 1986, the Toronto Star, one of the major newspapers in the country, had headlines three days in a row reporting from a peace conference in Edmonton, Alberta, that drew leaders from across the country. That has never happened before.

Peace seems to be gaining a broader base within Canada. It has a strong base within many parts of Europe, both East and West. The new nature of this movement has implications for the educational work we envision. For some, the new constituencies are difficult to trust. Years of struggle in a lonely area produce defences and cynicism which for long-time activists are difficult to deal with. But the tremendous work at building coalitions in cities and countries which has gone on over the past seven or eight years is giving us new experiences and ways of resolving these concerns.

The picture of course is not entirely optimistic. I am reminded of the 4th International Conference on Adult Education in Paris in March of 1985. Those of us working in that conference were dismayed by the fact that the word **peace** was nearly taboo in the official debates. Peace was associated, by the Western European countries, with being pro-Soviet each and every time discussion was promoted. We were told over and over again in both formal and informal settings that we should not promote peace education. This Cold War climate that permeates the higher reaches of governmental work is chilling and powerful. It sets the framework for self-censorship which is always the best way to control people.

Strangest Dream

Last night I had the strangest dream
I'd ever dreamed before:
I dreamed the world had all agreed
To put an end to war

(From an America folk song by Ed McCurdy)

ACTION AND EMPOWERMENT

Empowerment is the aquisition of more control over decisions which affect one's life. It is a term which has come into use amongst adult educators within the past 15 years. It refers to a combination of increased self-confidence, increased awareness of strategy and an ability and capacity to act. It is the antidote to powerlessness.

Some persons write or speak as though they believe that empowerment is something which adult educators or activists give or engender amongst people with whom they work.

My own sense of empowerment is that it occurs only through action. Individual or psychological power does not exist apart from action which is initiated to exercise more control or more influence in one's life. It is the combination of thinking, learning and acting which results in a sense of being empowered. It is the concrete confrontation or inter-action with forces, tendencies, organisations or persons apart from the person concerned which produces reaction which may or may not result in having a sense of more control or power. This reformulation of praxis, the combin-ation of reflection on theory and action or practice is particularly appropriate for peace educators or educational-ists within the peace movement.

The reactions to powerlessness seem to be similar in nearly all situations whether it is violence in the home, exploitation at work or racial hostility. We want to talk with other people who have the same experiences. We look for solutions. We try to solve the problem. Our difficulty with an issue as broad as peace is that it seems too large. We wonder at times whether or not violence is simply a genetic

177

flaw in humanity. It is too difficult for us to tackle. No one cares what we think.

So one of the challenges to peace educators is to try to link learning with specific possibilities for action. This means having some sense of where the larger peace movement is going. This means developing a sense of smaller step-by-step actions which will cumulatively build a sense of increased influence and control. It means seeing education in a far broader context than the straightforward presentation of information, important though that is.

One of the most exciting aspects of the peace movement has been the creativity and proliferation of peace eudcation initiatives. Teachers around the world have been trying out various kinds of peace curricula. The frustration around these outbreaks of peace however, is the sense that they are scattered, ad hoc and temporary. The bigger job of creating an entire curriculum for peace in all of our schools is far away.

The adult education movement itself cannot in any way be claimed to be in the forefront of peace education. While we have some remarkable exceptions, the potential impact of the adult education community on peace and development issues remains just that, potential. Reading the journals of many of the adult education associations one finds far more concern with the financing of adult education, the training of adult educators, the professional status of the field or yet another study on drop-outs in a community centre. The adult educators who are engaged in peace education are more often the volunteers, the activists, the informal educators or the marginal.

All of this means that there are some remarkable opportunities for educators within the peace movement and adult educators who would like to become involved in peace issues to act and create opportunities for others to act.

1. Work towards broadening and strengthening the educational committee or activities within your local peace coalition or organisation. It may be the single best strategy available to swell the ranks of the movement beyond the already converted.

2. Find out about the activities of others working in the field. The Peace Education Network of the International Council for Adult Education, Museokatu 18 A 9, SF-00100 Helsinki, Finland, produces a Peaceletter which is available to all interested subscribers. In it you

will find reports of activities from many parts of the world.

3. Start a course of peace, peace education or any related subject in your own centre, school, neighbourhood or university. The process of trying to get this started in and of itself will be an important way to reach other people.

4. Make links with the media. The television, newspapers and radio are the most influential educators in most of our nations. We ignore them at our peril. We have few skills for dealing with the media and we need them. We need joint action to counter the pervasive campaigns of misinformation which dominate.

5. Make links with groups that are involved in solidarity work and Third World work. These are natural allies as less money spent on arms means more money potentially available for other purposes.

6. Establish peace committees within your union, teacher's association or adult education association.

CONCLUSION

I am now finishing this article at my desk in the bedroom. I am glad to have had the chance to work on it. These few words have done nothing to change the fact of Nabila's murder. They have not made any difference to Canadian defence policy, much less to the policies of the United States, the Soviet Union or South Africa. But they have helped me to make at least mental links with many of you, with many people elsewhere who wish we had a more just and less violent world. Knowing that there are at least a few others authors who have joined together for this book gives me some encouragement. I hope you will accept this for what it is, a small and rather personal contribution to hope.

REFERENCES

1. World Association for Adult Education, Report of Conference Proceedings (Cambridge: 1929).

2. J. Roby Kidd, Tale of Three Cities: Elsinore, Montreal and Tokyo (Syracuse, New York: Syracuse University, 1973).

3. UNESCO, Report of the Second International

Conference on Adult Education (Paris: 1960).

4. Canadian Commission for UNESCO, Recommendation of Adult Education (Ottawa, 1976).

5. Murray Thomson, Learning and Peace, unpublished paper (Ottawa: 1986).

6. Finnish Association for Adult Education Organisations, Peaceletter, No. 2 (Helsinki, 1983).

7. Helena Kekkonen, A Window onto the Future (Helsinki: 1983), p.56.

8. UNESCO, Recommendation on Education for International Understanding, Co-operation and Peace Education (Paris: 1974, Article III.6).

9. Kekkonen, A Window, p.56.

8

Adult Education and the Women's Movement

Jane L. Thompson

For women, the re-emergence of feminism in the late 1960s has been one of the most important political developments since the war. Some women would want to link this with the consolidation of black consciousness and with the reclassification of lesbianism as a political and sexual choice rather than a congenital affliction. Others would mention the Peace Movement and an opposition to imperialism as related issues. Even women, who for a whole variety of familiar reasons, do not call themselves feminists, know that whatever else women's liberation means, it represents a standpoint that begins with women and with the intention of reconstituting the world for women as a better place. In terms of the distribution of the world's resources we know that women - half of the world's population - share 1 per cent of them.[1] And whilst this massive imbalance has an enormous amount to do with international capitalism, imperialism, racism and militarism, it is also embedded in the historical development of patriarchy which precedes all other oppressions, post-dates fascist, socialist and communist revolutions and seems to recognise no boundaries when it comes to cultural, regional and racial differences. It is not only that patriarchy is institutionalised in the major systems and apparatus of control in any given society, but it also structures the interpersonal relationships between men and women in their private and most intimate concerns.

The re-emergence of feminism in the 1960s is important for women because whatever other political struggles we might be engaged in, our subordination to men individually and collectively is a condition we share with all women irrespective of class, race and sexual preference.

In the 1960s feminism was a fairly middle-class affair - some would say it still is - except that in Britain, just as in the earlier suffrage, trade union and legal struggles around the turn of the century, working-class women have been strongly involved in campaigns to do with working conditions and wages, male violence, racism, childcare, housing and community action. Although a rich resource for trivialisation by the media, the women's movement in the 1970s succeeded in making issues to do with women's rights visible in ways they had not been for over sixty years. The launching of the United Nations Decade for Women began in Britain with the passing of Equal Pay and Anti-Sex Discrimination legislation, and so long as women's demands were not seen as too extreme, and were easily satisfied by a few minor modifications in the administration of sexual injustice, then the liberal socialist establishment seemed happy to make the appropriate gestures.

The main concerns of the women's movement at that time - job opportunities, pay, childcare, education and reproductive rights - were familiar topics of discussion and there was a sense in which ideas and attitudes were settling and. shifting into more enlightened grooves. But, of course, not all feminists were happy to settle for gestures or liberal attitudes without much serious commitment to social change. The New Left was in practice turning out to be almost as bad as the Old Left when it came to defining political priorities and treating women as the cheer-leaders, nurturers and sexual services brigade of the revolution. By which time the sexual revolution was also wearing a bit thin and became more to do with increasing women's availability to men than the sexual autonomy and control over our own bodies we had all been promised. And when the economy began to collapse and the political optimism of the 1960s and early 1970s began to tarnish, it was women who saw our jobs, our wages, our support services and our educational opportunities become the first and most serious casualties of the new depression.

Of course, no one else except feminists and women returned to the trenches and put under seige noticed what was happening. Returned to the invisibility of the home front, where we should have been all along, unaccounted for among the statistics of unemployment, stuck with the main responsibility for unpaid community care as the welfare state collapsed, women have seen the major characteristics of the depression of the 1980s depicted as male and youth unemployment, the destruction of men's jobs, small businessmen going bankrupt and resentment turning to violence on the streets. Women's response to poverty and unemployment remains an enigma, and whilst the inequality which leads to civil war between men on the streets is called a riot, the battles at home between unequals, in which the less powerful are also the losers, is dismissed as 'domestic violence'.

In these circumstances the voice of feminism has become more insistent and more angry on behalf of battered and abused women and against male violence in general. Increasingly patriarchy, racism and militarism have been named as the main enemy rather than the milder rebukes of the 1970s against red tape, prejudice and sexism.

And women have become more impatient with each other for allowing the divisions which men have created historically – class, racism and heterosexuality – to continue to divide us as women from finding ways of working politically that do not only liberate women but transform the systems of oppression themselves. Not surprisingly, the popular trivialisation of the women's movement in the 1960s and 1970s has now sharpened into a more concentrated and vicious backlash against feminism. The return of women to the homefront to live in varying degrees of poverty has been paralleled by an intensification of family-centred propaganda to remind us that women are the 'natural' homemakers, and that in difficult and unsettled times our prime responsibility is to make sure that our men and our children and our dependent relatives are properly cared for. Feminist ideas are presented as extreme, and women who hold them are described variously as unfeminine, man-hating, aggressive, ugly and perverted. In circumstances in which women's primary commitment to men can no longer be guaranteed, the attack on 'extremists', and especially lesbians, within the women's movement has increased. It is part of an attempt to deter potential recruits and to distract us from concluding that it is men who are the cause of women's oppression, not anyone else.[2] To crown it all, I now read in my newspaper that we are living in 'the post-feminist era' which I take to mean either that the battle is won – a view informed by the same kind of stupidity which once encouraged Macmillan to proclaim 'we're all middle-class now' - or that feminism is a spent force and has slipped back into obscurity for another sixty years of oblivion. Either way the notion is both ill-informed and ridiculous and it comes from paying too much attention to newspapers like the Guardian.

So far as adult education is concerned it would seem reasonable to expect some significant response to the women's movement given the close association between adult education and popular political movements in the formative years, and also because women constitute the majority of students, in current adult education provision. In practice, of course, this hasn't been the case, largely because the controlling influence in adult education historically, and those who monopolise the current debate and the definitions of issues in adult education are predominantly men. This is not the place to elaborate upon why the educational system we have inherited can be described as men's education or why, even in areas like adult and community education in which women outnumber men as students, and are employed in considerable numbers as part-time tutors and volunteers, the structures in which we operate are so effectively well grounded in male power and male values as to appear inevitable.[3] Except to say that women's entry into education generally was conceded reluctantly and belatedly a hundred or so years ago, long after the rules had been established and the parameters had been set. Our subsequent participation has been conditional upon our acceptance of the inevitable - a curriculum constructed historically as a reflection of men's ideas, assumptions and priorities, presented as objective truth: and a view of women informed by a range of ideologies collectively based upon notions of male supremacy. For women, education in the men's system has meant learning a lot about men in male ways and a lot about learning to be the women men have determined we should be.

In adult education, more than in schooling, and more than in higher education, the possibilities for resisting the inevitable are greater, because the learning relationship is not based on complusion in quite the same way and because there is less male power invested in it. And yet the evidence of radical initiatives on behalf of women, which seriously challenge patriarchal knowledge and control actually being seen to flourish and beginning to transform oppressive structures are extremely rare. Most of what passes for women's education and which is considered different in kind and emphasis from that which is usually provided in mainstream education for women, is, in my view, a transparent variation on a familiar theme. In circumstances in which the opinion leaders and policy-makers in adult education have responded to the women's movement at all, it has been to co-opt feminism into their platitudes, whilst at the same time seeking to deflect and defeat the radical intention of women's liberation as it might be applied in adult education and society generally.

If we examine the record of adult education in relation to the women's movement there seem to me to be four kinds of responses. The most familiar is that of <u>total ignorance</u>, in the sense of making no response at all, and which could also be said to be based on total ignorance.

The second is based on a <u>latter day philanthropy</u>, which like its nineteenth-century antecedent, muffles the iron fist of control in the velvet glove of sentiment. This kind of response is based on the view that women are one of those 'minorities' (sic) who are disadvantaged and for whom the mission of adult education is to provide the wherewithal to cope with their misfortunes.

The third response is more enlightened and less grounded in the liberal fixation with genetic and pathological explanations of deficiency when it comes to deprivation. But it still retains the liberal tradition of 'rescue' in its definition of responsibility. This response has incorporated the <u>respectable face of feminism</u>, concerned with 'equal rights', into its understanding and provision, with a range of initiatives intended to acknowledge the justice of equal opportunities. It is favoured by all those who believe that institutional practices can be changed by persistence and goodwill, and by those who understand that the best way to defeat feminism is to co-opt its radical and rebellious potential.

The fourth response is more to do with the response of the women's movement to adult education than the other way round and about welcoming adult education as just one more arena in the battle for women's liberation. It is based on the conviction that women's liberation is principally about personal and social change but that the opportunity for consciousness-raising and intellectual clarification of ideas and strategies, together with the consolidation that can come from collective support and struggle, constitutes really useful knowledge in the old radical sense.[4] But it is not just knowledge that matters in this view of women's education; it is control over the learning process. Radical feminists want <u>freedom from male control</u>. It is this version of the relationship between adult education and the women's movement which is at the same time the most challenging and the most precarious.

TOTAL IGNORANCE

It has taken a long time for those engaged in mainstream

adult education to attribute any significance to the Women's Movement. A few years ago, in the brief period of enthusiasm and expansion after Russell, those responsible for writing reports, conducting research, making recommendations, did so in a fairly jovial cavalier fashion that could be said to characterise the type of men who operated their way to the top in adult education. If the old guard could be depicted as slightly fusty quasi-academics, the 'new boys', who became the opinion leaders in the 1970s, with their retinue of henchmen and clones at local level, were more populist in their manner and opportunist in their principles. The inheritors of the liberal tradition, they reconstituted its principles and practice to legitimise their entrepreneurial concern with extending the influence of adult education, managing and professionalising the service, and advancing their own importance. All of this with no reference made to one of the most significant, popular, grassroots political movements of the time - feminism.[5]

Despite the fact that the majority of students in adult education are women, the majority of volunteers, part-time workers, detached workers, and assistant workers in adult education are women, those with key jobs in the career structure - mostly men - made no recognition of this fact, except in so far as it influenced their assumptions about 'relevant' curricula and enabled them to plan programmes which depended upon an enormous amount of female exploitation. In terms of their publications, their journal contributions, their conference papers, their committees and planning groups, women's existence and participation were both invisible and tokenistic. Just as it was extremely difficult to get the liberal establishment to take on board issues to do with social class in the 1970s[6] so too was it rare to hear feminism and the politics of gender discussed with any degree of seriousness or attention at any of their gatherings.

Today, the response based on total ignorance is still alive and well in circumstances in which even the limited attention given to gender discrimination in schools far exceeds its identification as an issue in the provision of educational opportunities for adult women. Most LEA programmes and the mainstay of WEA and extra-mural provision remains locked into the restricted notion of women as homemakers, or as consumers of male cultures and ideas. As ever, vigilant assessors of needs, and assiduous entrepreneurs in the pursuit of punters, the rhetoric of practice to be predictably familiar across regional and social settings. It is not unusual to find adult education centres, in the middle of provincial inner cities, for example, in which the majority of the provision is still a testimony to white, petit-bourgeois aspirations and hobbies, peopled by students who travel into classes by car from outside the immediate neighbourhood. Those who operate according to total ignorance about the women's movement also pay scant attention to social class and race as critical concerns in the content and teaching and provision of what passes as adult education.

Under pressure from government economic policies and spending cuts, the predisposition to rethink conventional provision is slight, except in so far as as competition for student numbers, effective teaching hours and fee-income intensifies the concentration on popular recreational and leisure pursuits, rather than innovative and developmental work in areas which cannot be relied upon to be lucrative.

The picture in extra-mural departments and the WEA is much the same, as the liberal tradition fights a rearguard collapse in the name of 'education for its own sake' in the face of enormous government and institutional pressure to become cost-effective. In these circumstances there is little visible money to be made out of feminism as such, although there are specific financial benefits to be gained by institutions from the identification of women as a deprived minority.

LATTER DAY PHILANTHROPY

One of the achievements of the British ruling class historically has been its capacity to deflect opposition and resistance by calculated philanthropy and by the concentration on individualism as an explanation of success and failure. It is less important that people gain sustenance from philanthropic benevolence than that gestures are seen to be made. It matters little whether there is much evidence of individualism creating achievement or loss so long as it is believed that it does. It is important if the interests and privileges of the ruling class are to be preserved that not too many people develop a sense of grievance, outrage or anger about the inequalities and oppressions which they experience. It is also important that agencies like education, the media, government and the legal system assist the ruling

187

class in preserving those interests. Great care has been taken in the current depression, for example, to construct the image of scrounging, fiddling, laziness and greed as characteristic of the unemployed who 'could find work if they really wanted to' or whose misfortune can be explained by 'the irresponsible pay demands and restrictive practices' of those still in work. The nineteenth-century notion of the undeserving poor and the deserving poor has been reconstituted - the former are effectively stigmatised, the latter become the focus of qualified liberal sentiment - the target group for crumbs of philanthropic consideration. Benevolence becomes the bridge between oppression and control.

The dissemination of these views in adult education is based not on a class or race or gender analysis of inequality but on notions of feckless, unconfident, incompetent individuals who, because of learning difficulties or lack of social and life skills, are inadequate in their day-to-day lives. They are seen not as the victims of social problems but as those who contribute to their own victimisation by their irresolution or fatalism or apathy. In the 'post-feminist era', equal opportunities are available to those women who 'get off their hands and knees and work for them'. Those who don't 'have only themselves to blame'. In the 1970s such individuals were called educationally and emotionally deprived or culturally disadvantaged, and a whole quasi-medical terminology of concern and cure became part of the intervention procedure of community workers, social workers and educationalists.[7] Today, the same individuals have become labelled as minority groups - ethnic, unemployed and women whose 'special needs' are the focus of limited intervention by the 'caring professions' including adult education.

Women who are identified as a problem are those whose isolation and poverty and poor housing affects their competence in childcare, domestic skills and coping with unsatisfactory circumstances. The cure? More domestication. Adult education's concern for them is mediated through community education outreach schemes based in neighbourhoods, community centres, clinics and mother and toddler groups. The emphasis is on contact and a chance to talk: non-formal activities centring on children, domestic skills and basic literacy. The philosophy underpinning such schemes is simplistic and patronising, concentrating on women's deficiencies rather than their strengths, their inadequacies rather than their capacities, their limitations rather than their possibilities. Education is rarely named by providers for fear of alienation and women are talked about in ways which make the hairs on the back of your neck stand on end. The role of the teacher/outreach worker is to guide facilitate, contain, but not to engage in critical social analysis or action. Although frequently the recipients of special grants, such schemes are understaffed and poorly funded, given the enormity of the resources which would be needed if women in such groups were to be genuinely compensated for their massive economic disadvantage and their political powerlessness. The schemes are also usually only short-term - six months, a year, two years at the most. But then, the intention is not to solve social problems so easily, only to acknowledge them. The recent history of liberal response to urban deprivation as it affects groups like women is littered with the unmet commitments and unfulfilled promises of such initiatives: each highly circumscribed; each mediated through the transitory commitment of part-time interlopers in communities in which they do not live, among women whose lives they do not share; and all controlled elsewhere. The best thing that can be said of them is that their contact with women is slight, the numbers who participate regularly are few, and whilst this reinforces the commonsense definition of poverty as being a result of apathy, it protects those who escape from the prescriptions of unperceptive need-meeters and from yet more management by misguided missionaries.

But it is also true to say that fashions in philanthropy change. The social isolation of women is not nearly as popular a cause for concern as it was in the 1970s. More recently, unemployment or 'education for leisure' have become the flavour of the month. In practice this means for men.

THE RESPECTABLE FACE OF FEMINISM

Of course, many workers in adult education are also feminists - they may be the anti-sexist male variety - but on the whole they are women who want adult education to respond to the concerns of the women's movement. (Whatever happened to liberation?) Adult education, unencumbered by the constraints of certification and examination, has been a popular breeding-ground for courses which focus on women's cultural and political ideas and activities. Workshops, day schools, short and more intensive courses about women's literature and history and psychology and health, for example, have become a feature of every self-respecting liberal studies programme; whilst courses in self-defence, assertiveness training, women's sexuality, welfare rights, peace studies and feminist politics have helped to reconstitute what is usually defined as a relevant curriculum for women. In the LEA sector women have been able to learn non-traditional skills like building, carpentry, motor mechanics and electrics. Some courses, especially those sponsored by the MSC like Wider Opportunities for Women, have been concerned with women re-entering the labour market. Others, like New Opportunities for Women, have provided the re-entry points into higher and continuing education for women whose choices have been restricted by marriage and childcare and lack of opportunity. The growth and development of new technologies and scientific knowledge have inspired programmes providing positive discrimination for women in areas concerned with science and computing. Some, encouraged by the EOC have offered Women into Accounting, Women into Management and Women into Public Life courses, aimed at women trying to break into areas of employment and influence usually monopolised by men. The variety is enormous as is the nature of the response to feminism which they reflect.

The characteristic that courses for career women, courses reclaiming the curriculum on behalf of women's history and culture, and courses providing useful knowledge and skills for women reconstitutung their traditional roles have in common is the recognition that some women at least have expectations, aspirations and preoccupations which are not well catered for in the mainstream provision of adult education. The assumption remains that most women will continue to be satisfied with conventional provision and that the others, the 'more liberated' perhaps, can choose women's studies options which now exist amidst the many other courses that go to make up a centre programme. The attraction of this approach is that most up-to-date and enlightened LEA centres, WEA branches and extra-mural departments can be relied upon to include some kind of women's studies in their provision which is different in kind from domestic education and men's education.

The problem with this approach however is that it is based on opportunism rather than commitment. So long as women's studies options exist, the rest of the curriculum which is not women's studies, and the structures in which knowledge is constructed, managed and transmitted, can remain unchanged. Issues about who comes to adult education, what knowledge gets transmitted, how the teaching-learning relationship is negotiated, who is in control, are all just as important questions for feminist education as the introduction of feminist content and analysis into the curriculum of some courses. And yet these are issues which the token recognition paid to the women's movement in adult education does not even begin to consider. The contradiction remains that in a liberal framework, feminism can be tolerated in a piecemeal way, and be claimed as evidence of enlightenment and progress, so long as nothing else - the rest - has to change.

Another problem with this view of reality is that it is more likely to respond to the respectable face of feminism than to women's liberation. So far as I am concerned, arguments that women's studies should include management training and courses to help women to be more assertive and successful in public life (like Margaret Thatcher?) don't have very much to say about how the majority of women live our lives. Courses which substitute female content for male content in the curriculum, but which continue to fragment subjects, which reflect the same criteria about what counts as excellence, and which construct language and theories which are obscure and elitist, all echo patriarchal ways of learning.

Just because courses are attended by women, taught by women and are about women, does not in itself make them feminist. With an educational heritage created and sustained by men, and in a context in which men control the employment of teachers and the allocation of resources, the constraints are enormous. In these circumstances the politics of penetration becomes the art of the possible. Women modify their demands and their language and explain their intentions in terms which will seem reasonable. Obvious flashpoints like 'women-only classes' and 'separatist politics' are avoided and terminology likely to be alarming like 'lesbianism', 'patriarchy', 'woman hating' and 'liberation', is diluted into 'sexuality', 'inequality of opportunity', 'sexism' and 'equal rights'. The price of a foothold in the system is compromise. The struggle, once a tiny space has been achieved, is to stay put. This can mean more compromise. The danger of compromise of course is that you forget what's been relinquished in the pursuit of what's been

191

achieved. The vision is translated into consequences which seem possible. The possible is dictated by the limits of men's tolerance. Men's intolerance is fortified by their power.

Some of the compromise has to do with money. Defined as a minority group with special needs, women's courses can attract - in adult education terms - quite large grants of money and special funding, principally from the European Social Fund and Manpower Services Commission (MSC).

European funding can be lavish but it is tied to cooperation with public bodies. Grants are not given into the control of women participating in the projects being funded. A more common relationship is that between adult education and MSC whose declared commitment to training of various kinds and social education in preparation for responsible citizenship is well known. The philosophy underlying the operation of MSC is also well known. It is rooted in conservative values of limited self-help, virtuous thrift and individualism. Courses can be instrumental or diversionary but not contentious. Students, tutors and the curriculum are supervised by representatives of MSC and unnecessary luxuries like crêches attached to women's courses are conspicuous by their absence 'in case women become dependent upon support services that will not be provided in the wider society'. MSC are opposed to schemes which can be defined by them as political or critical of prevailing government policy - in practice, this leaves courses for women which concentrate on traditional job skills and traditional job expectations - even though those skills are not valued in the present economic climate and the opportunities for women in the labour market are negligible.

Dependency on short-term grants and external funding is an excellent way of keeping women - as well as other disadvantaged groups - in competition with each other for scarce resources. So long as the energies of project workers and project participants can be distracted by the relentless search for short-term funding, the chances of any significant changes being achieved are minimal. Also, this form of poverty control and management is most susceptible to applications intended to pacify potentially disorderly groups. Projects directed at cooling the anger of the male unemployed or blacks in inner city areas are likely to be more successful than schemes seeking to increase women's access to employment or educational opportunities.

The picture so far presented, of feminism being restrained by this form of response to the women's movement, is not completely accurate, however. There are women holding positions of influence in adult education who have used their power to secure space and resources for women which would not otherwise exist. The consolidation of women's visibility and conspicuous presence in adult education means that the men with power must take us into account in ways which otherwise would not happen. In organisations like the WEA particularly, because of its grass roots and more democratic base, women have been able to take more control of their own learning and become their own teachers and organise themselves in ways which are less controlled by patriarchal infiltration. Although, as money runs out, the cost-effectiveness of non-traditional classes comes under greater scrutiny. For feminists who believe in coalition with other progressive groups and in the power of eloquence to change men's attitudes, then educational systems, like other institutions, can become the site of struggle in which concerted action might bring about changes in personnel and policies. It may be in these circumstances that moderation rather than liberation is more likely to achieve results, but it is a matter of interpretation whether the results achieved by good behaviour are worth the energy required. When feminism becomes respectable - and if the world hasn't been turned upside down as a consequence - the significance of our achievements needs to be examined carefully.

FREEDOM FROM MALE CONTROL

There isn't a great deal of historical precedent to support the view that patriarchy can be transformed by sweet reason and persuasion. It is more likely that the incorporation of radical ideas will contribute to their dilution and distraction. The definitions attached to strategies for change in educational institutions, as in other institutions, to do with becoming effective lobbyists, operators and competitors, are based on assumptions constructed over time about politics and power. Men have practised and perfected these strategies for centuries in different contexts. They may disagree with each other profoundly, and compete to outdo each other relentlessly, but they share the same notion of the contest and adhere, more or less, to the same rules. A change of emphasis merely replaces one group of men by another, as does revolution. The method is

193

as much a creation of their history and culture as is the priority given to the issues they compete about. Women wedded to men's systems, arguing for resources and significance, have little alternative but to accept the context as given and learn as effectively as possible, to pitch in with the rest. The problem with this, of course, is that, as in most sports, some competitors are nobbled from the start. They can never win, and when it looks like they might, someone moves the goal post. The odds against women beating men at their own game, without becoming amateur men in the process, are enormous. Access to men's institutions, with a transformation of the ways in which they operate, will not in itself assist women's struggle for independence. Given the resources available to men (99 percent of the world's resources) and the few available to women, and given the institution of male power in every dimension of the education system - grounded deep in the structures, the language and the social context of every exchange - it is unrealistic to imagine that individual women, men of good will, or students, however energetic, resourceful and determined, can change things single handed. If it were merely a matter of eloquence, or energy or conviction, the education system, like other male institutions, would have been transformed by women already. It's like expecting the class system to change once the workers have explained to the ruling class why they don't like poverty; or racism to go away once blacks have made clear why they find it oppressive.

Much better as women to put our energies elsewhere and to think in terms of guerilla action - to redistribute resources to women wherever possible; to asset-strip men's buildings of their space and facilities and resources on behalf of women; to expose male hypocrisy, corruption and oppression wherever it appears; to reserve loyalty for principles and for women not for institutions; and to concentrate on the subversion of men's ideas about themselves and about women by behaving badly and with irreverence to their rules. Adrienne Rich puts it precisely:

> The question facing women's studies today is the extent to which she has, in the last decade, matured into the dutiful daughter of the white patriarchal university - a daughter who threw tantrums and played the tomboy when she was younger, but who has now learned to wear a dress and speak

and act almost as nicely as Daddy wants her to. And the extent to which women's studies can remember that her mother was not Athena, but the Women's Liberation Movement, a grass roots political movement with roots in the civil rights movement of the 1960s; a movement blazing with lesbian energy whose earliest journals had names like, It Ain't Me Babe, No More Fun and Games, Off Our Backs, Up From Under and The Furies. In other words, how disobedient will women's studies be in the 1980s? And how will she address the racism, misogyny, homophobia of the university and of the corporate society in which it is embedded? And how will feminist teachers and scholars choose to practise their disobedience to white patriarchy?[8]

An education which does justice to feminist priorities is not merely a matter of curriculum innovation and change - although when women begin to rewrite the history and culture of societies in ways which include the diversity of women's experiences, and when women generate their own knowledge and become their own teachers - the consequences can be challenging to men's view of the world and their view of women. It is common to dismiss women's analysis and writing as tendentious, irrational, subjective, misguided, or more simply wrong. What it means, of course, is that very often we have different definitions of experience and reality from men, and that much of what we say is critical of men and about what they have done to women. Because of this, the Second Chance for Women courses[9] in Southampton have been continually investigated by local politicians, LEA advisers, university professors and HMI for signs of bias, indoctrination and extremism in ways which other courses sponsored by the university department have never been; and despite the lip-service paid to experimental learning and Freirian praxis in the rhetoric of our leaders this does not extend any encouragement or enlightenment about attempts to make space for feminist ideas in adult education. Increasingly, it has been necessary to think in terms of creating our own learning environment in a separate Women's Education Centre in which men as students, teachers or visiting authorities are unwelcome and in which women act independently for themselves. The rationale for women-only classes in adult education is often explained as a remedial excercise, in terms of women's lack of confidence and men's tendency to dominate and monopolise the educational exchange. Whilst this is undoubtably true - men, even when they're in the minority, take up proportionally more space and time and attention[10] than in equity they are entitled to - but it is not the reason why radical feminists argue for their exclusion. The most effective way in which any group, conscious of its oppression and concerned to change the relationships of oppression, can organise, is without the participation of the oppressors in the process of resistance. It is also empowering for groups who have long been powerless, downgraded, humiliated, patronised, deskilled and diminished to discover the strength of concerted action for themselves and on their own behalf. The same can be said for working-class, black and other oppressed groups. It is as true in political campaigns like Greenham and against male violence as it is in the reconstruction of an education which serves the concerns, reflects the values, and enhances the priorities of women. It means also the creation of a different kind of education in which the organisation and control is with women and in which the usual demarcation between teachers and learners, thought and action, fact and feelings, personal and public, becomes removed. It is not, on the whole, the kind of shift which men in education take kindly to. It challenges their authority and specialisms and notions of objectivity. It also raises critical questions about purpose, like: is the purpose of education to consolidate the logic of the present system or is it to challenge and transform it? The other reason why women should organise and educate separately is because we have more important work to do than to have our attention and energy continually claimed by men. Merely surviving in male systems, let alone trying to challenge them, is exhausting and frustrating in ways which drain energy away from more important issues. The re-emergence of feminism, which began as a flash of vision, and continued with an examination of the evils and gross distortions of patriarchy, and led to a whole variety of campaigns on behalf of women, now needs to concentrate on the differences between us as women which have divided us under patriarchy and which cannot be allowed to divide us as feminists.

The divisions, of course, are based mainly on class, race, age, politics, health and sexual identity, and of these class, race, and sexual identity are perhaps the most urgent in our immediate struggle.[11] Feminists who are also black, working-class or lesbian (or all three) have been as concerned as any other group to establish their own identity and to reclaim their own realities as women. But the women's movement, especially as it is represented in western-style education, is dominated by white, middle-class, heterosexual women. It has not been sufficiently sensitive to the issues which divide and potentially destroy us, or to the need to renounce the legacy of patriarchal relations in our own behaviour. Statistics aren't necessary to document what is painfully obvious. Working-class women live in increasing poverty and are more vulnerable than middle-class women to state interference and control.[12] Black women live and work in the poorest of circumstances and confront the penalties of white racism as a matter of course in every aspect of their lives.[13] Lesbian women can expect to lose their jobs, their children and their community support because they choose to love women in preference to men.[14] Audre Lorde reminds us of our differences and of the reasons why we need to overcome them:

> We are not as women living in a political and social vacuum. We operate in the teeth of a system for whom racism and sexism are primary, established, necessary props of profit... I am a lesbian women of colour whose children eat regularly because I work in a university. If their full bellies make me fail to recognise my communality with a woman of colour whose children who do not eat, because she can't find work; or a woman who has no children because her insides are rotten from home abortions and sterilisation; or if I fail to recognise the lesbian who chooses not to have children, or the woman who remains closeted because her homo-phobic community is her only life support; the woman who chooses silence instead of another death; the woman who is terrified lest any anger triggers the explosion of hers; if I fail to recognise these women as other faces of myself, then I am contributing to each of their oppressions, but also to my own. I am not free while any woman is unfree, even when her shackles are very different from my own. Nor are you.[15]

For the women's movement now this is one of the most

important issues we have to deal with - our relationships with each other and the eradication of all the opppressions we have inherited from capitalist patriarchy. The other major concern for women is about finding ways of living which give us more independence, more control over our own lives, and more self worth than is frequently the experience of women in subordination to men.

Men's opposition to women-only education, as with other women-only activities, is the fear of separatism and of men's exclusion from influence and control in our lives. This opposition, expressed in terms of adult education, seems out of all proportion given that most women can expect to spend at most three or four hours a week in women-only classes as against a lifetime in the world of men. And yet men do have reason to be concerned if, on these occasions, women find their lonely anger or isolated oppression is understood and shared by other women, so that personal struggles take on political dimensions. And if, in a woman-centred, woman-positive, pro-woman environment, women discover their affiliation and affection for other women, which raises critical questions about friendship and solidarity and love, and why we spend so much time and emotional energy on relationships with men which cause us so much pain.

Living and working separately from men, on our own, or with other women and children, as a conscious political choice and labelled separatism is not something the vast majority of women would identify as a possibility. It seems extreme and many women, for reasons of poverty, children and physical fear remain in unsatisfactory relationships without hope of change. But yet, the steady increase in the divorce rate over the last fifteen years or so is not the simple consequence of attending women's studies classes. The fact that women remarry is not surprising. What is more surprising, given the amount of pressure that goes into promoting compulsory heterosexuality and married bliss, and given the economic and social penalties imposed on single parenthood by the state, is that, increasingly, women are choosing to bring up children on their own without close relationships with men. Many women in this position today, sharing childcare and social support with other women, meeting in mother and toddler groups, in each other's houses, at the school gates, at the shops, are engaged in a kind of separatism. They are experiencing what women have always known - that the life-sustaining relationships that enable us to grit our teeth and pick our way through the mess made by men, to endure and to survive, are those we share with other women: our mothers, our sisters, our neighbours and friends. I have yet to see much validation of this support women give each other, especially in working-class communities, which recognise it as a political affili-ation, a movement. It is more common to associate what counts as politics in such communities with the labour movement - a movement which men have created and in which men meet to decide priorities and strategies. It is however an important part of the women's movement, which might lack the explicit analysis of male oppression and resistance, but is none the less an affirmation of women's allegiance to each other. The problem is, that because of the power of male definitions of reality in our culture, and because women are taught to accept these definitions too, the friendship and support which countless women give to each other can remain unacknowledged and invisible. The structural organisation of women's isolation in the home compounded by women's poverty doesn't help. And yet once these connections are made visible and acknowledged - often, in my experience, in the context of feminist education groups and meetings - the sense of men's signifi-cance evaporates. It becomes possible to imagine other ways of living. It becomes possible, if we remain committed to living and working with men, to identify the terms on which we shall participate and what re-negotiation must go on if these relationships are to be transformed.

The argument for feminist education, free from male control, is not as a remedial excercise, it is because we have important work to do together, from which we cannot afford to be distracted by the interference and destruction we know happens when men remain in control.

TRUE AND FALSE REBELLION

The problem we face as feminists is to understand the difference between true and false rebellion. White capitalist patriarchy will allow a certain amount of argument and independent thought. 'Women's Lib' has matured and has become incorporated into the language and into the super-ficial behaviour of most self-respecting liberal socialists. A good many educated women have used the ideology of economic independence, job sharing and role swapping to establish careers which bring satisfaction and economic rewards. Many have become lifestyle feminists with husbands and boyfriends who have cultivated the good-humoured acceptance of feminist ideas and who behave as non-oppressive, anti-sexist men, cooking the ratatouille, organising crêches at women's conferences, and turning a blind eye to untidy houses and piles of dirty washing. This is not the experience of most black and working class women.

In the academy, where a semblance of pluralism persists, it is perfectly acceptable to introduce elements of Women's Studies material into the curriculum which, during the last fifteen years or so, has also made space for Black Studies, the teaching of race relations and working-class history. None of these has posed any particular threat to the hagemony of traditional discipline and patterns of academic thought and women can be incorporated as easily as the rest.

In all of these circumstances women can wear their feminist hearts on their sleeves and the world will continue much the same. It's only when women refuse to tow the line, when we renounce the rewards of good behaviour and resist all attempts to be incorporated that true rebellion comes into its own. It is only when women cross the line drawn by patriarchy and choose to do things on our own and when our collusion with racism, homophobia and class oppression can no longer be guaranteed, that real resistance and real possibilities begin to emerge.

REFERENCES

1. United Nation's statistics. Women are one-half of the world's population, do two-thirds of the world's work, earn one-tenth of the world's wages and own one-hundredth of the world's wealth.

2. Although official figures consistently underestimate the true extent of male crimes of violence against women, it is well known that women and children are in more danger of domestic violence, rape and sexual abuse from male members of their own family than from strangers. The fears expressed by the general public about mugging, rape and child abuse are almost without exception a fear of men.

3. See Jane L. Thompson, Learning Liberation: Women's Response to Men's Education (Croom Helm, 1983).

4. Richard Johnson, ' "Really Useful Knowledge":

Radical Education and Working-Class Culture', in Clarke Critcher and Johnson (eds), Working Class Culture (Hutchinson, 1979).

5. Thompson, Learning Liberation.

6. The ideas of the 1970s opinion leaders are criticised in Jane L. Thompson (ed.), Adult Education for a Change (Hutchinson, 1980).

7. Ibid., Chapter 4.

8. Adrienne Rich, address to the National Women's Studies of America Annual Conference in June 1981.

9. Thompson, Learning Liberation, Chapter 10.

10. Dale Spender, Man Made Language (Routledge and Kegan Paul, 1980).

11. Thompson, Learning Liberation.

12. Beatrix Campbell, Wigan Pier Revisited (Virago, 1984).

13. Beverly Bryan, Stella Dadzie and Suzanne Scuse, The Heart of the Race (Virago, 1985).

14. See Lesbian Mother on Trial (Rights of Women Publication, 1984).

15. Audre Lorde, address to the National Women's Studies of America Annual Conference in June 1981.

16. The arguments presented in this chapter are developed in more detail, and with many illustrations from women who have been on the receiving end of men's education and who are now engaged in the struggle to develop alternative and independent education for women in, The Taking Liberties Collective, Learning the Hard Way - Women's Oppression in Men's Education (Women in Society, Macmillan), forthcoming.

9

Education and the Environmental Movement

Brian Martin

Education about 'the environment' played a vital role in the survival of the human species for many millennia. In gatherer-hunter societies, part of being a member of the society was learning about weather, climate, plants, animals, geography and other aspects of nature. Part of this learning was obtained by first-hand experience and part through stories, instruction, rituals and other intimate parts of the culture.

Many people with modern urban lifestyles are cut off from such traditional modes of interacting with and learning about the natural environment. Indeed, 'the environment' has become much more a humanly constructed one. People can directly experience some features of their environment, such as smelling exhaust fumes and driving on freeways, but many vital parts of modern life are normally only grasped through the medium of specialists, especially scientists. This includes many aspects of manufacturing, mining, energy systems, transport systems, chemicals, drugs, food production and communications. Assaults on humans in their humanly constructed environment as well as assaults on what is seen to be the 'natural environment' (which often has been extensively modified by humans) often require experts to establish or decipher knowledge. This includes areas such as the hazards of nuclear materials, threats to stratospheric ozone due to aerosols from spray cans, and the health effects of food additives. Much knowledge of the environment relies ultimately on the same division of labour and specialised expertise which is characteristic of the systems of production and social control which give rise to environmental problems.

In the late 1960s the modern environmental movement developed in the rich countries. It was a social movement built around concern for various 'environmental problems', including pollution and destruction of natural ecosystems. The environmental movement has been a typical social movement in most respects. At the core are the dedicated activists, devoted full-time to collecting information, organising groups and meetings, lobbying, speaking, writing and protesting. Some of these core activists are paid (often at a minimal wage) but many are not. The next level of participants are the active members: those who regularly attend meetings, write letters, join protests or otherwise give their energies to the issue. Then there are the occasional participants, those who may join a demonstration on a special occasion, or attend a public meeting now and again. Finally, outside the movement proper, are the passive supporters: people who support the goals and activities of the environmental movement but who do not participate themselves.

My focus in this chapter is on the relationship between the environmental movement and education about the environment. I start by looking at educational efforts within the movement and by the movement. Then, moving outwards, the movement has had an impact on the media and on various academic environmental programmes, which have also been influenced by government, corporate and professional groups with contrary goals. In particular I look at the relationship between experts inside and outside the movement.

In all these areas, knowledge about the environment has been the subject of struggles concerning its validity, meaning, implications, legitimacy and accessibility. Education about the environment is far from the learning of neutral facts. Rather, it is a political exercise at every stage.

When was the last time you obtained some information about an environmental issue? Most likely, it was through watching television or reading a newspaper, or perhaps reading a magazine, talking with a friend or listening to the radio. At least, this answer would apply to the bulk of the population. Only a small fraction of people actively keep up with environmental issues to the extent of regularly reading books or specialist journals, attending public meetings or participating in environmental action groups. Does this mean that the organised environmental movement is really peripheral to most public education about the environment?

I intend to deal with this question by concentrating on a particular case study: education about the issue of uranium mining and nuclear power in Australia. I choose this case because I was directly involved for many years, and also because, from what I know of other issues, the processes involved are typical. This account is not meant to be a full description of the debate over uranium mining, but simply enough detail to put educational aspects of it into perspective.

THE URANIUM ISSUE[1]

Although the British government tested nuclear weapons in Australia in the 1950s and there had been uranium mining in the country since the 1950s, the major debate about the nuclear fuel cycle did not begin until the 1970s. A major impetus for concern came from overseas, particularly the United States. An enormous expansion of nuclear power programmes was underway, and this triggered a parallel expansion of opposition.

The first nuclear power plants were constructed in Britain, the United States and the Soviet Union in the mid-1950s. Nuclear power was an offshoot of nuclear weapons programmes, relying on technologies and expertise developed under military auspices. In the 1950s, nuclear power was heralded as a peaceful application of nuclear technology and was supported by people from all parts of the political spectrum.

The environmental movement became a mass phenomenon in western societies in the late 1960s. There have been environmental problems for centuries, and they have particularly affected members of the working class. In the 1960s the environment became a cause for some members of the middle class, as the impact of the industrial production and consumer society affected the lives of the more affluent members of the community. Also involved was the upsurge of social concern in the 1960s which was manifest in the student movement, the black movement and the women's movement.

The early environmental movement drew upon many precursors, including various conservation societies, scientists who had been studying the problems for years, and scientist-writers such as Rachel Carson. The interaction between scientists and activists in the anti-nuclear power movement has been typical of the process.

In the United States, there were citizen protests against some of the early nuclear power plants. These local opponents were able to draw on a few scientists and other experts who produced findings critical of nuclear power.[2]

Several factors made nuclear power a prime target for opposition. The rise of the environmental movement meant that the existence of any environmental impacts of a technology made it vulnerable to attack. Nuclear power was particularly vulnerable because it was not yet entrenched, as was, for example, the automobile. Therefore nuclear power could be opposed outright, as well as regulated to make it safer. Nuclear power was associated with nuclear weapons both technologically and conceptually, and this became a more important negative factor in the 1970s after the signing of the Nuclear Non-proliferation Treaty. Finally, nuclear power has always been a technology which necessarily flaunts its dependence on experts and powerful political and economic interests. Unlike television, which insinuates itself into people's homes as a personal technology (even though there is centralised control of programming), nuclear power became categorised as an alien technology.

These factors are not just of historical or sociological interest in explaining why nuclear power was opposed. They also have influenced the way in which information about nuclear power has been used by the anti-nuclear power movement.

Especially in the United States, the early opposition to nuclear power was almost entirely on environmental grounds: thermal pollution, reactor accidents, release of radiation during shipments, radioactive waste disposal. The environmental movement had made such concerns socially legitimate, whereas opposition on issues such as proliferation of nuclear weapons or centralisation of political power did not have the same social resonance. The result was a gradually widening concern about the environmental impacts of nuclear power both by citizen opponents and by a few scientists who had studied the issue.

The issue developed in Australia partly in response to concern developing overseas and partly in response to events in Australia. There had been only one nuclear power plant proposed for Australia, and that had been aborted in 1971 on cost considerations. The main social issue debated at the time, in the late 1960s, was whether the plant would provide a basis for Australian nuclear weapons. The environmental impacts of nuclear technology received much wider attention in Australia in the early 1970s with popular opposition to the French government's testing of nuclear weapons in the South Pacific.

Because of its large reserves of cheap coal, nuclear power has never been a viable economic proposition in Australia. But the Australian continent also has large and rich reserves of uranium, and so it was the issue of uranium mining and export which became the focus of the nuclear power debate in the country. The uranium market began an upturn in the early 1970s due to the expansion of nuclear power programmes worldwide. Because Australian uranium deposits are far from urban populations, the main direct effects of mining are on the miners themselves and on Aborigines and the local environment. Hence much of the focus of the Australian anti-uranium movement has been on the global concern of proliferation of nuclear weapons, to which uranium mining would be a contribution. This is in striking contrast to other countries where most protests against nuclear facilities have been built initially around the concern of local residents.

A few activists within the environmental movement helped to bring the uranium issue onto the movement agenda in the early 1970s. Some of them had been in the United States and were familiar with the new group Friends of the Earth (FOE), which had been founded in 1969 by David Brower who had broken with the Sierra Club on its refusal to take a stand against nuclear power. Friends of the Earth groups were established in Australia, and among other things took up the uranium issue.

Also involved at the beginning of the anti-uranium movement in Australia were some trade unions. Trade unions in Australia have a history of activism on social issues outside the immediate interests of their members, most notably the green bans in the early 1970s.[3] This applies to only some unions some of the time, but nevertheless the potential for an alliance between trade unionists and environmentalists is much greater than in most other countries.

EDUCATION WITHIN THE MOVEMENT

A vital first step for any movement is internal education. At the very least, a core of activists must become knowledge-able about the issues so that the case can be presented and argued to the wider public through leaflets, talks, letters, broadcasts and so forth.

The earliest anti-uranium 'experts' were mainly self-taught. They read the technical and political writings on the subject, and in many cases contributed to this literature through their own investigations. These experts included a number of scientists and academics and also some full-time activists who became knowledgeable without a background in any way related to nuclear power, in the fashion of US anti-nuclear intervener Dan Ford, an economist who became a formidable expert on nuclear reactor safety.

The self-learning process was encouraged by an 'informal college' of leading anti-uranium figures: those who wrote articles and leaflets, who testified at public inquiries and who debated the issues with pro-nuclear opponents in public meetings and the media. The stimulus and testing ground for learning was public debate. The informal college operated then as it does now by exchange of writings, personal discussions (for example, at national anti-uranium meetings) and many telephone calls. The subjects discussed included technical points (can nuclear weapons be made from reactor-grade plutonium?) and political points (how are Aboriginal communities responding to the uranium debate?) The learning was always directed. It was to be used in the public debate, not for academic essays. When the other side came up with a 'fact' or a new argument, then there would be efforts made to formulate a response. 'There are now reactor programmes in 35 countries.' 'Yes, but it was the governments and not the people who made the decisions in those countries. We need a full public debate before participating in the nuclear fuel cycle.'

On many environmental issues, there are only a few movement experts who do most of the public speaking, appear regularly on the media and give most of the testimony at environmental inquiries. Relying on a few experts has the advantage of always putting forward people with experience, confidence and a public reputation. But it has the disadvantage of making the movement vulnerable to the loss of those people, and giving them undue influence over the public image and direction of the movement.

In the Australian anti-uranium movement in some places there has been considerable dependence on a few movement experts, but in other places there has been a conscious attempt to spread the expertise to as many people as possible. Partly this preference for broadening the knowledge base grew out of FOE-Australia's more radical grass-roots orientation: a belief in decentralised decision-making and sharing of skills within the movement. This contrasted with FOE-US and FOE-UK where national offices have played a major role in defining directions, providing materials and employing key figures, and where the issues have been tackled more by lobbying and providing a 'respectable' alternative than by popular mobilisation and direct action.[4]

'Spreading the expertise' has many ramifications. It means getting as many people as possible to be involved in writing letters and leaflets, in speaking to groups of all kinds and in attending movement conferences. For example, at the peak of the uranium debate, in 1977 and 1978, there was a heavy demand for speakers at schools, Rotary clubs, church groups and so forth. In some places a concerted attempt was made to train new people to do some of this speaking. By this stage a mass of new anti-uranium groups had been formed, usually under the name Movement Against Uranium Mining, and a host of new people involved, such as academics and members of political parties. These new people brought new sets of viewpoints, knowledge and experience in activism, and added to the mix of expertise in the movement.

Also important in the learning process within the movement were the numerous movement newsletters, petitions, leaflets and correspondence, all of which were circulated to other groups on a routine basis. The FOE national magazine Chain Reaction and some shorter-lived publications also provided valuable sharing of material.

EDUCATION BY THE MOVEMENT

The transition from education within the movement to education by the movement is not a sharp one. Typically, a newsletter produced by a local group goes out to all paid members, and often is passed out free at rallies and other events. Some of the paid members are activists who regularly attend meetings, but others joined to 'support the cause'. The newsletter is a prime source of information for them. Often it includes reprints of local or overseas articles as well as local news and copy written by local activists.

The front line of movement information has been the leaflet. These slips of paper, passed out freely and often thrown away by recipients, range from scrappy arguments quickly rushed into print to carefully worded arguments developed after anguished efforts to reach agreement. Leaflets are passed out at rallies, bookstalls, talks and any other available opportunity. They have the advantage of being easy and cheap to produce locally, of being short enough for most readers to digest, and of being a satisfying enterprise for some activists: preparing copy, collecting cartoons, laying out and arranging printing.

Books have also played an important role in the debate, in providing depth of argument for those who wanted it. In the early years the amount of detailed local anti-uranium material was limited, and there was heavy reliance on a few overseas books such as Lovins and Price's Non-nuclear Futures (1975) and Patterson's Nuclear Power (1976). The short Australian book Red Light for Yellowcake, published by FOE in 1977, filled a gap and sold tens of thousands of copies. Even Red Light included a major portion by US writer Denis Hayes. In later years many further books were published, leading to surfeit rather than scarcity of materials.[5]

The closest thing to the leaflet's verbal counterpart is the talk. Anti-uranium activists have given talks to church groups, Rotary clubs, political party branch meetings, school classes and all sorts of other groups. Talks give an added dimension: a reasonable-looking, reasonable-sounding person is arguing the case against uranium mining. The speaker as a person is part of the message. Also used with talks were slide shows (including several good ones made by movement activists), films (including the ubiquitous The War Game, used to show the consequences of nuclear proliferation) and leaflets.

The movement may have emphasised education and information, but it frequently seemed that many members of the 'public' wanted to know only enough to make up their minds - which often was to oppose uranium mining. Bookstalls, which were set up at shopping centres, public meetings and rallies, would typically contain two categories of material: information (books, magazines and leaflets) and symbols of opposition (badges, stickers and T-shirts). The usual experience was a brisk business in selling symbols with little interest in the information, even that provided free.

There are two typical strategies used by social movements to utilise the information and arguments at their disposal. One is to lobby government or corporate decision-makers. For this purpose it is usually considered important to be either 'respectable' and authoritative (since the information seldom speaks for itself), or to be known to be speaking on behalf of a formidable pressure group - or both. The anti-uranium movement used lobbying to some extent, but concentrated on a different strategy: mobilising grass-roots opposition amongst the public and especially within the labour movement. In 1976 it was consciously decided to 'take the issue to the public', through campaigns such as a national signature drive, a national leaflet to be distributed to all households, and rallies, public meetings, bookstalls, publicity stunts and all sorts of other means.

It was believed by movement activists that once people knew the full range of arguments, both for and against nuclear power, most of them would oppose it. Ironically, many of the proponents of nuclear power believed the same thing, except that 'real knowledge' would convince people to support nuclear power. Of course, the content and style of the 'information' disseminated by the two sides was quite different. Both sides subscribed to the belief that knowledge by itself would lead to changes in attitudes and behaviour. Actually, it was knowledge in conjunction with some sort of active involvement with the issues - discussions, personal contact with nuclear opponents, participation in rallies -that swung many to oppose nuclear power. The anti-uranium movement was more successful at this since it was a movement from the grassroots, unlike the pro-nuclear forces.

As well as aiming to educate 'the public' about the case against uranium mining, the movement focused on several groups, such as schools, churches, professions and, in particular, the labour movement. Labour was seen as crucial to stopping uranium mining. Trade unions could take direct action against mining, and a Labour government could legislate to prevent or stop it. A concerted attempt was made to reach the grassroots of the labour movement, for example through speaking to shop floor and Labour Party meetings. This effort had spectacular success in 1977 when both the Australian Council of Trade Unions and the Australian Labour Party adopted policies opposing uranium mining.

THE MEDIA

The mass media have played an important role in disseminating information about nuclear issues. Some of the owners and editors have been highly resistant to reporting the case against uranium, but ultimately the strength of the movement turned much of the media into allies, unwitting or otherwise.

Until 1975, the wisdom of uranium mining was virtually unquestioned by anyone, including all political parties. At this stage in the 'debate', the very existence of opposition was newsworthy. The coverage of rallies and bike rides organised by FOE emphasised the scruffy, 'ratbag' image which did indeed fit many of the protesters. Some members of the movement played on this image through outrageous stunts, such as when one activist, wearing a skeleton suit, sat on a table next to where the leader of the Country Party, a leading supporter of uranium mining, was giving a talk.

As opposition developed, a more serious discussion of the issues was included in the media. Several events aided this process. The Labour government in 1975 set up an inquiry into uranium, and the Liberal-Country Party government which came to power in November that year felt obliged to wait for the findings of the inquiry, which were in October 1976 and May 1977. Thus there was a real decision to be made, which did not seem entirely prejudged. The rapidly expanding anti-uranium movement, a massive advertising campaign by the pro-uranium lobby, the debates within the labour movement, developments in the uranium market overseas, plus overseas opposition - all these generated a large amount of media attention. Newspapers were inundated by letters to the editor. Some refused to print letters in opposition, but many did, and this helped air the arguments and reveal the existence of opposition.

Some journalists were sympathetic to the anti-uranium cause, while others just became attuned to a change in 'newsworthiness' which meant that nuclear issues were worth reporting. The uranium issue was more readily brought to the attention of anyone who read newspapers or watched television. Even the slightest nuclear accident became a story. Once this transition had occurred, the movement had succeeded in its effort to take the issue into the mainstream. But this was far from having won its demands.

Increased media attention to the uranium issue was not completely beneficial to the movement. By itself media coverage didn't bring all that many people into the movement: personal contact remained the key factor in recruitment. Treatments in newspapers and especially on television turned the issue into a spectacle, something 'out there' to be watched and concerned about but not directly involved in.[6] Jerry Mander argues that television as a medium is inherently unsuitable for conveying a feeling for the environment.[7]

The anti-uranium movement seldom used paid advertising. The main reason was its high cost. Movement organisations were usually in debt as it was. Uranium, as a political issue, did not stimulate the outpouring of monetary contributions which have occurred when the issue was whaling or the flooding of the Franklin River. For the cost of a one-page ad in a major daily paper, an organiser could be employed for several months (at low wages, to be sure).

There is also an ideological reason for avoiding advertisements: they are not a grassroots method. They are one-directional, and do not involve either activists or the public in actively debating the issues. Furthermore, the usual anti-uranium advertisement that did get organised was based on signatures of well-known people, thus emphasising authority rather than the issues. Advertisements are not an effective investment by a movement with little money and numerous supporters willing to contribute their labour. The pro-uranium lobby, with enormous funds but little mass base, has relied on advertisements extensively.

FORMAL EDUCATION

The anti-nuclear power movement has put some effort into institutions for formal education, by talking to school classes, putting on occasional adult education courses and encouraging academics to study and research the issues. Sometimes this effort was systematic and directed, as when approaches were made to teachers' unions. But by and large the introduction of discussions of nuclear power, renewable energy and related topics into education systems has come as a spinoff of the movement's general activities. Once uranium became an important topic for public debate, with treatments in the media, teachers and academics promoted treatment of the area on their own initiative. A few have been members of anti-uranium groups, but most simply came to believe that here was an issue worth discussing with their students.

The availability of information on the subject made this

process much easier. Once books and magazines were available, some librarians would order them and some teachers would use them to prepare lessons. (The pro-nuclear lobby for its part produced quite a few materials which were distributed free to schools.) Some new texts for science and social science courses would include treatments of 'the energy question'. A few of the teachers invited anti-uranium speakers along to talk to their classes, show slide shows and pass out leaflets, but eventually this became superfluous: the issue had entered the mainstream of political discourse.

Although the uranium issue was no longer stigmatised as only the latest preoccupation of a few greenies, at the same time the legitimating of the issue also meant its partial deradicalisation. The more strident pro- and anti-uranium claims are usually softened or omitted in textbook presentations. The important political and social aspects of the debate - such as the likelihood of attacks on civil liberties in the nuclear society, and the changes in lifestyle which might accompany either a soft or a hard energy future - tend to be avoided in favour of accounts of the hazards and efficiencies of different energy sources.

While the development of formal environmental educat-ion owes much to the initial and continuing stimulus of the environmental movement, there is little discussion of social movements and of the powerful institutions implicated in environmental problems in most educational writings on the environment, which usually present the environment as a neutral subject cut off from political and economic con-troversy. It has been a continual amazement to me to see how little material from formal environmental education is of any use to environmental activists. This is because the structure of the educational system encourages passive absorption of information rather than social action.

Academic environmental studies programmes have largely been set up in response to the rise of the environ-ment movement and the popularisation of environmental concerns.[8] These programmes are important beyond their size in that a sizeable proportion of full-time professional intellectuals who deal with environmental issues are found in them. It is not so much that these intellectuals do a lot that others couldn't do, but that any work they do has a much higher status because of their position.

Some academic programmes are technocratic in content and style. They bring together experts from a variety of fields, such as biology, physics, chemistry, engineering and so forth, to deal with technical problems related to environmental issues. Much of this work is of the technical fix variety: setting water pollution standards, examining traffic flow problems, looking at 'safe' mining practices.[9] Once the environment became a 'socially significant' area, lots of scientists joined the bandwagon by relabelling their research - for example, surface physics became a contribution to solar collector research - in the same way that scientists have relabelled a multitude of projects as cancer research.

Technocratic environmental research is an adaptation of research work to the standard pattern of specialisation and professionalisation which makes most science selectively useful to governments and corporations (or just the scientists themselves). Community groups seldom have have any use for such research. Technocratic environmental researchers, if they enter public debates at all, are careful to distance themselves from the 'political' advocates. The researchers are political themselves, but this is hidden behind the mask of neutrality and objectivity.

Other academic programmes take a much more critical perspective on environmental issues, emphasising the wider poltical and social factors and the different ways in which the issues can be approached. Whether or not they have direct ties to environmental groups, they draw on and feed back into the environmental concerns felt by many people. Programmes of this sort often face difficulties in the academic system. One example is the Human Sciences Programme at the Australian National University. From its first mooting in 1970 it has been the object of attacks by powerful figures in the ANU hierarchy. Typical complaints are that it is not sufficiently 'rigorous', that it is unnecessary and that there are deficiencies in its running. The Programme has been vindicated by several reviews, but that has not stopped the attacks. There was an attempt to deny tenure to Jeremy Evans, one of the key members of the Programme, and a long-term whittling away of staff numbers, undercutting the viability of the Programme. Other such programmes have suffered similar attacks.

The real reason for the attacks is that transdisciplinary environmental studies programmes pose a serious threat to the academic system of power, which is built on hierarchy and knowledge specialisation. Academics build fiefdoms on exclusive claims to bodies of knowledge, usually amalgamated around 'disciplines' such as biochemistry or history and specialities within them. This division of knowledge allows particular disciplines to be tied to particular outside groups, such as engineering to corporations and law to the legal profession. The more 'pure' subjects such as physics and philosophy provide status for academia as a whole; specialisation and jargon separate them from the general public. Transdisciplinary programmes pose a double threat. They trespass on the knowledge territories of several disciplines, and they also organise knowledge in a fashion which can be useful to non-elite groups either practically or to legitimate their concerns. As long as the relevant social movement is strong, critical academic programmes can survive. Otherwise, many of them will be attacked and/or become more cautious and conservative. This applies to areas such as women's studies and peace studies as well as environmental studies.

Critical intellectuals with insider status are always threatening to the powers that be. In its rallies, leaflets and lobbying, the environmental movement can be dismissed by many people as being uninformed and 'emotional'. But when professionals from corporations, government or academia speak out, this is not so easily ignored. One of the most powerful blows to the authority of the nuclear industry was the resignation of three nuclear engineers from General Electric in 1976.[10]

Attempts are regularly made to silence critics who have some formal status, by smear campaigns, blocking tenure or promotion, or dismissal.[11] In 1971, Clyde Manwell, Professor of Zoology at the University of Adelaide, and his wife Ann Baker made some criticisms of the South Australian government's fruit fly spraying programme. This led to an attempt to dismiss Manwell from his post, a case which was not resolved until 1975. It is revealing that several 'members of the public' had publicly criticised the fruit fly spraying programme prior to Manwell and Baker, but they had not been attacked in state parliament or at their jobs. The attacks were launched precisely because Manwell, as a professor, had much greater status and hence credibility.

At the Australian National University in the early 1970s, Richard and Val Routley wrote a book, Fight for the Forests, which was very critical of forestry planning and practice, and which was to be published through the Research School of Social Sciences where Richard Routley

215

worked. There was an attempt to block publication of the book, instigated from within the Department of Forestry at the ANU. After the publication of the book, Richard Routley was barred from using the Forestry Department library for six months. The Routleys are philosophers; if they had been in the field of forestry it is unlikely they would have survived in their professional positions. I have been informed of numerous cases of suppression of dissidents within forestry.

These and other cases show that knowledge about the environment is not something that simply develops as a result of neutral processes of research and education. There are active political interventions into knowledge creation, certification and dissemination. The dominant formal power lies in the hands of institutions which cause environmental problems, mainly corporations and governments. Against this, the environmental movement has sometimes tried to muster logic, counter-expertise and inside connections (the respectable approach) and sometimes tried to mobilise grassroots action. Both approaches have their strengths and weaknesses. The 'respectable' approach has a good chance of success when the demands made are widely popular and do not challenge powerful vested interests. Whaling could be stopped in most countries because the whalers did not muster sufficient political clout against popular concern - though even in this case massive campaigns had to be mounted. Stopping whaling does not pose any fundamental questioning of the systems of capitalism or industrialism, and even the connections with the domination of nature were not developed at the time.

The nuclear power industry is a much more formidable opponent, and the critique of the 'hard energy path' raises crucial questions about centralisation of energy sources, energy-intensive lifestyles and destruction of indigenous cultures. The 'debate' has always been at cross-purposes, with proponents and opponents raising different concerns, because ultimately different values and social interests have underlaid different views on the subject. More revealing than the ostensible 'arguments' have been the political dynamics of the debate. Nuclear dissenters from within the establishment have been transferred, dismissed and denigrated. At stake is the unanimity of 'expert' opinion, with expertise defined as nuclear expertise rather than expertise in the wider value judgements about what energy futures are desirable. The anti-nuclear movement has provided the encouragement and support for dissent by insiders and has also developed its own critical understanding. But more important has been the spreading of knowledge to all sorts of people, beyond the small circle of 'counter-experts'. In an immediate sense this has been done to mobilise opposition, but it has a deeper aspect. It has been an attempt to undercut the very value of specialist knowledge as a resource that can best be wielded by experts. By spelling out the wider values involved in the debate and the way they relate to the technical issues, some activists have hoped to build a different basis for social decision-making, in which expertise is at the service of the people rather than the elites. This goal is vague enough, and the degree of success in moving towards it has probably not been all that great. But an important part of the anti-nuclear power movement has been the very attempt to move in this direction.

DECLINE OF THE ANTI-URANIUM MOVEMENT

The peak years of the Australian anti-uranium movement were 1976-79. In August 1977 the government gave the go-ahead for mining, but with significant reservations made in response to popular opposition. It took the government a year to manipulate acquiescence of the Aborigines required by its own legislation, and mining began in 1979. In that year the anti-uranium movement had planned several major campaigns, including promotion of nuclear-free zones, a boycott of the Australia New Zealand Bank which has close links with the uranium industry, and collection of signatures on a 'statement of defiance' to the harsh provisions of the law under which uranium mining proceeded. All these campaigns provided an interaction of direct action and education. For example, in order to promote the boycott, people would need to be informed of the financial aspects of the nuclear industry and as well as reasons to oppose the industry.

While these campaigns were in many ways the most coherent ones yet planned by the Australian movement, the outcome was quite different. The movement went into a rapid decline due to demoralisation brought about by the beginning of mining. Only the nuclear-free zones campaign had much success. Most of the activists did not have a sufficiently long-term perspective on the issue to be able to maintain energy during the short-term failure to stop

217

mining.

One of the problems was that the movement had staked a lot on the election of a Labour government. But Labour was soundly defeated in 1977 and 1980. 'Education' of the public and the labour movement was successful as far as it went, but it did not provide an alternative strategy to election of the Labour Party.[12] Another problem was that the media tired of the issue, and many activists lost enthusiasm for an issue no longer in the limelight.

The years 1980-82 were quiet ones for the uranium debate. With the election of a Labour government in March 1983 there was a resurgence of activity: now was the chance to implement the party's anti-uranium policy. But Labour Party elites who had always favoured uranium had not been napping. In 1982 at the Party's national conference the anti-uranium platform was watered down in a clever move which by-passed grassroots opposition to uranium in Party branches. Once in government, key Labour elites further sabotaged the platform and among other things allowed Roxby Downs, potentially the largest uranium mine in the western world, to proceed.

The successes of the movement are not as apparent as the failures, but remain large. The prospects for nuclear power, uranium enrichment or reprocessing are slim in Australia: moves to introduce them would trigger a groundswell of opposition. Even uranium mining is encountering many obstacles, including major direct actions at Roxby Downs and continuing trade union resistance in the Northern Territory. These successes owe a lot to the education campaigns in the earlier years of the anti-uranium campaign. While the organised movement has dwindled in size and energy, the concern about the nuclear issue has spread further and further, especially via schools and the media.

In summary, the role of social movement organisations is especially vital in the early stages of an issue, when few people know that there is an issue at all. Dissemination of information, developing arguments, questioning established truths, formulating alternatives - 'education' in the widest sense - is of central importance for movements. For the movement to have an effective base, rather than depending on a few experts, education within the movement is crucial. The very existence of the movement, plus its own efforts, leads to education of wider publics. At all stages, the credibility of proponents on either side of the 'debate' is the subject of struggle, and this is manifest in attempts to suppress experts who support the movement.

This is a pretty picture which hides some less attractive sides to the role of 'education' in social movements. The biggest problem is that 'knowledge' is frequently subjugated to the short-term needs of the movement. Those arguments and claims which gain the greatest media attention are played up. In the nuclear debate this has often led to fearmongering about cancers and genetic defects and lack of attention to the more politically-oriented objections to nuclear power, based on proliferation, threats to civil liberties and centralisation of power. Seldom have movement activists openly criticised anti-nuclear figures such as Helen Caldicott for their exaggerations and technical errors. While a focus on the hazards of nuclear power sometimes can bring more people into the movement, its danger lies in diverting attention away from long-term strategies to challenge the institutions promoting nuclear power. Trumpeting the dangers of a technology does not in itself provide a way of overcoming it, as the case of nuclear weapons shows.

Related to this is the lack of internal criticism in the movement. Certain dogmas develop, such as that it is impossible to dispose of high-level radioactive waste 'safely' or that renewable energy sources have been neglected entirely because of subsidies to conventional sources. The pro-nuclear arguments are studied by only a few in the movement, and even then the strengths of the pro-nuclear case are hardly ever acknowledged. (It is no excuse that the same criticism applies with even greater force to the supporters of nuclear power.) Internal criticism is difficult to sustain in a movement in which much activism is based on moral outrage, but in the long run the lack of critical thinking weakens the movement, since arguments are not sufficiently tested and improved. Focusing on the less political safety issues opens the movement to challenge. Most members of the general public would probably name radioactive waste disposal as their key concern about nuclear power, whereas those who have studied the issues in more depth typically see proliferation, political hazards of a nuclear society and other arguments as equally significant. The issues of safety are more vulnerable to solution by technical fix, such as a new improved method of waste disposal. Those familiar with the issue believe that the technical and political aspects of waste disposal cannot be separated, but these subtleties gain little circulation.

The quest by environmental organisations for 'respectability' poses another threat to the wider discussions of issues: the suppression of radicals within the movement. The anti-uranium movement, a much more radical movement itself within the wider environmental movement, has not been subect to this problem to a great extent, but I know of two cases in which paid workers in Australian environmental or consumer organisations have been dismissed because of their radical stands.

What happens in the course of many campaigns is that information becomes a 'resource' which is used to promote the cause rather than to enlighten people so that they can judge the issues for themselves. In the narrow sense people always do judge the issues for themselves, but the question here is whether they are encouraged to grasp the full range of evidence and arguments. When movements produce glossy brochures or pay for large newspaper advertisements, as in the case of the campaign to stop the flooding of the Franklin River in south-west Tasmania, they are still providing information, but that information is often mobilised to sway emotions rather than encourage critical thinking. It is typically argued that these methods are essential to support a valid cause, and that in any case the other side is using even less edifying methods, such as the promise of large pay-offs. That may be true, but it remains yet another case of the ends allegedly justifying the means. Those issues which lend themselves to this sort of promotion are the 'goody-goody' ones of wilderness and rare species. Less spectacular issues such as soil degradation or the build-up of carbon dioxide in the atmosphere receive less attention. The dissemination of information, development of strategies and hard thinking necessary to deal with this sort of issue are neglected when information becomes a commodity used to sell the latest environmental concern.

This orientation is one reason why there are seldom more than a few people with a depth of knowledge about any given environmental issue. In the uranium debate, the number of people on either side with a wide grasp of the arguments has always been quite small. This is a more serious weakness for the environmentalists, since they seldom have the formal endorsement of professional bodies to provide 'authoritative backing' for their views - and therefore they rely more on the arguments themselves.

The availability of knowledgeable people to the

movement is also a major factor here. Only a relatively small fraction of those with a grasp of the issues are willing to openly identify themselves with the movement. These are the ones who develop the arguments for public debate. There are others, such as quite a few scientists, who know a lot about the issues but who do not want to become open partisans on one side or the other. Academics often fall in this category: they decline to 'descend' to the sordid arenas of newspapers, radio programmes and dinner club talks. Thus there is a sizeable reservoir of potential expertise which remains untapped by either environmentalists or their opponents. The detached observers of the debate will rarely approach environmental organisations offering to help, while activists often can't be bothered seeking out reluctant scientists and academics.

Another category of knowledgeable people lost to the movement are those who enter the parliamentary or bureaucratic arenas. In about 1977, several of the most knowledgeable and effective anti-uranium activists took up jobs working for Labour Members of Parliament in Canberra. Similarly, with a Labour government in Victoria in the 1980s, a number of key environmental activists in that state have joined the Victorian public service to implement environmental programmes. In a few cases these activists remained effective campaigners within the Labour Party or the state bureaucracy; in all too many others they adapted their spots to the party or bureaucratic power structures. What was lost in most cases was a continuing interaction with the outside movement. This is inevitable to some extent: it is very difficult to be both a prominent activist and a credible voice inside a bureaucratic organisation. Once again, the fault lay on both sides. Those moving 'inside the system' became oriented to bureaucratic imperatives and lost the incentive to keep in contact with outside activists, while the outside activists became disillusioned with those they saw as partly or wholely coopted by the system.

When the links between insider and outsider activists can be maintained, the results can be very fruitful. This was one of the strengths of the anti-uranium movement for many years: community activists and labour movement activists supported each other and exchanged invaluable information and campaigning suggestions. In more recent years, this linkage has weakened. In the non-violent direct actions held at Roxby Downs in 1983 and 1984, there was relatively little mutual support between workers and protesters. (Significantly, the managers did everything they could to prevent contact between the groups). The polarisation between workers and environmentalists has been much greater in other campaigns, notably in forestry. Some environmentalists have engaged in a virtual cult of protest and direct action without laying the groundwork of developing sound arguments and programmes and undertaking education campaigns to reach workers who, superficially at least, are threatened by environmental demands.

This recent tendency in the Australian environmental movement reflects a more basic difficulty in most social movements, namely the orientation to reactive protest and the failure to develop long-term perspectives and campaigns. A long-term perspective immediately highlights the need for developing expertise, spreading knowledge and laying the basis for continued commitment. The Freire approach among others provides a way to develop strategies of this sort.[13] The continuing difficulty is to engage people in long-term efforts. There is a core of dedicated activists who might undertake such programmes, but they are typically pressed to act on the latest urgent issues and are prone to burnout. Those who are not so heavily involved are less likely to commit themselves to an issue sufficiently. When the current concern fades from public view, they are likely to take up different, more 'trendy' issues. Finally, institutionalised education about the environment carries on, but seldom with a strong orientation to action: it is education for individual understanding, not education for social action.

REFERENCES

1. Accounts of the Australian uranium issue include M. Elliott (ed.), Ground for Concern (Hardmondsworth: Penguin, 1977); J. Falk, Global Fission (Melbourne: Oxford University Press, 1982); B. Martin, 'The Australian anti-uranium movement', Alternatives, vol. 10, no. 4 (Summer 1982); T. Smith, 'Forming a uranium policy', Australian Quarterly, vol. 51 (December 1979).

2. See for example R.S. Lewis, The Nuclear Power Rebellion (New York: Viking, 1972); D. Nelkin, Nuclear Power and its Critics (Ithaca: Cornell University Press, 1971).

3. R. J. Roddewig, Green Bans (Sydney: Hale and Iremonger, 1978).

4. P. Lowe and J. Goyder, Environmental Groups in Politics (London: Allen and Unwin, 1983).

5. A.B. Lovins and J.H. Price, Non-nuclear Futures (Cambridge, Mass.: Ballinger, 1975); W.C. Patterson, Nuclear Power (Harmondsworth: Penguin, 1976); D. Hayes, J. Falk and N. Barrett, Red Light for Yellowcake (Melbourne: Friends of the Earth Australia, 1977).

6. P.M. Sandman, 'Mass environmental education: can the media do the job?', in J.A. Swan and W.B. Stapp (eds), Environmental Education (Beverley Hills: Sage, 1974), pp. 207-47.

7. J. Mander, Four Arguments for the Elimination of Television (New York: William Morrow, 1978).

8. D. Rose, 'New laboratories for old', in G. Holton and W.A. Blanpied (eds), Science and its Public (Dordrecht: D. Reidel, 1976), pp. 143-55.

9. B. Martin, 'Academics and the environment', Ecologist, vol. 7, no. 6 (July 1977).

10. L.J. Freeman, Nuclear Witnesses (New York: Norton, 1981).

11. B. Martin, C.M.A. Baker, C. Manwell and C. Pugh (eds), Intellectual Suppression (Sydney: Angus and Robertson, 1986).

12. B. Martin, 'Environmentalism and electoralism', Ecologist, vol. 14, no. 3 (1984).

13. An excellent treatment is given by I. Watson, Environmental Education and Community Action (Canberra: Canberra and South-East Region Environment Centre, 1985).

10

Workers' Education and the Crisis of British Trade Unionism

John Field

Until perhaps twenty years ago, it would have been pointless to speak of a radical tradition in British adult education in isolation from the organised labour movement. The precise nature of the relations between adult education institutions and organised labour has always been problematic, and usually unsatisfactory, but that there should be a close and organic relationship was never questioned by adult educators who saw their work as part of a broader movement towards social emancipation and change.

If we look at the context of Tawney's 1957 address to the extra-mural department at London University, we find that the idea that all serious educational movements in England have also been social movements was no intellectual abstraction.[1] Tawney's argument placed 'the world of Labour' explicitly before his audience, at a time when he and they were concerned about the WEA's drift towards the middle class - a drift that any radical, like Tawney, would have regarded as an unqualified loss, an opting for the 'line of least resistance'.[2] The radical tradition, from the Chartist Sunday Schools of the 1840s through to the WEA and extra-mural department situated its practice firmly within a labour movement paradigm that increasingly placed the organised working class - defined above all as the active members of the trade union movement - at the heart of its endeavours. Since the late 1960s, though, organised labour has been displaced from its focal position at the crux of education for social change, and a growing rift has opened up between those who work in education for trade unionists and those who work in community-based forms of radical adult education.

A remarkable silence, to take one salient example, has greeted a heated debate among trade union educators about the nature and purpose of their work. In two recent books which attempt to examine the philosophy and practice of a radical adult education, the only substantial references to education for trade unionists are historical;[3] yet both books were conceived at a time of unparalleled expansion in trade union education, underpinned by a sizeable government grant and the first statutory entitlements to paid educational leave for working-class people that Britain has ever experienced. For their part, trade unions showed little or no interest in the new community-based movements that emerged from the late 1960s, and saw little to interest them in the educational work that developed around community struggles.

The consequences of that rift have been thrown into sharp relief by the present crisis. It is above all a crisis of and for British capitalism, but it is one in which the working class and its organisations have been unable to mount an effective resistance, let alone develop an effective struggle for a socialist solution: Conservative ideas and values may not be pervasive amongst working-class people, but they were sufficiently popular in 1983 to deliver 32 per cent of trade unionists' votes to the Conservative Party.[4] Ways of organising struggles that were appropriate to a phase of economic growth and full employment must now be reviewed and revised; although the scope and diversity of trade union education have remained admirably broad even under the impact of the crisis, defence of past achievements must as ever be supported by an appraisal of shortcomings and deficiencies.

TRADE UNION STRATEGIES IN THE 1980s

Struggles that were limited to the workplace or the neigh-bourhood brought real, if limited gains, up to the 1970s. Nor are they now dead: limited and sectional actions can still bring results, both for trade unionists and for community groups.[5] Clearly, though, the scale and the nature of the crisis have altered the context in which struggles occur, and have set constraints on the effectiveness of inherited patterns of organisation and action.

Most disturbing, for socialists, is the profound unpopu-larity of trade unionism and trade union action, combined with a very real decline in working-class involvement in union organisation. Ten years ago, evidence of the gap between organisations and members was generally hailed, on the left, as a conflict between stodgy bureaucrats and heroic workers; today, the left is likely to be on the

receiving end of complaints about unresponsiveness, paternalism and manipulation. For its part, the Trades Union
Congress has recognised the gap; but its response has been
primarily cosmetic, couched in terms of a public relations
campaign which leaves power where it already is, and fails
to address the crisis within the movement itself. A strategy
document circulated internally in 1984 treated the problem
largely as one of presentation:

> The vital task facing trade unions at the present
> time is to sell trade unionism - to convince trade
> union members that they belong to a beneficial,
> positive and essential organisation.[6]

The far greater challenges - transforming union organisation
and government in ways that involve members in actively
making their own decisions and implementing them - have
been taken up only by a minority of unions, such as NUPE,
the TGWU, the Society of Civil and Public Servants and -
arguably - the Electricians and the Engineers.

It would be foolish to claim that the unions have done
nothing right since 1979. The movement remains remarkably
strong: despite all that the government and economic
collapse have done, TUC membership is still above the ten
million mark, and many unions enjoy the loyalty and energetic commitment of tens of thousands of active members.
For many working-class men and women, their union is still
the most effective and open means of participating in a
democratic organisation belonging, not to the state or the
employer, but to them. In spite of the onslaught, at local
and national level employers have no option but to engage in
collective bargaining with union representatives; an index of
their effectiveness is that, in general, wage settlements are
still (for those in work) running ahead of inflation. Finally,
there have been some striking public successes, notably in
the highly effective campaigns to defend the political levy,
which have even produced ballot results in favour of
political funds in unions like the Hosiery and Knitwear
Workers or the Inland Revenue Staffs Federation which have
never previously had them. Unions continue to make a
vigorous and robust contribution to the defence of working-
class interests in a hostile society; but, especially since the
unsuccessful conclusion to the miners' strike, there is no
escaping the problems facing the movement.

In the bitter climate of the 1980s, the organisation,

operation and quality of trade union education are hardly likely to be decisive. It might be able to make a valuable contribution, as is suggested by the part played by the organisation of dayschools and weekend conferences during the political fund campaign in enabling unions to hold close discussions with active members, provide clear and detailed information, and build up a grassroots movement. But the question of education cannot be dealt with in isolation from the wider and urgent need to develop forms of union organisation and action that will rebuild the movement and protect and advance working-class interests.

THE ROLE FOR TRADE UNION EDUCATION

One response to the effects of the crisis upon trade unionism is to suggest that it needs a more politicised education. It should shift away from narrow economic and workplace concerns to embrace a broader view. This raises as many questions, though, as it answers. Most obviously, what kind of politics? What interpretations of the wider issues should it consider? Which trade union members should engage in such wider learning? With a membership deeply divided in its views, will a politicised curriculum be divisive? On its own, the call for a broader and more political curriculum leaves untouched vital questions of scope, purpose, organisation and control. The implications of the crisis for union democracy, including control over union education, and for forms of organisation and education that will encourage a more popular and campaigning trade union-ism, have their parallels in radical educational initiatives elsewhere.

Since 1979, the rapid expansion of union education in Britain has gone into reverse. From a peak of almost 44,000 students in 1979, the TUC's day-release courses had declined by 1983 to some 31,000. Many trade union studies units in colleges of further education have now closed; trade union tutors from colleges, extra-mural departments and the WEA are now spending all or part of their time in organising and teaching courses for unemployed people and others.

The catastrophic fall in union education mirrored a wider malaise in the movement as a whole, as the assumptions that underlay existing strategies started to crumble, The TUC's own education programme is a case in point; it expanded rapidly from 1975, after an internal review of educational services showed that the average workplace or branch official enjoyed half a day's education a year,[7] but it did so on the basis of government funding combined with statutory entitlements to day release for workplace representatives. From the government's point of view, the settlement complemented the 'Social Contract' between unions and state; it accorded the unions considerably more leeway than the joint management-union training scheme proposed in 1972 by the Commission on Industrial Relations, with the stated purpose of 'improving industrial relations' through corporatism in the workplace,[8] while setting limits on the scope and nature of the expansion.

While the TUC adamantly rejected direct employer control over union education, as proposed by the CIR, its independence was compromised by the legislation and agreements of the mid-1970s. First, legislation allowed paid release only for certain stipulated categories; these were for the most part workplace stewards and health and safety representatives. Second, it was open for employers to challenge the content of courses where they felt that it was irrelevant to industrial relations (an option increasingly taken up by employers in the past five years). Third, partly for reasons of cost, almost all the expansion was taken up by fairly short courses (five to ten days, with limited options for follow-on courses of a further ten days), largely taught in local authority technical colleges. Fourth, the grant depended on continued government goodwill; in 1983 it was cut, and part of the rest was allotted only to courses jointly approved by employers. Finally, the TUC consciously sought to confine course content to workplace issues, encouraging tutors to rely upon centrally produced materials and not to apply any specialist knowledge of their own.

The debate among trade union tutors has concentrated almost entirely upon the content and organisation of the TUC day-release scheme. Doug Gowan, of the TUC Education Department, argues that the courses are intended to develop skills and techniques rather than transmit abstract and academic knowledge; the TUC has tried to dissuade tutors from thinking in terms of 'subjects' or 'disciplines', and instead to shift towards 'student-centred educational methods' which shift away from classroom styles towards something more like a trade union meeting or office discussion:

One of the asumptions that underlies a traditional

approach to the role of the tutor is the idea that more effort, direction, control, leadership, motivation and so on by the tutor is better. But the more tutored a course is, it is likely that the less self-reliance and self-activity are produced in the students.[9]

The non-hierarchical, participative styles of teaching now common in community-based adult education made particular sense for the TUC, given its decision to use existing public educational services to deliver the courses rather than educators whom it employed and controlled directly, combined with its suspicion of the more independent 'service organisations' (WEA, extra-mural departments and residential colleges). Similarly, the TUC's exclusive concentration on learning from experience in the workplace resembles much of what now passes for experience-based learning in progressive adult education elsewhere.

From 1979, a number of trade union tutors started openly to criticise the TUC's preoccupation with methods and its failure to enable trade unionists to grapple with wider and more analytical issues. Paradoxically, the critics have appeared at the same time more radical and more conservative than the TUC. More conservative because they clearly derive inspiration from the old WEA extra-mural model, of the tutorial class seriously, conscientiously, and at length coming to grips with conceptual insights and analytical frameworks which appear remote from the workplace, and because they insist upon the vital contribution of the professional educator. More radical, because they insist that what is needed is a trade union education that recognises the political and economic causes that underly workplace concerns, and that brings together and questions the common experiences of a range of working people. John McIlroy, most persistent of the critics, argues that

Skills are important but in the harsh world of the 1980s the basic 'battle of ideas' is even more vital. Core TUC courses do not deal with the ownership of industry and managerial control of the workplace, the historical development of trade unions and their present predicament, the economic context or the poltical dilemmas. TUC Education creates its own sealed world; its overwhelming

229

focus on plant bargaining is like using bows and arrows to combat nuclear technology.[10]

The TUC's response to such criticisms has been character-istically heavy-handed: McIlroy was barred from teaching on TUC courses, and it is alleged that attempts have been made to stifle debate.

Outside the TUC, individual trade unions have their own education programmes which are not always hampered by the same constraints. Some unions, notably the EETPU, organise joint courses with employers and invite manage-ment to contribute to teaching. Others, including NUPE, GMBATU and the TGWU, have moved towards more wide-spread membership education (including an ambitious distance learning programme in the case of the TGWU), involving shop stewards as lay tutors, and developing more politically aware forms of education that are related to active campaigns around particular issues.[11] The mine-workers have always preferred lengthy day-release courses for active members, usually organised through extra-mural departments of the WEA and pre-dating the 1975 entitle-ments, to the more limited TUC courses (more limited in three senses: they are shorter, they are role training, and they are only for representatives).[12] Trades councils organise seminars and conferences, branches hold discus-sions or pay tuition fees for members attending evening classes and workshops; there are study tours and exchanges with overseas comrades.

The debate over the TUC's programme has missed much of this diversity and pluralism; in particular, it has ignored the extent to which many trade unions run a broad programme of courses and resources for members as well as representatives, both directly and through organisations like the WEA. The debate has also failed to question the way that union education is organised, particularly where 'service organisations' with some degree of independence from the unions and from the state are concerned.

There have been real gains in trade union education in Britain, through the TUC and through individual unions. As a forum it involves larger numbers of working-class men and women than any other form of adult education in Britain, and it appeals to them as representatives of a wider movement of working people, banded together into continuing and accountable organisations. One study of day-release trade union students found that the most important benefit they identified from the courses was not simply enhanced skills and smoother communications with management, but a general gain in confidence; judged by the 'needs-meeting' paradigm, it was an overwhelming success.[13]

Clearly, individual gains, in terms of meeting individual needs, have important collective consequences in a trade union. But judged by the needs of the collectivity - whether the union or the wider community of working men and women - union education has a number of deficiencies:

1.   Trade union education, particularly where opportunities are limited to representatives who enjoy day-release facilities, can simply highlight the differences between the active minority and ordinary members.

2.   There are far too few structures for democratic representation and control over union education, so that decision-making depends mostly on a smaller number of individuals.

3.   The 'front-end loader' model of initial training ignores the changing and continuing needs for representatives and other workers to learn how to cope with new challenges and demands in the workplace.

4.   Other than in mining and one or two other industries, there is still a massive gap between the best day-release work and the advanced courses on offer at the residential colleges or higher education institutions like Middlesex Polytechnic.

5.   The labour movement has made hardly any use of its own scholars and intellectuals, and gives them little support, so that many drift through higher education into roles that have little relationship with their origins and aspirations.

6.   No satisfactory relationship exists with 'service organisations' like the WEA, extra-mural departments and residential colleges.

7.   Trade union horizons rarely rise above the economistic, and fail to address the political and cultural aspects of the crisis that working class people are living through.

8.   Most day-release is concerned with socialising representatives into forms of collective bargaining which are under challenge, and carefully avoid encouraging creative thought about representatives' role in generating and sustaining organisational change.

The old slogan, carried on many union banners and enshrined in rule books, holds that 'Knowledge is Power'; the present weaknesses of British trade union education call into question its ability to support those active members who are trying to resist and counteract ideological dominance, let alone revive the old ambition of a learning that would emancipate the oppressed and engender social change.

SOME ALTERNATIVE APPROACHES

Internationally, most trade union education looks remarkably similar, in its main purposes and structures, to the British pattern (apart from in certain non-capitalist states). An education which is both liberating and informed by an alternative conception of society is rare, and educational opportunities which are extended beyond representatives to the wider membership is rarer still. Even in South Africa, for instance, most union training is organised for shop and shaft stewards, and the curriculum is workplace-based; there is, though, a recognition of the national struggle and of the role of multinational capital.[14] The same insistence upon a curriculum which goes beyond a narrow conception of role initiation may be found even in North America, where trade union traditions are relatively apolitical but not all union education is as blinkered as that offered by the British TUC.

In Canada, where the government agreed a $2 million annual grant in 1977, the Canadian Labour Congress decided only to accept the money on a 'no strings' basis, taking its traditional view that labour education must be controlled by labour. The view, ironically, has a reactionary provenance; the Canadian WEA was strangled by Candian universities and trade unions precisely because they could not control what they saw as its promotion of class consciousness,[15] but the resulting empahsis upon a 'do-it-yourself' labour education enabled Canadian unions to avoid the academic drift that characterises labour education in the USA.

In 1977, the CLC chose to make its own educational system, creating a national Labour Education Studies Centre and developing materials and courses for regional use. In the first two years, the LESC ran 76 courses on 31 subjects, ranging from Occupational Health and Safety to public relations and Labour Journalism, Socio-Economic Planning, Labour Economics and International Affairs. Traditional 'tool courses' were left to the existing Congress programme, or preferably to affliated unions.[16] In other words, basic steward training was not financed out of additional funding, which was devoted instead to a union-controlled programme which tackled more advanced issues. The response, it was said in 1979, suggested 'a considerable backlog of interest in obtaining training at advanced levels'.[17]

Some individual unions have gone much further, notably the Steelworkers, who have responded to the collapse of steelmaking in Canada by recruiting in high-technology industries and the service sector, including fast-food chains. The Steelworkers, financing their programme through a 1 per cent levy on union dues, provided training for reps in fighting union-busting methods in the early 1930s; by 1985, they had developed a full two-day residential course on 'Facing Management', which includes introduction exercises, and a role play ('Handle with Care') on productivity bargaining; the course also looks at Japanese management methods, quality circles and technological change. Over a two-day residential course, it is possible to start with recent trends in the workplace, go on to analyse a variety of management styles and approaches, consider strategies, and then develop what the course manual describes as 'a sense of solidarity and optimism in "Hard Times"'.[18] Canadian labour education is by no means a model of good practice, but if it is possible for unions with far weaker traditions of political affiliation and shopfloor militancy than in Britain to stray beyond the circumscribed perimeters of the workplace in their training, then it is harder still to accept the myopic parochialism of much current British practice.

It makes even less sense in view of the collapse of the TUC's regional day-release programme. Currently, the TUC's regional education programme is shifting steadily in favour of courses even shorter than the ten-day representatives' courses, not organised coherently as part of a process of recurrent union education but arranged on a more or less ad hoc basis around single issues. And, as the old manufacturing heartlands decline, so participation in TUC courses is increasingly drawn from the public sector unions, representing women and men whose labour processes and relationships with employers set quite different constraints to effective struggle from those affecting private-sector workers. Trade union education has, for the most part, barely started to grapple with the implications of the growing importance of public-sector trade unionism: in 1972, for example, 6.6 per cent of all TUC membership belonged to NUPE or NALGO alone; by 1982, the equivalent figure was 14.1 per cent.

The growth of public sector unionism raises starkly the

issue of alliances between workers as producers and working people as consumers. For any adult education movement which addresses itself seriously to education for social change, such alliances are of profound importance - as arenas within which really useful knowledge can be learned, as subjects for learning from, and as sites of practical intervention in the form of participatory research and independent analysis. As yet, though, these alliances - many of which, by their nature, will be localised and often short-lived - constitute an underdeveloped agenda.

In Britain, a number of projects developed in the 1970s with the objective of bringing together socialists, trade unionists and community activists. Most initiatives arose from the 'movement left' - that amorphous network of local groupings, cultural ventures and autonomous campaigns that was the legacy of the libertarian revolts of the late 1960s and early 1970s - rather than from within the existing labour movement (apart from the Institute for Workers' Control, which in the mid-1970s looked as though it might become a major national forum for the newer movements of the 1970s and the earlier generation of intellectuals and trade unionists who had quit the Communist Party after 1956). A number of locally-based trade union and community resource centres were established, often with support from trades councils and the WEA, only to be subsequently proscribed by the TUC as 'unofficial'.

Coventry Workshop, one independent research, education and advice centre, founded in 1975 out of the Home Office-sponsored Community Development Project, tried to service a range of community and trade union organisations. On the principle that 'the job of winning control has to start where the powerless are', it supports struggles at grassroots level over health, housing, wages, health and safety, and employment.[19] Its role was partly that of a forum, partly a catalyst, and partly that of an intellectual resource which feeds in ideas and information; over the years it has developed an outstanding reputation for encouraging and sustaining an informed dialogue between local movements. But its principled insistence upon grassroots-level work, criticising labour movement official-dom where necessary, has also produced difficulties: its inability to win sustained trade union support at regional level, over-reliance on the now abolished West Midlands County Council for core funding, and the instability of many of the community groups it serviced, have placed its future at serious risk.

Even more ambitious attempts to bring trade unionists and community activists together in educational settings have taken place at Northern College. Opened by the four Labour-controlled local authorities of South Yorkshire in 1978, the College was deliberately intended to be rather different from existing residential colleges. Whereas they all currently specialise either in advanced academic credit-bearing courses of one or two years, or in short courses for groups who often have little or no contact with each other, Northern College's founders hoped to combine long courses with ten-week courses so that students would benefit from having the continuity of learning associated with the long courses alongside the fresher experiences and perceptions of students on short courses. It was also intended that a wide range of groups and individuals would take advantage of both types of course; trade unionists, school governors, people intending to be councillors, voluntary organisations, and people intending to apply for higher education or vocational retraining were all mentioned in the final planning paper in 1978,[20] whereas the other long-term colleges concerned with education for social action were either, like Ruskin, largely trade union-oriented or, like the Cooperative College, intended for cooperators. Finally, by the time that the early group of tutors was appointed, there was a strong concern not to be caught up in the academic drift that, we felt, had tugged Ruskin away from its labour movement roots.

Plans for ten-week short courses were never realised: the longest is the five-week course for the Yorkshire and Derbyshire Areas of the NUM, the average is around one week, and many are only a weekend. Like course content and organisation in general, length is negotiated with organisations before they come in. Moreover, trade union students, at around a fifth or a quarter of all short-course students, are a smaller proportion of the total than we hoped.

The College has provided an important forum and resource for a wide variety of groups and individuals from working-class backgrounds. During the miners' strike, for instance, it hosted dayschools and conferences for ordinary NUM members and miners' wives groups, which allowed them to discuss the direction that events were taking. It also ran a series of weekend schools for the women's groups, mostly taught by College staff, offering the women the opportunity to situate their own struggles in a wider historical, political and economic context, and develop a more strategic purpose for their actions as well as identify continuing needs for further educational work. But this work also had its flaws and weaknesses.

The College was unable, during the dispute, to continue its ordinary programmes with Yorkshire and Derbyshire miners. While this might have been expected, neither did it explore alternative ways of allowing mineworkers to use its educational resources. The opportunity for a serious educational intervention was missed: a sad contrast to the rapid organisation of adult education lectures by Yorkshire WEA and Nottingham University during the 1926 miners' lockout,[21] especially in the light of the College's unambiguous commitment to a working-class adult education that is independent and emancipatory, that analyses and seeks to explain the structures of inequality and power that operate in British society and elsewhere.[22]

Of more long-term concern is the degree to which the frontiers between trade union and other courses have or have not been broken down. The intention was always to develop the College as a learning community, which deliberately sought to emphasise the common experiences of working-class people through the full use of the residential setting by

> the mix of students - men and women, old and young, black and white, on long and short courses, from many different backgrounds and parts of the country, studying on different courses - with a common interest in learning from each other's experience.[23]

In a society which fragments and alienates working people from one another, the process of learning from differences is as difficult as the more intellectual learning from analysis and explanation on the course. It has not, though, been addressed nearly as carefully.

On the other hand, Northern College has established the basis for a new type of working-class adult education, by providing a shared educational and residential resource for people who are active in their unions, their communities or in neighbourhood-level adult education. Its contribution has in part been developed through its critical understanding of what a working-class adult education might be, drawing on the best elements of the liberal adult education tradition to produce an education that respects people's culture and experience, but also subjects it to analysis and questioning.

The celebration of working-class culture on its own can be simply an acceptance of oppression, a refusal to recognise the often racist and male nature of that culture, a romantic blindness to rapid change in the social composition of the working class. Trade union education can only contribute to the regeneration of the movement; first, if it is prepared to subject what now exists to sustained debate and analysis, and if its development is tied to a thorough and far-reaching commitment to more campaigning, participatory and decentralised forms of trade union organisation and action.

COMMUNITY, DEMOCRACY, AND THE TRADE UNION MOVEMENT

Trade union education in the 1970s developed in a world of its own, cut off from many of the new developments in community-based adult education and from its own origins in the committed and politically alert work of the WEA and Labour College movement. But the advocates of radical community education bear part responsibility for this caesura between different attempts to develop an education which will inform and support effective social action.

Many of the community-based projects were developed by libertarian socialists, formed politically in the 'alternative' social movements of the 1960s and 1970s, who rejected hierarchical and bureaucratic forms of organisation and who celebrated cultural rather than economic struggle.[24] With the exception of the tiny Trotskyist groups, libertarian socialists - even in the Communist Party - regarded trade unions with suspicion or even contempt (conveniently forgetting that these were institutions that working-class people had themselves built up and developed). For their part, trade unions mostly ignored community-based groups as irrelevant, self-appointed and ephemeral; they seemed unaware that they were becoming increasingly remote from the people who belonged to them, especially to women (as members, and even more so as unwaged workers).

The new forms of organising had, therefore, at best a tenuous relationship with organised labour. Some projects did attempt to establish trade union links at grassroots

237

level: organisations like Coventry Workshop bring together people from a range of causes and struggles in a common endeavour to build connections and analyse the wider context. Their successes highlight the failure of vision elsewhere.

The current crisis places a new agenda before trade unionists and community groups, and it is an agenda on which many of the items are common to both. Deindustrial-isation and job loss, and proposals for economic renewal and growth, are shared concerns, and urgently so. Health is another, whether in the form of workplace hazards that pose broader dangers or in the form of struggles to defend the health service. A third is the defence of public services more generally. A trade unionism that is paralysed by an obsession with parliamentary lobbying and television training for general secretaries can scarcely expect to win the wholehearted support even of its own members, let alone women engaged in domestic labour, part-time workers or the unemployed.

The 'gulf ... between the formal structures and machinery of government of the unions and the rank-and-file membership', combined with traditional union hostility towards what it sees as parallel organisation, is a major cause of the current crisis of trade unionism in particular, and the predicament of the working class more generally.[25] The miners' strike revealed the range of new movements and organisations which have been arenas, if complex and con-tradictory, for the development of working-class culture and working-class consciousness, promising to broaden traditional conceptions of the composition and objectives of the labour movement yet also portraying the unions' capacity to ignore that potential when it stepped beyond the domestic and controllable to stake its own claims for recognition.[26]

For working-class people, the crisis - economic, political or cultural - is being experienced above all at the local level yet is the outcome of unprecedentedly global forces. The role of adult education networks and institutions whose mission encompasses a strong social purpose is now an urgent issue. What is urgently needed is forms of education which open up resources - intellectual and material, critical and role-supporting, analytical and committed - to sustain a dialogue between people engaged in different kinds of struggle: a dialogue that respects the differences, while seeking to generalise out of practice at local level to reach an understanding of the power structures against which struggle takes place.

Ultimately, it is necessary to develop forms of trade union education which tackle, as well as the collective bargaining framework and negotiating tactics, issues of control and power. And that includes the major issues of change and development within the labour movement itself; the most serious indictment of all involved in trade union education in the past fifteen years is their failure to inspire a regeneration of the ideology of labour as a collective movement for democratic advance combined with the widespread dissemination of a modern organisational competence. A trade union education that is - as some have rightly advocated[27] - open to members as well as representatives, broad-based and educational rather than narrow and role-specific, continuing and recurrent rather than ad hoc and disparate, will itself produce limited and ephemeral results unless working people can see that what they learn is also practised in their own organisations.

REFERENCES

1. R.H. Tawney, 'The Workers' Educational Association and Adult Education', The Radical Tradition (Pelican, 1964), p. 84.

2. The phrase comes from Tawney's presidential address to the 1936 WEA Conference, reprinted in The Highway (February 1936), p. 106.

3. J.E. Thomas, Radical Adult Education: Theory and Practice (Nottingham University, 1982); J.L. Thompson (ed.), Adult Education for a Change (Hutchinson, 1980).

4. I. Crewe, Guardian, 13 June 1983.

5. B. Spencer, Workplace Trade Unionism: Making it Work (WEA, 1986); M. Terry, 'How Do We Know Shop Stewards Are Getting Weaker?' British Journal of Industrial Relations, 24, 2 (1986), pp. 251-61.

6. TUC Strategy: Union Communications (1984), p. 12.

7. Trades Union Congress, Annual Report (1975), p. 189.

8. J. Fyrth, 'Industrial Studies and the Labour Movement', in E. Coker and G. Stuttard (eds), Industrial Studies 3: Understanding Industrial Society (Arrow, 1980), pp. 145-7.

9. D. Gowan, 'Student-centred approaches revisited', Trade Union Studies Journal, 6 (1982), pp. 4-7.

10. J. McIlroy, 'Goodbye Mr Chips?', Industrial Tutor, 4, 2 (1985), p. 4.

11. R. Bickerstaffe, Trade Unions and the Future of Socialism (Northern College, 1984), p. 7; for the TGWU, see F. Cosgrove, 'Redesigning Trade Union Education', Industrial Tutor, 3, 8 (1983); and J. Fisher, 'Some Recent Developments in Trade Union Education in the United Kingdom', International Journal of Lifelong Education, 3, 3 (1983); for NUPE, see Education in NUPE: An Executive Council Discussion Doument (n.d. but widely circulated in 1982), and A Report on the NUPE Basic Skills Project, 1979-1983 (Adult Literacy and Basic Skills Unit, n.d.).

12. For the National Union of Mineworkers' day-release schemes in their heyday, see particularly M. Barratt Brown, Adult Education for Industrial Workers (National Institute of Adult Education/Society of Industrial Tutors, 1969); and J.E. MacFarlane, 'Getting the Message Through to the Coalface' (Times Higher Education Supplement, 31 October 1975).

13. J. Killeen and M. Bird, Education and Work: A Study of Paid Educational Leave in England and Wales (National Institute of Adult Education/Society of Industrial Tutors, 1981), p. 79; also D. Robertson and T. Schuller, 'Stewards, Members and Trade Union Training', Centre for Research in Industrial Democracy and Participation Discussion Paper 6 (University of Glasgow, 1982).

14. South African Labour Bulletin, 9, 8 (1984), p. 27 (a reference I owe to Judy Favish).

15. I. Radford and J. Sangster, 'A Link Between Labour and Learning: the WEA in Ontario, 1917-1951', Labour/Le Travailleur, 8/9 (1981/2).

16. A.M. Thomas and D.S. Abbey, Labour Canada's Labour Education Program: Preliminery Evaluation (Ontario Institute for Studies in Education, 1979). For the USA, see J. Brown, 'Trade Union Education in the USA - a comparative note', Industrial Tutor, 3, 3 (1980).

17. Ibid., p. 65.

18. United Steelworkers of America (Canadian Conference), Facing Management (1985).

19. See Coventry Workshop Bulletin (November/December 1985).

20. 'Proposal to establish a Northern Residential College of Adult Education' (1977).

21. G. Mee, Miners, Adult Education and Community Service, 1920-1984, (Nottingham University, 1984), p. 5; J. Field, Education for a Tolerable Society: The WEA in the

Dearne Valley (Northern College/South Yorks WEA, 1986).

22. M. Barratt Brown, 'Trade Union Education and the Residential Colleges', Industrial Tutor, 3, 9 (1984); A New Approach to Adult Education (Northern College, 1983).

23. Ibid., p. 32. See also B. Fryer, 'Trade Union Studies at the Northern College', Trade Union Studies Journal, (1984); A. Goodwin and J. Field, 'Teaching Media Studies to Trade Unionists', Industrial Tutor, 4, 2 (1985).

24. See the brief critique in C. Landry et al., What a Way to Run a Railroad: An Analysis of Radical Failure (Comedia, 1985), ch. 1.

25. B. Fryer, 'Trade Unionism in Crisis: The Miners' Strike and the Challenge to Union Democracy', in H. Beynon (ed.), Digging Deeper: Issues in the Miners' Strike (Verso, 1985).

26. D. Massey and H. Wainwright, 'Beyond the Coalfields: The Work of the Miners' Support Groups', in Beynon (ed.), Digging Deeper; for a slightly more pessimistic view, J. Field, 'Police and Thieves', Radical America (19, 2/3, 1985), pp. 17-21.

27. E.g. the TGWU's exciting proposals for 'Paid Release for Trade Union Education', summarised in Cosgrove, 'Redesigning Trade Union Legislation'.

11

Adult Education with Unemployed People

Richard Taylor and Kevin Ward

INTRODUCTION

The 1930s and the 1980s

> January 1936: In South Wales, particularly in the
> Rhonda Valley the tramp of thousands of feet was
> heard day after day. Even the shopkeepers closed
> their doors and joined the demonstrations. They
> knew what this new attack would mean to them,
> that more little shopkeepers would be driven out of
> business by the poverty of the people and their
> inability to purchase goods. Doctors also marched:
> they knew that the new [unemployment benefit]
> scales meant increased difficulties for them in
> their desperate efforts to protect the health stand-
> ards of the people against the ravages of poverty.
> Teachers, who had the difficult problem of endeav-
> ouring to educate half-starved children, knew that
> their task would become still more onerous under
> the new scales: so they too joined in the demon-
> strations. Employed workers, who found that they
> were being compelled to maintain their
> unemployed relatives out of their meagre wages
> joined with the unemployed. Reactionary trade
> union officials who had steadfastly declared that
> they would not stand on a public platform with
> revolutionary workers, found themselves caught up
> in the stream and carried forward to participation
> in great united front unemployed demonstrations.[1]

These demonstrations were organised by the National Unemployed Workers' Movement, and their actions illustrate
one of the major differences between responses to unemployment in the 1920s and 1930s and current responses.

Unemployment in the 1980s is generally regarded as one of the most important political issues facing all major capitalist economies. In Britain, the problem has been particularly acute and all political parties are agreed that the phenomenon of unemployment is not only a centrally important political issue but raises also profound economic, social and moral questions.

Unlike the 1930s, however, there is a dramatic contrast between this generalised macro-concern, and the manner in which unemployment and its effects on millions of people's lives are, in practice, marginalised and hidden. Unemployment in the 1920s and 1930s, partly through the types of demonstrations outlined above, was highly visible. In the 1980s, unemployment is often invisible and there is no organisation of unemployed people themselves to highlight the problems.

The 1930s and 1980s <u>are</u> similar in that a wide variety of institutions, both voluntary and statutory, were involved in both decades in work with or for the unemployed. In both periods, churches, charitable bodies, voluntary organis-ations, the Trades Union Congress (TUC), central and local government, and, more particularly in the context of this chapter, a variety of adult educators responded to un-employment.[2] Whilst it is not possible in this chapter to provide a detailed comparative analysis of the two periods it is important to outline the context within which adult education responses to unemployment in the 1980s take place.

ADULT EDUCATION RESPONSES TO UNEMPLOYMENT IN THE 1980s: AN OVERVIEW

During the 1980s there has been a proliferation of schemes, courses and activities for unemployed people in many parts of the country organised by a wide range of adult education agencies and voluntary organisations.[3] McDonald has sum-marised the objectives of the programmes specifically designed for the unemployed:

> These may aim to provide ... basic education, English as a Second Language (ESL), second chance, and in-fill (to existing courses). They may be concerned with helping people to formulate their educational needs. They may be concerned

with helping people to face up to unemployment and make choices for themselves, including the acceptance of alternatives to unemployment. They may be intended to help people to be more aware of their own interests and abilities with a view to taking the first steps towards any of these possibilities.[4]

Overall it is clear that two parallel developments have been taking place in adult education for the unemployed. Adult educators in all sectors have attempted to make access to existing facilities easier; and/or special programmes have been developed. McDonald comments that in the course of her enquiry, 'there was much evidence of concern for the needs of special groups and much imaginative development of outreach and provision to satisfy them'.[5]

The combination of these factors - increasing evidence from projects and reports about the educational needs of the adult unemployed, allied to increasing concern generally in education about the financial and ideological predominance of the Manpower Services Commission (MSC) - led the Department of Education and Science (DES) to take some initiative. Thus, despite continuing major cutbacks affecting all adult education agencies, it was announced in Parliament on 5 March 1984 that a three-year DES initiative (subsequently entitled REPLAN) costing £2.5 million would be launched to improve educational opportunities for unemployed adults. This is not the place for a detailed critique of REPLAN,[6] but elements within it (such as the National Institute of Adult Continuing Education (NIACE) local development project) are currently at a crucial stage. Projects in different parts of the country have gained valuable experience and useful lessons have been learned. Staff and participants involved in them are now asking critical questions about the future of such projects. If the projects themselves and the questions which have been raised are quietly shelved and ignored, many adult educators will be severely critical of NIACE (as the managing agent) and the DES (as funders) for establishing ad hoc, token gestures towards the educational needs, in the broadest sense, of unemployed adults.

Before describing some examples of current or recent educational work with unemployed people, it is necessary to explore the objectives of various kinds of provision.

MODELS OF DEVELOPMENT: OBJECTIVES OF PROVISION

In this section, five models, with differing underlying objectives are examined. These are the training model, the therapy/social control model, the liberal model, the social purpose model and the socialist/community action model.

Training model

Reference to training inevitably raises questions about the role of the Manpower Services Commission (MSC) which has emerged as the major institutional vehicle for government schemes to cope with unemployment. Whilst the MSC is not the main focus of attention here it is important to refer to the gross disparity of resources - financial, human and political - between the training agencies, represented by the MSC, and the educational providers.[7]

What, then, is the nature of the current 'training model' in provision for unemployed people? The first priority for most unemployed people is obtaining a job: and training or retraining courses are one seemingly obvious route to this end. Yet there are, of course, severe problems. As far as adults are concerned it is important to note that the overwhelming emphasis within MSC is upon the 16-19 age group. (The problems of YTS et al. lie beyond our scope here: but the hostility with which such schemes have been greeted from many parts of the political spectrum is indicative of their questionable value.) Nevertheless, both MSC and other agencies are involved in training schemes for adults, and it can be argued that this is the most appropriate form of 'educational' provision for the unemployed. Nobody could deny that, in a rapidly changing society, retraining has a centrally important role. An exclusive emphasis upon such approaches, however, is fallacious, and would be a misuse of AE resources. First, the 'Thatcherite' myth of a leaner, fitter economic structure, engendered via market forces, and producing at some unspecified future date a buoyant economy with full employment, has been exposed as a myth, from numerous ideological standpoints.[8] To pretend, therefore, that unemployment is a temporary phenomenon, which can be cured by a combination of retraining and market forces, is at best naively optimistic and at worst politically dishonest. In this context, then, approaches to education

245

must begin from the notion, articulated by André Gorz and others,[9] that ours is a post-industrial society where paid work on a full-time basis is no longer to be seen as the norm, and where 'education for life' rather than 'training for jobs' should be the objective. Second, the training model assumes that all criteria are economic and unilinear, and rejects, by implication, the validity of social, cultural and indeed human concerns. Changes of social and geographical, as well as occupational, location are simply assumed, taking no account of the often very strong existing attachments (let alone more mundane issues, such as differential house prices and rental charges). Third, a purely training model is inherently mechanistic and conservative: the task to be accomplished is given, assumed; the training consists of instruction as to how best it is to be accomplished. No discussion or anlaysis - except in terms of efficient achievement of the given task - can enter into such a process. No questioning of the validity or desirability of the task can be permitted to intervene in the process. And no open-ended discussion, in the wider social, economic and political contexts, of possible alternatives or possible criticisms of the assumptions, can be undertaken. In all these senses, therefore, the exclusively training model performs no educational function at all. Indeed, it reinforces the status quo, closes off discussion and analysis, and restricts rather than expands popular consciousness. For these reasons it is no exaggeration to claim that the increasing drift to training at the expense of education, in adult education as elsewhere, represents a very real threat to a democratic society.

Therapy/social control model

From a similar ideological stance as the 'trainers' are those who see the purpose of adult education with the unemployed as being either therapeutic - easing the process of adjustment and thereby acceptance - or controlling - ensuring that potentially disruptive elements in society are neutralised. The level of unemployment, at least in the short to medium term, is likely to remain high; therefore, so the argument goes, it is essential that unemployed people, in both their own interests and those of the wider society, do not drift into alienation or even 'subversion'. The role of adult education, in this respect, is therefore twofold: to provide leisure or recreational courses to enable unemployed people to fill in their increased 'leisure hours' with personally satisfying (but cheap) activities; and to ensure that in a variety of ways unemployed people are 'reintegrated' into society, brought within the norms of the dominant culture, and protected from deviant modes of thought and behaviour.

Three aspects of such approaches are worthy of particular note. First, they depend upon a pathological view of unemployment: that is, it is implicit that 'being un-employed' is indicative, at least in part, of some personality deficiency or lack of ability or drive (cf. Tebbit's 'on your bike' attitude), and is also akin to a social disease. There is no hint here of <u>structural</u> explanations, still less of critical analyses of alternative political and economic strategies which might be held to ameliorate, if not cure absolutely, unemployment. Second, such approaches contain an often explicit, and always implicit, element of ideological and political control. In its milder forms this can be articulated as 'giving people what they want' - in reality, providing what the lowest common denominator commerical culture dictates; but, in a significant number of instances, the element of 'social control' is quite explicit - the refusal to allow politically controversial topics to be discussed in government or local authority funded centres, for example.[10] Finally, such approaches are, again, inherently conservative in that they underpin the prevailing common sense about the nature and causes of unemployment, they foreclose discussion on any alternative analyses, and they integrate and undermine potentially 'deviant' political stances amongst the unemployed.

The liberal model

The traditional liberal approach to adult education as exemplified in the University Extension and WEA move-ments (from the 1870s and 1900s respectively) formed the core of the approach of the responsible Bodies (RBs: that is, University Adult Education (UAE) Departments and the Workers' Educational Association (WEA)) in the inter-war years, and, in their period of greatest growth, from the 1940s through until the late 1970s. The liberal tradition is hard to define briefly, both because it is a 'conceptual continuum' rather than one specific stance, and because its practice - its organisational application - has varied widely over both time and institutional location.[11] However, it is safe to assert that it has always had a strong emphasis upon personal development and upon the intrinsic worth of education _per se_; and, equally, that a critical, open-ended and analytical approach, and a 'democratic' teaching mode, have characterised the provision of the RBs for many years.

Such precepts have underlain some of the provision made by the RBs for the unemployed. Most RBs (as Local Education Authorities - LEAs) have introduced fee reductions for unemployed people attending their 'mainstream' programmes; and some Departments have introduced specially targeted provision (see next section below).

The problems with such an approach can be divided broadly into two: those relating to the nature of RB provision _per se_; and those relating to the underlying educational perspectives of the liberal tradition itself. On the first count, it is significant that a very small proportion of RB programmes is concerned with developing work with the unemployed[12]; moreover, much of this work is concerned not with the working-class unemployed (who, of course, form the large bulk of unemployed people in Britain),[13] but with the unemployed middle-class or professional people.[14] Moreover, much of this latter work is much closer to a 'training' than to a 'liberal' approach. All this reflects the RBs' increasing concerns with middle-class education; and, in the case of the UAE Departments, with an increasing emphasis upon professional, continuing, and post-experience work. Whilst there may well be every justification for such developments, which have been growing steadily since the 1950s but with increasing rapidity over the last decade, these emphases do undermine the notion of RBs as being wholly concerned with _liberal_ adult education. The DES's New Formula for grant aid, which is complicated but based essentially on a head-count of students attending courses as the future basis for allocation of grant (the grant having, anyway, undergone a global reduction), exacerbates considerably such tendencies. In future, the best way to secure grant will be to provide popular, undemanding short courses, aimed at the 'soft end' of the market - the already educationally integrated middle class.

The scope for adult educators to develop liberal AE for the unemployed is thus severely limited in the 1980s - and is, of course, further curtailed by the continuing UGC cuts. But, moving on to the second of the problematic areas indicated earlier, the liberal mode itself is open to question, irrespective of its organisational context. The traditional 'neutrality' of the tutor, syllabus content and presentation have tended, de facto, to result in orthodox viewpoints predominating. And the orthodox pedagogic practice of the liberal tradition - the imparting of an established body of knowledge by the tutor to the students - has also tended, in practice, to predominate. These characteristics have applied to much of the RB liberal provision for the unemployed. Often, provision for the unemployed has consisted largely of mainstream courses based in educational institutions, with virtually the only distinctive feature being a reduced fee. Not surprisingly, the result has been to recruit predominantly middle-class unemployed people into mainstream programmes.

The net effect of the application of the liberal model for developing work with the unemployed is thus somewhat muted and minimal.

The social purpose model

As was noted earlier, the liberal tradition should be viewed as a continuum; and, at the radical end of the continuum, has existed as a continuous, albeit minority, strand: the commitment to collective, social purpose Adult Education.[15] In the long history of workers' education the role of the RBs has an important place: from the early days of University Extension, through the founding of the WEA, and the development of Trade Union education, the idea of 'education for citizenship' to enable a genuinely participative and egalitarian democracy to emerge, has been central.[16]

The point need not be laboured, as this aspect of Adult Education history is, rightly, much emphasised and is well known. What is noteworthy, here, however, is the two contrasting legacies of this tradition for contemporary Adult Education practice in work with the unemployed. The first is that the social purpose framework - of raising collective working-class consciousness through critical, liberal educational processes - has been of central importance in the development of community adult education practice in Britain. And this development has been the key to such successful innovation in the field of work with the unemployed as has so far been accomplished.

249

On the more negative side, however, the social purpose tradition of workers' education has been concentrated overwhelmingly on the white, male, manual, working-class trade unionist, to the virtual exclusion of other sections of the working class. Thus, as we have argued at length in a recent book,[17] 'doubly disadvantaged' sections of the working class - the unemployed, women, black people, the retired, and the disabled - have especially acute educational needs. Moreover, such groups require innovative and community education approaches if adequate and relevant social purpose education is to be provided.

Socialist/community action model

It is also the case that, in practice, social purpose Adult Education has frequently concerned itself exclusively with the small minority of politically active, leftist members of the working class, usually, though not always, via trade union education. Such groupings respond more readily, naturally, than the great mass of the working class, to institution-based, and social studies-oriented, courses. There is a strong case for 'educational vanguardism' of this type. Moreover, there have been successful schemes which have combined this approach with that of community activism (see, for example, the Liverpool programmes in the 1960s and 1970s).[18]

A related, though significantly different, approach has been developed since the 1960s in the community education movement. (Examples of this include the Northern Ireland work pioneered by Tom Lovett,[19] and the Leeds Pioneer Work programme, discussed briefly below.) Here, the objective has been to involve the local community, first, in awareness of its own problems, provision of access to relevant information about them, and the alternative solutions that might be constructed to solve them; and, second, in the development of local community groups, concerned partly with further analysis and discussion, partly with building community consciousness and collective involvement, and partly with community action to improve conditions and ameliorate problems.

Some of the work with the unemployed has taken place within this context. There are, however, considerable problems with such approaches, however desirable radical adult educators may consider them to be. There is no

necessary connection between community activism and progressive or radical politics: indeed, quite the reverse may
well be the case, as is to be expected in a predominantly
conservative society (cf. working-class racism). How far,
then, are radical adult educators prepared to engage in a
fully democratic community education? In a context where
unemployed whites think that unemployment would be
solved by 'repatriation' of black people and, generally, the
adoption of National Front-type policies, are the facilitating
roles of community education to be used? Obviously not: but
how does this tally with community control?

Much more problematic, in practical terms, is the
resistance by public bodies to funding what are seen as
subversive cliques. Nor is this a problem for the authorities
alone: how far should adult educators, qua educators, engage
in activism as opposed to education? The dividing-line may
be difficult to draw but most would agree that it must be
drawn somewhere.

Perhaps most important of all is the clear and simple
fact that the vast majority of the unemployed do not want
'political' classes. Here, the Leeds approach, for example,
may be instructive. Rather than classes on directly social or
political topics, the emphasis has been upon issue-based
provision, in the first instance, as a means to develop work,
where appropriate and possible, with a broader scope (hence
courses in Housing, Welfare Rights, Health Care, etc. rather
than in Social Policy, Politics etc.).

Within working-class communities generally, and
perhaps amongst unemployed people in particular, there is
an undestandably negative attitude towards 'education' in all
its forms. If significant provision is to be made it must be on
the basis of a genuine negotiation and interaction between
educators and the community, involving both social understanding and careful curriculum development to meet the
needs of each particular group.

From the viewpoint of the radical adult educator there
is also a need for a reinterpretation of the liberal approach
to adult education. In a society where there is a hegemonic
bourgeois culture pervading all sectors, including that of
education, it is essential that the ideals of critical, open-
ended analyses that are at the core of the liberal approach,
are upheld. This entails a 'positive discrimination', in ideological terms, to give a full explication of deviant ideological perspectives within the educational process. This is
not to advocate socialist or any other sort of indoctrination,

but to stress the importance of studying - via community education provision - alternative perspectives on reality - socialist, libertarian, feminist or whatever - in order to counteract the prevailing orthodoxies portrayed through the media and other agencies of socialisation.

Whilst such experimentation in community education may be small-scale it does provide the opportunity for adult education to demonstrate in microcosm the potential for change that inheres within the adult education framework, given the right political context.

These are points to be returned to in our concluding section. All that need be noted here is that, whilst none of these approaches is unproblematic, it is within the latter two perspectives that radical adult educators will find the most potential for development. Equally important, it must always be emphasised that all approaches, here as else- where, are underpinned by a series of ideological assumptions and arguments. Even the most seemingly neutral model has in reality strong ideological orientations. A brief review of some recent experience in the field will serve to amplify in specific and practical detail some of the more general points made in the foregoing section.

SOME EXAMPLES FROM PRACTICE

Five current examples of adult education schemes for unemployed people, from different settings in Britain, indicate the potential and the problems of this kind of work. These examples are located in: a local authority-funded employment project; a Local Education Authority Institute of Adult Education; a College of Further Education; a university adult education project for unemployed people; and the work of the Trades Union Congress Centres Against Unemployment.

These examples have been chosen not because they are necessarily typical or representative but because they illustrate interesting practices which are now underway to a greater or lesser extent both across different areas of adult education, (Local Education Authority, mainstream provision, Further Education colleges, the Responsible Bodies) and outside the formal boundaries of adult education (an employment project, and the Trades Union Congress Centres).

An Employment Project[20]

The Braunstone Employment Project (BEP) is based in a shop on a large council estate which is situated on the edge of Leicester. The estate, with 2000 houses, has an unemployment rate of over 50 per cent.

The workers devised detailed outreach strategies (based on surveys, including a local talent survey, and community consultations) which taught them a great deal about the skills and experiences in the area, and attitudes to unemployment. With the residents, they applied successfully for finance throug the Inner Area Programme to establish the Braunstone workshops on the estate. These provide a car repair workshop and facilities for woodworking, metal working, the construction trade and textiles.

These resources, however, needed sympathetic staff to work with groups of residents. The BEP staff therefore approached two Colleges of Further Education and they began to provide courses on the estate. One example is a course on building and construction skills which makes use of 'in-fill places' but is run on an outreach basis by the College using Braunstone Training Workshops as a base. These courses are jointly planned by the College and the residents' training groups.

This project has focused on training and 'employability'. Through the involvement of local people, resources have been secured which are based on their needs, and made available in their area. The College's resources have been deployed on the estate, and jointly controlled by staff and residents.

BEP illustrates the possibility of linking together a training/employability approach with an educational orientation. The surveys and the detailed discussions with local groups ensured that questions of training resources (and the control of them) were raised, but within the context of unemployment as a more explicit, live, local issue.

A Local Education Authority Institute of Adult Education[21]

The Southwark Adult Education Institute, London, has developed special provision for unemployed people, as well as being sensitive to the needs of unemployed people on its mainstream programme. This work may be representative of much LEA adult education activity with unemployed people, but unfortunately the paucity of action-research evidence means that this must remain a hypothesis.

The specific provision at Southwark includes a basic education programme located on one particular housing estate. Run on an open-access basis, it includes very basic literacy/numeracy skills, to 0-level standard. A large number of students are enrolled for City and Guilds and RSA certificates.

These qualification-based courses may assist some people in gaining employment, but staff feel they are perhaps more important for personal development and self-confidence. This liberal model was articulated by one of the basic education tutors in the following way: 'To see the look of joy on someone's face when they pass, when they've never passed anything else in their lives, is wonderful... And the change in self-image is remarkable... a big boost in confidence.'[22]

The Southwark programmes attach heavy priority to work with ethnic minorities and with women. On one estate basic education and general classes are held in various premises after staff have developed contacts through outreach. The unemployed, then, are broadly defined to include the unregistered unemployed, particularly women.

Other specific provision includes an ESL (English as a Second Language) initiative which seeks to help unwaged individuals from ethnic minorities to look at the skills involved in setting up small businesses or entering self-employment.

These specific initiatives, however, represent neither the only nor the main use which the unemployed make of the Institute's resources. 'A recent in-house survey showed that almost exactly 10% of the students in the mainstream provision were unemployed (1300 out of 13,000).'[23]

Many adult educators, particularly in inner city and working-class areas, would probably argue that they are already working with unemployed people, like the Southwark Institute, through their mainstream programme. The critical questions which remain unanswered relate to the objectives of this approach. Clarity is needed about which of the five models (the training model, the liberal model, the therapy/social control model, the social purpose model or the socialist/community action model) is being adopted and evidence is needed about the outcomes of the work as seen by participants.

A College of Further Education[24]

Valuable lessons should be available from specific community-based programmes aimed at unemployed people; an exclusive focus on these initiatives, however, can deflect attention from the need for Colleges of Further Education (with much more subtantial resources than community-based programmes) to confront the issue of long-term structural unemployment.

The Leicester project illustrates that college resources can be taken to the community and their use jointly negotiated and controlled with local residents. Even where this does not happen, colleges can still make courses more accessible to unemployed people by experimenting with the timing and publicty for courses and supporting them with creches and easy access arrangements.

Tile Hill College in Coventry has attempted to do this through its courses which are specifically geared towards the unemployed (MSC-funded), and general courses which by their nature and structure attract the unemployed.

The MSC courses in 1985 included a Pre-Tops 'Breakthrough' course, a Business Skills Workshop, New Skills courses, and Adult Preparation Training (funded through the Adult Training Strategy and using a modular approach).

Unfortunately, many non-waged people are unable to benefit from these MSC courses since they are only available for those with UB40 cards.

The courses are obviously based on a training model, and all colleges running such courses should evaluate longitudinally whether participants do in fact secure subsequent employment or further education and training. It is also important to evaluate other outcomes of these courses. Do they lead to increased self-confidence, and if so, is this deliberate or unintentional (the liberal model)? Do they implicitly reinforce particular views about paid work and the inevitability of unemployment (the social control model)? Are the general courses (the non-MSC ones) based on a similar training model? These included a computer programming course and an Open-Access course (aimed at ethnic minorities and acting as a bridge into higher education). Or, are they explicitly broader than MSC courses and based on the liberal or social purpose model; and if so, to what extent are issues of unemployment brought into the course and stereotypes challenged?

These broader, qualitative questions must be raised and

255

examined as courses for unemployed people continue to proliferate. It is probable, however, that many colleges may not, as yet, be examining even the organisational issues about such courses, far less the more complex qualitative questions raised above.

A university Adult Education Project with unemployed people[25]

Although much of the provision for unemployed people is organised through the local education authorities, this university project illustrates that the RBs (referred to earlier in the liberal model) can also play an important role in developing this work. By systematic monitoring and evaluation, they can produce guidelines about approaches, recuitment methods, curriculum and outcomes.

Since a project at Leeds University was established in 1982, more than 400 short courses have been organised with various groups of unemployed people. The vast majority of participants have not had previous experience of higher or adult education, and had left school at the minimum age.

The courses are neither qualification-based nor training-oriented. They are primarily issue and community-based, and could be described as 'education for everyday living'. They have included Welfare Rights, Interest Courses (Photography, Video, Art, Local History), locally-based courses with tenants groups (Housing, 'Know the System', 'How the Council Works'), and Women's Courses (Women and Health etc.)

There are no restrictive enrolment procedures for these courses, which are all free, and held in locations away from the University (e.g. in unemployed centres, community centres etc.)

The process for organising these courses involves detailed discussions with core groups of interested people, and the courses emerge from their concerns and interests. These may be members of local community groups or unemployed centres and/or paid staff of particular projects or paid staff working in the community.

This process of negotiation is crucial, since one of the principles underlying the work is a belief in the potential participants to plan jointly and control their own learning and the way in which it is provided.

A two-year research programme is currently in progress

which is examining the outcomes of these courses. Based on detailed interviews with unemployed people who have attended courses, it should provide valuable information about the effectiveness (or otherwise) of the provision and the extent to which the liberal model, the social purpose model and/or the socialist community action model are implemented in practice.

Such projects, then, can produce important lessons, but there is a danger of temporary, inadequately funded special projects being seen as the sole response of adult education to the unemployment crisis.

The TUC Centres against Unemployment[26]

There are currently 210 TUC centres against unemployment in Britain, and there is increasing evidence that much adult education is organised with unemployed people in such centres.

The TUC Guidelines for these centres list three objectives: (i) to provide advice (eg. on welfare rights) and counselling; (ii) to provide a focal point for unemployed people; (iii) to develop a 'representation' role (eg. promote concessionary schemes for unemployed people.)

The rapid development of these centres during the 1980s in different parts of the country has led to different emphases being developed in practice (some are mainly advice centres, other social centres; others combine these roles with elements of campaigning work). Educationally, it is clear that a wide variety of provision has been developed, mainly in 'coping' (welfare rights, staying healthy on the dole) and 'interest' courses (photography, art, hobbies, DIY, etc.) More recently, users and staff have been meeting at regional and national courses sponsored by the TUC which have examined the political and organisational issues about these centres and unemployment generally.

Given the absence of any organisational focal point for unemployed people in the 1980s, it is obviously important for adult educators concerned about unemployment to utilise such centres and work jointly with them. Any educational intervention in these centres, however, must be carefully monitored so that the effects of different models of education can be assessed more accurately than is possible at the moment.

The five examples outlined above illustrate the proliferation of schemes and courses which have been developed
for unemployed people in the 1980s. They indicate that
much imaginative work is being developed, and that different types of provision have been established. Many lessons
have been learnt (including the need for outreach, pre-
course negotiations, free and relevant courses, and inter-
agency collaboration) but considerable challenges still
confront the major institutions of adult education - the
LEAs, the RBs and the Colleges.

CONCLUSION

The persistence of long-term structural unemployment is
now generally accepted, albeit not explicitly stressed, by
politicians, planners and government ministries. Thus, the
Manpower Services Commission (MSC) stated in 1985 that
'the best assumption for planning purposes is for a
continuing high level of unemployment throughout the
period (1985-89) and for a level of long-term unemployment
remaining at around the one million mark.' In this context,
adult educators have responded with a variety of
educational and vocational training measures, some of which
were discussed earlier in this chapter. There is a gross
disparity between the size of the unemployment problem
and the miniscule educational resources available to make
adequate provision. Such miserliness is nothing new for adult
education, of course. After all, the concept of mass
working-class adult education organised and taught from
within existing institutions and existing budgets, is
inherently unrealistic.

Over and above resource problems, however, there are
several more fundamental ideological and structural
problems. There is, to begin with, a complex of institutional
problems. Although an increasing amount of community
adult education development involves small voluntary
organisations, the crucial full-time staff involvement comes
from the major adult education institutions. Moreover, the
funding for part-time staff involvement and administrative
and clerical back-up is also provided from these institutional
sources. And yet these institutions are concerned only
marginally with working-class adult education, and still less
with the specific field of adult education for the
unemployed. Despite all their marked differences (in scale,

perspective and perceived functions) most of these agencies have in common their commitment to institution-based and qualification-oriented programming. Moreover, they are all, in different ways, linked both structurally and ideologically to existing patterns of provision and to the dominant culture and its assumptions.

Closely related to these institutional problems are the pedagogic concerns raised by the development of community adult education in general, and work with the unemployed in particular. Is it possible - and if so is it desirable - that the institutional, professional control of the curriculum and of the whole teaching context should be shared with the participants? How far is a 'Freirean model' of adult education a practicable proposition? It is essential for radical adult educators to provide coherent and positive answers to such questions if a viable practice is to be constructed.

Most fundamental of all, however, is the question of the political context of adult education of this type, and the delineation of aims, objectives and relative priorities. We need here to return to our discussion of the social purpose and socialist/community action models, in order to explore these problems in more depth. Adult education for the unemployed, as with other areas of working-class adult education, must be concerned centrally with developing both individual intellectual awareness and collective community consciousness. These general principles have long lain at the heart of the social purpose approach: and they are no less relevant today than in the 1900s. Moreover, such educational concepts are integrally related to political commitments to a radical and decentralised democratic social and political structure. If we are to produce a genuinely participative and educated democracy then adult education - untrammelled by 'establishment ideology' - has a central role to play. All this, however, is not enough. In a society so deeply divided by class (and gender and race) inequalities, and increasingly dominated by the privatised technological culture of late capitalism, the social purpose orientation alone is now inadequate, however admirable it may have been in the past.

The 'educational' problems of the unemployed are but one dimension of a range of negative factors -psychological, economic, environmental, and so on. And the unemployed themselves are but one section, albeit an important and prominent section, of the 'disadvantaged' in our society.

Problems of inequality and disadvantage are thus, in one sense, too big and too fundamental for education per se, let alone adult education, to resolve. Nevertheless there are possibilities within the adult education system (some of which have been indicated, at least in their potential, earlier in this chapter). If really significant progress is to be made, in the educational context, however, there must be radical changes at both the structural and pedagogic levels.

Structurally, adult education for the unemployed must be seen as part of a wider reorientation of priorities within the education system as a whole towards the 'disadvantaged'. Priority, in terms of funding, staffing and programming, must be given to the educational needs of the large majority of the population who do not at present have access to educational resources beyond minimum school leaving age. Such a reorientation requires, first, political will, and, second, institutional restructuring (by, for example, universities and polytechnics in the higher education sector) to facilitate the sort of programming discussed in this chapter (and similar developments in analogous fields).

Pedagogically, there must be a similar change towards an outreach and needs-oriented educational delivery system. Whilst this requires considerable political and structural change to achieve full success, potentially important beginnings can be made through educational programming that is based in the community, that recognises community needs, and is attractive and relevant to adults in the community. To demonstrate the viability and utility of such approaches is a significant, though of course partial, advance towards the more macrocosmic political change. What must be emphasised here is the absolute need to achieve such a reorientation if adult education with the unemployed and analogous work with other 'disadvantaged' sections of the population, is to move beyond a marginal and merely 'symbolic' aspect of adult education provision.

REFERENCES

1. W. Hannington, Unemployed Struggles, 1919-1936 (Lawrence and Wishart, 1977), p. 309.
2. For details about adult education responses in the 1930s, see H. Marks, 'Unemployment and Adult Education in the 1930s', Studies in Adult Education, Vol. 14, September

1982.

3. See Education for Unemployed Adults (UCACE, 1982); J. McDonald, Education for Unemployed Adults: Problems and Good Practice (DES, 1984); A. H. Charnley, V. K. McGivney and D. J. Sims, Education for the Adult Unemployed: Some Responses (NIACE/REPLAN 1985).

4. J. McDonald, Education for Unemployed, p. 22.

5. Ibid., p. 26.

6. For further details, see K. Ward and R. Taylor (eds), Adult Education and the Working Class: Education for the Missing Millions (Croom Helm, 1986), Chapters 2 and 3.

7. For more detailed analyses of the MSC, see H. Salmon, Unemployment, Government Schemes and Alternatives (ACW, 1984); also Ward and Taylor, Adult Education, Chapter 2. For details about the MSC's programmes and finances, see Corporate Plan, 1985-89 (MSC, 1985).

8. Thus not only socialists of all hues, but also Liberal and SDP analyses are now wholly critical of Thatcherite economics, as indeed are the CBI most prominent economists, and increasingly large sections of the Conservative Party.

9. André Gorz, Paths to Paradise, on the Liberation from Work (Pluto Press, 1985).

10. TUC Centres for the Unemployed have been informed that they must not engage in campaign activities. Centres at Sheffield, Newcastle and Bristol had their funds withdrawn for refusing to follow the MSC's guidelines.

11. For discussion of the liberal tradition in Adult Education, see R. Taylor, K. Rockhill and R. Fieldhouse, University Adult Education in England and the USA: a reappraisal of the liberal tradition (Croom Helm, 1985).

12. See the useful survey conducted by the UCACE in 1984/5, UAE Provision for the Unemployed, UCACE, 1985.

13. Whilst definitions of 'working class' are contentious, it is clear that with significant exceptions (especially at the UAE Departments at Leeds and Liverpool and in the Northern District of the WEA), the bulk of RB work with the unemployed is with those who have had some experience of education beyond minimum school leaving age.

14. See the UCACE Report.

15. See R. Taylor, K. Rockhill and R. Fieldhouse, University Adult Education in England and the USA.

16. See R. Fieldhouse, The WEA: Aims and Achievements 1903-1977 (Syracuse: University Publications, 1977).

17. K. Ward and R. Taylor (eds), <u>Adult Education and the Working Class: Education for the Missing Millions</u>.

18. B. Ashcroft and K. Jackson, 'Adult Education and Social Action', in Jones and Mayo (eds) <u>Community Work One</u> (Routledge and Kegan Paul, 1971); and K. Jackson, 'Adult Education and Community Development', <u>Studies in Adult Education</u> Vol. 2, No. 2 (1970).

19. See T. Lovett, 'Adult Education and Community Action: the Northern Ireland Experience', in Fletcher and Thompson (eds), <u>Issues in Community Education</u> (1980); and T. Lovett, C. Clarke and A. Kilmurray, <u>Adult Education and Community Action</u> (Croom Helm, 1983).

20. Details about this project are taken from K. Ward, 'Outreach in Practice - Some Examples of Community-Based Projects', <u>Replan Review</u> (DES, 1986).

21. For more details about this project, see A. G. Watts and E. G. Knasel, <u>Adult Unemployment and the Curriculum: A Manual for Practitioners</u> (FEU, 1986).

22. Ibid., p. 74.

23. Ibid., p. 93.

24. Watts and Knasel, <u>Adult Unemployment and the Curriculum</u>, p. 88.

25. For full details about this project, see K. Ward, <u>Beyond Tokenism: - Unemployed Adults and Education</u> (University of Leeds, 1983): and K. Ward and R. Taylor, <u>Adult Education and the Working Class</u>.

26. For more information about the development of these centres, see K. Ward and K. Forrester, 'Organising the Unemployed?: The TUC and the Unemployed Workers Centres', <u>Journal of Industrial Relations</u>, Vol. 17, No. 1 (1986).

27. Manpower Services Commission, <u>Corporate Plan 1985-1989</u> (MSC 1985), p. 6.

12

Worker Ownership:
An Opportunity to Control the Production of Knowledge

Frank Adams

EDUCATION AND WORKER-OWNERS

Workers who own the means of production, then use the principles of democracy to manage those businesses, are refashioning the meaning of education, moving, if ever so slowly, to end the educational dualism which promotes one kind of learning for those who own capital and another for those who only own their labour. While the number of such persons is miniscule worldwide worker-ownership is a growing movement catching the attention of working people in industrial and developing nations alike. For adult educators the movement for workplace democracy poses historic possibilities.

The idea of worker-ownership is easily understood, almost self-defining, and can be traced through antiquity to virtually every culture. In practice, however, when labour hires capital, which is a bond common to these often disparate enterprises, economic tradition in place since the Industrial Revolution is upended, challenging the ideologies of both capitalism and state socialism. And, when the principles of political democracy are joined with this economic heresy, it is little wonder that workers, owners and managers alike often have difficulty making worker-owned firms profitable and democratic. Most of them, if not all, come to these new workplaces with no previous similar experience to build upon. What schools have prepared them for such responsibilities, or such dramatically altered workplace roles?

As workers, collective self-interest dictates a desire to govern the job, controlling labour themselves rather than being dominated by capital, or the state. As owners, the demands of production require that jobs be performed predictably and uniformly in accord with organisational authority. As humans, more often than not socialised to accept the lot of an employee rather than an entrepreneur, these emerging labour-managed firms require fundamentally altered self-concepts. Borrowing from the institutions of political democracy to govern economic institutions is analogous to that moment each New Year's Eve when past familiarities give way to the uncertain future.

Worker-owners are testing all manner of ways to give substance to the practice of workplace democracy and in the doing (even in limited, often virtually unnoticed ways) are slowly yet dramatically redefining what is meant by adult education, where it is practised and by whom. But there are no certainties about this emerging pedagogy, or that if such theory and practice will even come into being. The effort to fashion useful learning experience within these firms is already underway, deriving chiefly from the impluses of workers themselves but, as well, from the relative handful of adult educators who support their struggle. The experience of Almarinda Souza, a seamstress from Fall River, Massachusetts, who is chair of her production cooperative's education committee, is typical. 'Years ago, when I first started working for the other company, I went to the boss and said I had an idea I thought would save the company money. He told me, "Almarinda, your job is to sew, not think". From that day until we took over the company, I kept my mouth shut. Now, if I don't think, I don't get paid. That's why I accepted the job on the education committee. I want to learn.' Souza, like many worker-owners, realises that the labour-managed cooperative must devise its own educational programmes, ensuring that what is to be learned grows from their collective needs and interests, and that they collaborate with competent teachers in carrying the task of learning forward.

Some have argued that the organisation of work determines the shape, form and substance of education as surely as night follows day. Others argue that societies set forth their productive needs then, after tracing the processes necessary to meet those needs, schools are established to reproduce needed labour. Worker-owners draw from both traditions, yet require freedom to choose, reorganise, conceptualise anew. Since the introduction of the first flying shuttle, the common nail, or Darby's notion for smelting iron with coal, work has been increasingly categorised and cultures have been shattered, often at tragic social costs, in accord with the needs of industrial capitalism, or later, in reaction, by central governments. More often than not the owners of capital, individual or state, determined the substance and administration of education. Since worker-owned and managed enterprises are neither capitalist nor socialist, but rather are labourist, then reliance on the pedagogy undergirding one or the other may not suit either the short or long-term interests of worker-owners. Even a brief glimpse of the rich social history of education emanating from workers' struggles to control their labour outlined in previous chapters in this book suggests as much.

However, there is no clear, formulated understanding yet articulated about the relationship between production and education within a labour-controlled enterprise. These firms are like Janus, the Roman God whose name turns the calendar annually: they borrow at once from capitalist and from collective economic realms. On the one hand, a labour-managed firm, like any business, is measured by the return on investment of labour and capital. Here, it would seem, functional education would suit. On the other, the firm must be measured by the quality of the decisions taken, and their impact on the worker-members. In the labour-managed enterprise, the quality and reliability of the decision-making process is crucial. The extent to which worker-owners participate in the decision-making process must be defined within both economic and political limitations. But to use the curriculum, methods, etc., which have evolved for the use of capitalism, or those from socialist economic reproduction willy-nilly, could prove destructive of the labourist economy.

The historical experience of British worker-owners is instructive.[1] In 1844, after months of discussions among themselves about remedies 'for the evils of society' 24 jobless weavers in Rochdale formed the Society of Equitable Pioneers. This was a period known as 'the Hungry Forties', because of widespread unemployment and industrial dislocation. Their aim was 'to arrange the powers of production, distribution, education and government' in the interest of and under the control of cooperative membership. They had been reading Dr King's papers. Some were followers of Robert Owen. They held their meetings several times weekly, often including readings from literature. A Manchester cloth cutter who was active in the cooperative movement visited Rochdale, recorded their activity:

As soon as the men assembled to discuss how their

affairs were to be best managed, their minds received new impluses, new ideas, new motives, and new objectives. They had to exercise their judgements, to weigh and balance probabilities, and they could not do so without becoming men of knowledge. They would have to acquire knowledge of the commodities in which they traded and of reasons for the variations of prices, and as they commenced manufacture and invested capital, 'higher knowledge' would be forced upon them.[2]

After months of discussion, and of saving two pence a week, the Pioneers opened a tiny shop on Toad Lane, near most of their homes, selling consumer goods - flour, candles and the like. Soon they rented a second room, and then a second floor, which they turned into a classroom and library. R.H. Tawney would begin his distinguished teaching career there learning, he wrote later, his methods had to change because his 'students' knew what they wanted to learn and were asking difficult questions.

The rules formulated by the weavers proved sound for the operation of a consumer cooperative but, when applied to the production process, were wanting. In 1850 the Pioneers opened a woollen mill. They sold shares to anyone who was willing to buy between two and twenty of them, regardless of whether they worked in the factory or not. Initially, the majority of persons who bought stock were workers, and for nine years, the cooperative prospered and the workers controlled their labour. But in 1859, faced with the need to expand, stock was sold to persons whose principle interest was return on their investment. By 1862, the cooperative had become a traditional capitalist firm. Labour no longer hired capital. Its failure as a cooperative was used by friend and foe alike for years to discourage similar efforts 'to arrange the powers of production ... in the ... interest of the members'.

The collapse of the woollen mill was a failure for worker-centred learning, as well. The weavers, relying chiefly on their own experience or focusing on Dr King's paper, fashioned a body of knowledge which was their own and which, when put to the test of the marketplace, worked.

By the time the woollen mill started, that lesson had been lost on the Pioneers. The many educational activities carried on at Toad Lane were organised by a sympathetic organisation, the Workers' Education Association, but it was an organisation not directly controlled by worker-owners. The Rochdale Pioneers had forfeited control of the production of knowledge.

MONDRAGON - A MODERN INITIATIVE

The lessons of the Rochdale mill were examined years later by a young Basque priest, Father Jose Arizmendi who, in the wake of the devastating Spanish Civil War, an equally disastrous World War II and the emergence of Franco, was exploring ways Basque's labour could control and use capital. He was searching for ways to rebuild the shattered economy of the Basque provinces, while facing the restrictions of Franco's dictatorship and the strictures of the Catholic Church.

Father Arizmendi had been assigned to serve a war-ravaged mountain town deep in the Basque Province after World War II. He looked to cooperatives as had others before him as an alternative to capitalism or state socialism, both of which were criticised by popes in encyclicals. In the experience of the Pioneers the priest recognised that ownership carried responsibilities beyond participation. And while he started applying these lessons through the establishment of a technical school in Mondragon, a small industrial town in the mountains, it was by accident that some of the school's graduates eventually founded a cooperative.

Starting in 1956 with 23 worker-members the firm grew, helping spawn other producer cooperatives; including a vital central bank, health care system, a string of consumer cooperatives and a system of schools which commence with day care and continue through post graduate studies in engineering and business administration. The Basques, through the physical growth of the successful Mondragon cooperatives, made a significant contribution to the emergence of a cooperative pedagogy.

They incorporated the factory system of production in their factories, including with it the hierarchical organisation of work. However, by building educational practice on a tradition of cooperation within the Basque culture and history a spirit of collective cooperation rather than competitive individualism was nurtured in the schools. No doubt Basque nationalism and the oppressive Franco regime played a part. But as Ana Gutierrez-Johnson, a

267

student of that history has written, they fashioned a doctrine of labour entrepreneurship which, in addition to participation in decisions and enjoyment of profits, includes taking risks with one's capital, husbandry of productivity, and the search for new profitable business opportunities. Significantly, it also involved elaborating an educational system which is integral to the firms, the group of producer cooperations (which now numbers over 100) and to the Basque region. Although buffeted at times by demands from state and church that they alter educational practice the Basques never lost control of their schools. And, she continued, 'The difference in labour-entrepreneurship lies in the active role assumed by the associated workers, the collective decision-making process and the labour-based vision of development. Labour-entrepreneurship transformed the traditional concept of the cooperative as a private, closed, corporation into a concept of broader social enterprise.'[3]

As has been seen in this abbreviated history of the role of education in worker-ownership it fits neither the functionalist model, nor the Marxist paradigm. It takes from both yet demands independence. Historically, no modern social movement which has brought about fundamental social change has been without some self-elaborated, independent educational effort. This is the opportunity for adult education. The education which serves capitalism has evolved over many years, that which serves socialist states in much less time. In the case of Yugoslavia, with its state-controlled system of worker-run enterprises, an appropriate pedagogy emerged in less than four decades. Examination of what sort of education will support a labour-based vision of economic development is just beginning. Will that pedagogy be founded on the experience and beliefs of worker-owners and controlled by them? Or will practictioners unmindfully borrow hither and yon from the overarching ideologies? And what role will adult educators negotiate with the growing number of worker-owners who recognise the need to produce knowledge as well as goods, services, and economic democracy? Recent American experience may offer some tentative answers to these questions.

THE AMERICAN EXPERIENCE - AN EMERGING PEDAGOGY?

As the movement for workplace democracy has gathered momentum in America so too has the recognition that education is a vital part of that movement. When Vermont Asbestos was organised, no intentional effort was made to fashion a suitable way to transfer the knowledge needed by labour in that early attempt to manage production and own capital, or to spark the transition in self-concept from employee to owner. The want of education was one of several factors causing the demise of that pioneering attempt. Today however, as economic democracy has spread to workplaces throughout North America, significant energy is devoted to teaching and learning in worker-owned enterprises. But the question arises: does emerging pedagogic practice suit a democratic labour-based vision of economic development?

The Industrial Co-operative Association is one of several American firms which consults on worker-ownership exclusively. ICA has one full-time workplace educator and one working part-time. Additionally, five business analysts, two attorneys, the director of public policy, a staff economist, and staff director all teach as circumstances dictate either incidentally, as they assist workers or managers establish labour-managed enterprises, or informally, during specially arranged workshops, conferences, or through papers, position papers, seminars, and related public forums. The ICA works nationally with business start-ups, conversions, or buy-outs. Its educational efforts and materials are generic to the principles of labour-managed enterprises and are not industry specific. The organisation relies principally upon experimental educational theory and practice.

In operation seven years as a technical assistance organisation, time and its agenda have given the ICA an opportunity to evolve a tested comprehensive methodology and curriculum appropriate to most start-ups, conversions, or buy-out situations, especially as related to workplaces with large numbers of blue-collar and minority persons. A handbook describing the ICA experience and practice is being written, as are inexpensive, easily reproduced materials devoted to the role and skills which characterise a worker-member, board member, company officer, manager, and operational aspects such as the internal membership accounts, organisation charts, etc., and legal questions. These educational materials are being framed for use in the well-tested context of study circles, a tool long used by democratic unions.

With particular worker-owned firms ICA devises, with worker-members or elected managers, appropriate educational programmes suited especially to the needs of the individual firm, its work history, and surrounding culture. These workplace-specific programmes evolve through dialogue with worker-members, managers, and the ICA staff, and are formalised by a contract for services.

A third focus of ICA's educational programme has been to encourage and support education devoted to worker-ownership within other organisations. This has taken two directions: with other technical assistance providers, throughout the United States, England and Puerto Rico, and with progressive, but formal educational institutions, particularly Roxbury College, New Hampshire College, the Guilford College programme on Democratic Management, or annually at the North American Students of Co-operation, and at Tufts University. The ICA is a worker-managed firm with each fully vested member having one vote in all policy matters. The board of directors currently is composed of the entire membership. That body, in turn, employs a manager to govern daily affairs.

EDUCATIONAL TYPOLOGIES

Generally, ICA offers education within situations where workers are attempting to found from scratch; to prevent a business from being closed by its owners; or when workers attempt to buy out a firm to convert it to worker-ownership. Each situation has its own peculiar dynamics, just as each firm possesses a unique cultural history. Further, experience has taught that, within these distinct situations, most workers who would be owners go through three phases: the anxious exhilaration of starting in business for themselves; the sobering reality born of ownership's rights and responsibilities that making the business prosper requires more skill than was initially acknowledged; and, finally, the recognition that, if the founders' vision is not to be lost, a new generation of leadership must be nurtured.

For the most part, ICA has laboured with business either in the euphoric or start-up phases or as their workforces become more established and begin searching for additional savvy. For a host of reasons only a handful of worker-owned firms have yet faced the questions posed by second-generation transitions. On one level, organisational policy dictates how educational work is carried out; on a second level, however, ideology plays a part. Geography, time constraints, and strategic questions are all factors in how ICA teachers intervene.

Their approach to learning can best be seen against the educational categories set out by Rolland G. Paulston of the University of Pittsburgh.[4] Paulston has described four basic components in the way people organise learning in any given society: informal, non-formal, formal and international. Informal learning takes place intentionally, but is self- or group-directed, neither prompted nor carried out by teachers or schools. As Paulston puts it, informal learning derives in a non-systematic manner from generally unstructured exposure to cultural facilities, social institutions, political processes, personal media and the mass media. Both on the job, through invisible work groups, and off the job in clubs, bars or unions, workers have used informal learning as a tool to control their lot.

Non-formal learning is also intentional, but is carried systematically by a school or teacher outside the school as workshops, seminars, or similar short-term activities aimed at transferring knowledge, changing attitudes or behaviour. Most union educational activities, and much of the work done by ICA, falls in this category. Formal learning, according to Paulston, takes place in, and through, age-graded (or other) hierarchies which predetermine what is to be learned, when, where and how. Formal education has little to do directly with ICA's educational work.

International learning takes place outside national boundaries and results chiefly through travel, attending conferences, etc.; activities seldom open to most workers unless they belong to unions or are very well paid. Nevertheless, international education is important, chiefly because it forces comparisons, opens new situations or models, and offers differing cultural or political perspectives. ICA encourages worker-owners to learn in this manner, but does little itself beyond encouraging participation.

Paulston's otherwise comprehensive typology omits one critically important learning source: work itself. This might be described as incidental learning, an activity which takes

271

place unintentionally as work goes on, and is derived from the task itself, or the way the task is organised within the enterprise. Historically, steel-workers, glassmakers, farmers, and countless others have sparked social reform from lessons incidentally resulting from work. ICA has found work to be a valuable source of education which leads to social and personal change.

With these reference points in mind, it becomes possible to probe more deeply into the approaches used by ICA. ICA has extensive non-formal educational experience and has done this in a wide number of industrial settings evolving an approach, style and materials effectively suited to the start-up, conversion or buy-outs of any firm. This has been done by devising principles, methods and materials which are generically vital to any firm, then tailoring them to the unique requirements of the labour-owned enterprise at each worksite.

To date, while themselves mostly well-schooled, the ICA staff has only infrequently turned to academia for substantive advice on particular problems within specific worker-owned firms. However, ICA staff frequently serve as resources for single classes, or entire courses, at several colleges and universities. And, frequently, these are able to send students to ICA-related enterprises for study. ICA has also worked with several academic institutions in the formulation of programmes aimed to prepare future worker-members.

Within the incidental, informal and international categories, ICA has devoted little or no systematic thought to experimentation, except to insist that direct participation is the means by which the principles of democracy are best learned, both in the economic and political governance of the firms. What is learned from a job, how it is learned, and consequently how the specifics of that job are translated by workers into a universal vision of their economic lives has yet to be examined. The role of the invisible work group is understood in terms of political power within workplaces, but how that power can be translated into educational activities has yet to be explored. A careful examination of the way learning occurs within the omnipresent groupings at work, and how that might affect workplace democracy remains an opportunity to be taken up. Understandably, since ICA itself lives on the margin of profitability, there has been scant time or money to promote international travel. Nevertheless, historic patterns of isolation among workers can be tackled through cross-cultural exchanges among peers.

A FOUNDATION OF BELIEFS

ICA is an expression of a set of beliefs which guide teachers' activities in the labour-managed workplace. Some of these beliefs are overt; others are sublime. Here, while the emphasis and phrasing are mine, as are the beliefs themselves, it can generally be assumed they are shared by most ICA staff.

At the peak of the beliefs shared generally is an affirmative respect for each worker, especially those individuals who have been excluded from ownership, or from an equitable share of the value their labour adds to the production of goods or service delivery. Each shares a belief in the intelligent capacity of a majority to decide how to govern their economic lives using the tools of a political democracy.

Further, we share the assumption that all individuals have the right to adequate food, shelter, clothing, and medical care, but, in addition to those indispensable needs, the enjoyment of wants, which change and which make possible the development of the whole person culturally and intellectually. And, while it is recognised there is no equality in physical or psychological terms, equality does have a claim on pedagogic behaviour regardless of sex, race, class, national origin or political persuasion. Thus, without trumpeting the fact, we endorse the Bill of Rights, and certainly would expand the constitutional guarantees afforded workers. Work is seen as an activity which can be an invigorating form of positive self-expression. The notion that the term 'worker' suggests menial position, inferiority of class, a being without culture or history is the antithesis of ICA's collective values. Worker-ownership becomes a means to end the dualism which promotes one kind of education for those who own capital and another for those who own only their labour. A new conception of labour, and hence pedagogy, remains incomplete.

In the formal way ICA has organised our own work, sometimes as a cooperative and at others as a collaborative, expresses the belief that individual well-being is the result of collective, interdependent exertion. Neither computers nor groceries are produced without a division of labour.

Group work leads naturally to group activity. The end logic of worker solidarity is worker-ownership. That axiom informs most, if not all, the teaching and learning activities carried on by ICA. Finally, growing from these beliefs is the operative assumption that workers' education is one means by which a labour-managed vision of economic growth can evolve, and by which the term democracy can be enhanced. Learning is the instrument by which ICA can vitalise the commonly shared beliefs while seeking to paralyse the influence of beliefs we reject.

These seem to bear most directly upon educational outcomes. As this essay is already growing to some length, I will not set forth in detail those characteristics of any ideally organised labour-managed enterprise, save to say ICA would agree that each worker must enjoy the franchise as a personal right derived from labour participation rather than as property right based upon provision of capital. The supply of capital confers no management rights, participation in self-governance does. The common bond is labour, not property, and labour hires capital.

WHY A PEDAGOGY FOR THE DEMOCRATIC WORK-PLACE?

The activities carried out by ICA, the beliefs upon which they are founded, and the structures they nurture turn economic tradition upside down. Worker-ownership raises serious challenges to the traditional way we teach and learn about work. Worker-ownership is neither capitalist nor socialist but is, in fact, a still evolving alternative to both, a third way for which a fully elaborated descriptive language is just starting to be fashioned, at least in America.

Worker-ownership is labourist. For teachers trained and seasoned to transfer knowledge which aims to reproduce the means of production, or to recruit and train new labour prepared for work within one ideological system, to mention but two of the historically sanctioned roles for education, this fact poses problems, not least of which is American capitalism, culture, history, and experience. For example, capitalism everywhere, but to new extremes in America, has sought to monopolise knowledge for the profit of those who own capital or property, or those who manage on behalf of owners. Elsewhere, the state has monopolised knowledge for those who govern through party affiliation. In theory, at least, worker-ownership will democratise knowledge. A labour-managed economy requires ever-increasing knowledge, broader skills and fundamental, yet steady growth in self- and group-consciousness for all who work. The experience emerging from the Mondragon experiment demonstrates this fact. The artificial barriers as to who gets to learn what must fall aside if cooperation is to flourish as the organising medium for production.

At the risk of oversimplification, the distinctions are sharpest when seen against five basic characteristics of traditional American adult education, or by education which has been devised by the conventional, mainstream trade union movement within American capitalism. Starkly drawn to heighten distinctions, they are:

1. With respect to value added: traditional adult education adds value to capital by improving individual skills which then can only be used in workplaces where capital controls labour. Labour union education has added value to workers' collective capacity to coerce capital but, in the final analysis (at least to date in America) mainstream unions accept capital's permanent domination of labour education in the framework of economic democracy adds value directly to labour's ability to control and manage capital.

2. With respect to worker solidarity: most traditional adult education has fostered individual competitiveness, and powerlessness with regard to one's economic destiny, while perpetuating the distinction between earning a living with one's hands or with one's head. Most labour education institutionalises the adversarial relationship between capital and labour, elaborating, if not extending, government's mediating role which ultimately always favours capital. Education in the democratic workplace by definition nourishes mutual aid and cooperation between workers and managers, and between other worker-members.

3. With respect to ideology, traditional adult education has inherently taught job scarcity and Social Darwinism. On the other hand, labour education has taught the ideology of class, job consciousness, the closed shop, and the means to preserve hard-won privilege - often at the expense of fellow workers. The democratically-managed workplace itself teaches the necessity of expanding political and economic

opportunity, and of widening privilege - if the worker-owned and democratically managed firm is to prosper in a free market.

4. With respect to social logic: while adult education implicitly has taught the logic of self-aggrandisement, labour education perforce has taught the logic of collective benefits. To date, at least with respect to the evolving experience in the Mondragon Group, workers' education has taught the logic of democratic social transformation, inherently if not overtly.

5. Finally, with respect to the function of adult education: in America, at least, most schooling for adults rests on the assumption that learning is a way out of the working class. For the union movement, education has been seen as a way to move the working class into improved social strata while strengthening the loyalty of members to union leaders. In the democratically-managed, worker-owned firm, education can be seen as one means by which to achieve labour solidarity, as well as a labour-mananged company; recent Polish history testifies to this assertion.

In American culture and history non-traditional adult education usually has been taken up by emerging groups contesting oppressive restrictions on their aspirations for power, participation and ownership. Farmers, workers, Blacks and Hispanics, women and others have created non-formal education to imbue each other with the skills necessary for the changes they seek, and, as well, the ideology of their movements. Brookwood, the Work People's College, Highlander Folk School are but three examples of where adult education has been collectively fashioned to serve social change. As yet, there is no similar 'school' for worker-owners.

SOME PERSONAL EXPERIENCES

Like most American teachers, I have been seasoned to transfer knowledge which aims to reproduce the means of production, or to recruit and train new labour prepared for work within capitalism: one of two ideological systems which dominate economic discourse worldwide, and which shape educational work. My own experience in worker-owned firms since 1979 indicates the labourist enterprise requires a pedagogy which derives from the needs, interests, history and culture of labour - the workers, the job they do, and the necessity for workers to control capital in the fullest sense. The historic, elitist rationale for dividing knowledge into two broad, hierarchical categories - one for the head and one for the hand - is inherently subverted by the organisation of the labour-managed enterprise itself, and eventually by worker-owners.

The structure of a worker-owned firm itself provides additional sources for education. Persons who otherwise have had little practice, or use, for the tools of civic democracy must learn how to apply them to an economic institution. Those tools usually are embedded in the by-laws of most, if not all, worker-owned firms: freedom of speech; the concept of one person, one vote; the right to free assembly, or of voluntary participation; and safeguards for the rights of a minority. Verbal literacy has long been recognised as important for the survival of a political democracy. Economic literacy is essential for the survival of worker-owned firms. For example, workers who are unable to read the balance sheets of the companies they own risk the loss of both labour and freedom. Failure to learn about their markets, or regulations, about contracts, and other bodies of knowledge can hazard an investment of labour and capital as quickly as any natural disaster. Marge Bonacci had clerked in a grocery store 23 years when the owners suddenly announced the business was being closed. Bonacci and others bought the place, turning a marginal company into a profitable firm. 'When it first started out', she told a Wall Street Journal reporter, 'I thought, Oh, my God, we'll never be able to do this. We're not smart enough. They said to me, "You're on the governance committee." I said, "Who me?" My God, I was a deli person. I sliced meat. How do I know what a manager does"?'

In a few worker-owned firms, decision-making has been democratised, or shifted from traditional unilateral, hierarchical systems to bilateral, horizontal systems where management and workers share in taking decisions, solving problems, setting corporate goals, even affecting wages and the basic conditions of work, starting at the shopfloor level and working through the firm. In effect, workers produce the knowledge necessary to continue the company's growth. Collaborative, or participatory, educational processes deriving from historically progressive adult educational practice are used by worker-owners themselves to identify

277

issues, discuss options, and test solutions. For instance in Seymour Specialty Wire in Seymour, Connecticut, nearly 250 workers and managers themselves redesigned the means by which production decisions are taken.

A strong United Auto Workers local, which represented employees before they purchased the firm, took an active part in the formation of the bilateral, participatory programme which was called the Workers' Solving Problems programme. It evolved during company-wide meetings, a nine-member working group dominated by workers, not managers, then adopted by Seymour's board of directors. As Mike Kearney, President of the United Auto Workers local at Seymour said, 'Trains don't run on one track. I see this company like a railroad track. Hourly people and salaried people here are tied together, and this programme gives us a way to work in the same direction.'

To establish a cooperative working relationship between all worker-owners it was agreed that any problem under the control of a work unit, or department, could be discussed and a decision reached by the worker-owners in that unit, provided the proposed action did not conflict with the union's contract with the company, or the company's fiduciary responsibilities. Work units on each of the company's three-shift, round-the-clock operations were trained in decision-making, problem-solving, dispute-resolution skills. They were encouraged to pass as few problems along as possible, testing each decision however by the impact it would have on fellow workers in other parts of the sprawling wire mill, and for its impact on the company itself.

Each work unit elected a chair who, during a one-year term, ran formal, half-hour, bimonthly decision-making meetings. In a reversal of roles, work unit foremen took notes, recorded decisions, and ensured that fellow owners had accurate, complete information upon which to formulate and decide on a course of action. All work unit members were expected to attend and participate in the bimonthly meetings. It was part of their job. If for whatever reason a decision could not be reached at the shopfloor level then the elected chair, who came from the rank and file, and the foreman took the matter directly to the department superintendant. Should the three of them reach no decision, then they took the issue to Seymour's president, and sent the originating shopfloor unit a written status report. Each step was flexible, but stated time-limits to ensure that problems were resolved, not ignored. Should action be required by the board of directors, the elected shopfloor chair, shopfloor foreman, department superintendant, and president presented the issue and when action was taken, issued a written report to the originating shopfloor unit. Workers and managers at Seymour fashioned a direct and easily understood means to solve problems, while holding worker and manager alike democratically accountable.

To commence the participatory programme, Seymour's worker-owners assumed the responsibility for work-time and assignment, performance standards, working conditions, and interdepartmental coordination, shifting dramatically the role and authority of management while perforce democratising knowledge within the firm. It is expected additional areas of concern will be added as the programme evolves, and workers gain more experience with its operation.

These changes did not come at Seymour without pain, either for management or union members. Nor were they the result of accidental learning without educational intent. For me, as an adult educator thrust in the midst of the opportunity presented at Seymour, or similar worker-owned companies in the United States, the concept of participatory learning has taken on significantly altered dimensions in the worker-owned firm. Three unoriginal principles form the basis of my work. First, I listen a lot, attempting to learn what worker-owners are interested in learning, both individually and collectively. Learning how to keep my own mouth shut in these situations has been difficult. Teachers are supposed to talk. Second, while we as Americans take narrow nationalistic pride in the legal guarantee of free speech, open, free, candid dialogue among equals has yet to become a hallmark of American working life. Workers have ample historic and economic reason to know that honest talk which is important to them usually meant trouble. I try to find ways to encourage workers in groups to talk about what matters most to them as owners. Third, using what I hear, I pose problems deriving from the immediate situation, but which have bearing on the long-term aim of developing labour-managed enterprises.

The experiences of worker-owners themselves taught one of the theoretical founders of the contemporary drive for worker-ownership, Jaroslav Vanek, the importance of education. He opened a paper written in 1977 titled 'Education for the Practice of Self-Management in the

Control of the Production of Knowledge

United States', saying:

> The Rochdale pioneers, forerunners of all co-operative movements today, were well aware of the significance of education for the liberation of the worker. When they wrote down the fundamental principles of their movement some one and a quarter centuries ago, they knew it was the ignorance of the wage earner of how to do things, how to organise production, that enslaved him. Thus, they resolved to allot some portion of their meagre resources to education ... Education, and more generally the transformation of the human consciousness, is the precondition and the very life-blood of any successful and lasting effort to bring about self-management and economic democracy.

Thus, one vision which propels some of the education work being undertaken in the growing number of democratic workplaces is a Kantian one, albeit a collective, or group, struggle to use knowledge without direction from others.

REFERENCES

1. G.R. Lockwood, The New Harmony Movement (New York: D. Appleton & Co., 1905); T.W. Mercer, Co-operation's Prophet. The Life and Letters of Dr. William King of Brighton with a Reprint of the Co-operator, 1828-1830 (Manchester: Cooperative Union, 1947).
2. L. Jones, as quoted in A. Bonner, British Co-operation: The History, Principles and Organisation of the British Co-operative Movement (Manchester: Cooperative Union, 1970), p.43.
3. A. Gutierrez-Johnson, 'The Mondragon Co-operative Model', in Changing Work, Vol. 1 (1984), p.40.
4. R.G. Paulston, Changing Educational Systems: A Review of Theory and Practice (Washington, D.C.: World Bank, 1978).

13

Adult Education and the Third World:
An African Perspective

Retta Alemayehu

THIRD WORLD: A DECEITFUL TERM

It is probably helpful, in this chapter, to draw a rough
picture of what we mean by the term 'Third World'.
Although it may sound slightly outside the scope of this
chapter, we shall attempt to find out who or what is
responsible for creating the condition(s) which has forced
more than half of humanity to lead a 'third'-grade life akin
to sheer proverty. This attempt may shed some light on the
'why' and 'how' of a 'three world' division on the same planet.
The raison d'être for writing this chapter would not be
adequate in this context unless we take a brief look at the
Third World and how its socio-economic and political
machinery (as part and parcel of the global whole) play their
part in the reproduction as well as reinforcement of the
global socio-economic and political structures which were
mainly crafted to ensure and guarantee the safety and
survival of the international status quo.

The question that interests us most here is, what are
the political, social and economic components which
constitute a relatively recent phenomenon of underdevelopment politely referred to as 'developing' or the 'Third
World'? In order to answer this question one may need to
browse through contemporary economic and political
publications, United Nations documents etc., only to
discover that they all give slightly differing meanings based
on their own levels of understanding of the whole problem.

Many authors, from the 'developing' or the 'developed'
world, for instance, use such terms as emerging nations,
developing countries, ex-colonies, less developed countries,
underdeveloped nations, underprivileged nations, poor
countries, newly freed countries, primitive, etc., to signify
the 'Third World'. Authors who are using these terms often
vary as much in their outlooks as in the aims and purposes of
their writing. Some of the terms sometimes reflect the

ideological/political and economic arrogance or perhaps the
innocently naive views of the users on such delicate issues.
Terms such as 'developing' - no matter how 'nice' they may
sound - would always embody the real meanings: material
poverty and technological underdevelopment.

All the terms listed in the preceding paragraph, it was
hoped, would help in drawing our attention to the socio-
economic conditions of most African, Latin American and
Asian countries. Among those who write very differently
from the conventional ways on such issues are the Paddocks
who made some effort to point out clearly the extent of the
social and economic plight of the masses of people in the
Third World. With no intention of communicating a
derogatory message, they referred to the 'Third World' as
'hungry nations'. The following is taken from their
elaboration on their statement:

> A more exact term than 'backward' is 'hungry'
> ...[we] shall refer to these 'undeveloped', 'less well
> developed', 'poorest third', 'emerging' nations
> simply as hungry.
> They are hungry for food, they are hungry for
> stability, they are hungry for international
> prestige, for education, for health, for housing,
> culture. They are hungry for the twentieth
> century.[1]

For the Paddocks the opposite of a 'hungry nation' is a
'comfortable nation' the people of which do not have to
suffer from the harshness of Third World social and
economic realities.

As we shall also see later on in this chapter, it is hard
to draw meaningful geographical, cultural, economic and
linguistic lines of demarcation between the 'First', the
'Second' and the 'Third' Worlds so as to be able to point our
fingers at a distinct geographical region called the 'Third
World'. One thing is quite clear, though, in people's minds:
the term 'Third World' evokes nothing but an image of
material 'poverty' and an 'undeveloped' scientific and
technological capacity.

Many economists and planning experts generally agree
that the 'Third World' is anything outside of the 'Capitalist
West' (sometimes referred to as the First World) and the
'Communist East' (sometimes referred to as the Second
World). Max Beloff, for instance, holds to the view that 'the

Third World can be regarded as simply a residue: what is left when one has subtracted from the world as a whole the industrialized West... and Communist... East.'[2] It seems to this writer, though, that the Third World First World division has a lot more to do with the socio-economic and cultural development of a certain class(es) in society than with distinct geographic, linguistic and political entitites. This is so partly because we see a good section of society (for instance, the poor in the West) not benefiting from the fruits of the astoundingly high level of scientific and technological advancement in society. This means that those who live below the poverty line in the West cannot even dream about the life of affluence of the few wealthy individuals in many developing countries. Therefore, the notion that the 'Third World' is out there, not here, proves to be either a naive belief on the part of the people leading lives largely similar to that of the 'Third World' while still being legitimate members of the 'First World'. Or, it may also be a reflection of a propaganda 'gospel' designed by the rich and powerful in the wealthy nations who foster the conditions for keeping the poor below the poverty line.

One thing which may not cause a lot of dispute about the 'Third World' proper, is the fact that there is one commonality between almost all Third World countries: they are either colonies or ex-colonies of European colonial powers. In just the same manner, the undeveloped areas and peoples of the 'First/Second World' could be seen as 'Third World' by the virtue of their being internal colonies.[3]

The 'Third World' covers a large area of land and includes slightly over three-quarters of the inhabitants of the planet and, if the number of human beings is taken into consideration, it is a power to be reckoned with. As of January 1982, according to Finer, there are 127 states in the Third World (including China, which is now a nuclear power). Of these countries 86 attained their independence only after 1945 and therefore are very young as nation-states. Of those which got their independence after World War II, 16 became free in 1945-55; 38 in 1956-65; 23 in 1966-75; and 9 gained their independence from 1976-81.[4] There are still Third World areas which are fighting and paying dearly with the lives of their peoples to regain the independence which they enjoyed before the coming of slavery and colonialism.

WHY IS THERE A NEED FOR WIDER PROVISION OF ADULT EDUCATION IN THE THIRD WORLD?

Before answering this question we have to survey briefly the socio-economic and cultural conditions of the 'Third World' so that we argue from the point of view of meeting the basic needs of the people. Major problems of the Third World can be summarised as illiteracy, disease, poverty, famine and militarism, which are directly or indirectly caused by either the local or by the global economic and military powers.

Concrete examples will be necessary if we are to understand the magnitude of the problem. According to numerous UNESCO reports, in 1967, there were about 700 million illiterates in the world.[5] UNESCO had also projected that illiteracy would completely be wiped out by the year 2000.[6] Unfortunately, however, according to a 1983 World Bank Report, and despite the tremendous efforts made to expand primary school education and adult literacy programmes, the number of illiterates grew from 700 million in 1967 to 1.2 billion in 1983.[7]

Providing the basic minimum of adult literacy is 'expensive' partly because of the inadequacy of resources as a result of the economic trap which left most Third World countries in 'vicious circles of poverty' - the characteristic features of which, according to Angelopoulos, are:

1. A high proportion of the working population employed in agriculture using primitive farming techniques...;
2. chronic nutritional deficiency in large sections of the population;
3. chronic unemployment and underemployment;
4. high rates of population growth;
5. deficient infrastructure and inefficient industrialisation;
6. low levels of scientific and technological know-how;
7. low savings and investment levels and limited accumulation of capital;
8. underutilisation of natural resources;
9. structural imbalances and economic dualism, ie., the coexistence of modern and primitive economic sectors;
10. excessive dependence on foreign trade and capital inflow;
11. low income and living levels.[8]

The Third World: An African Perspective

Let us see how these characteristic features of poverty vividly manifest themselves across the maps of most Third World countries. According to one World Bank report, in 1981, about 850 million people in the developing world had little or no opportunity to receive even rudimentary schooling... Most of them are among the 770 million absolute poor.[9] Perhaps that is precisely why some writers, when they refer to the Third World, want to remind us that 'the world map of poverty is almost identical to the world map of illiteracy'.[10]

The misallocation of resources is appalling. In a world where US$ 1.3 million of the public treasury is being spent on the world military budget, 30 children die for lack of food and shortage of vaccines at the rate of a tick of a minute.[11] It had been estimated in 1983 that about two billion people (most of whom are in the Third World) did not have a reliable supply of safe drinking water, and hence were vulnerable to preventable diseases. In a world where more than half of humankind have no answer to the problems of meeting their basic needs such as food, shelter, safe drinking water, health care etc., nearly 'one-fifth' of the world's best engineers and scientists are busily engaged in perfecting the tools of death.[12]

As a result of borders drawn between former colonies and conflicts triggered by former colonial powers, Third Word countries are increasingly becoming intolerant of each other. These countries tend to spend more on arms imports. In 1978 alone developing nations spent 'five times as much foreign exchange for the import of arms as for agricultural machinery'.[13] The Iran-Iraq war which entered its 7th year in 1987 is an example of this: '...the first five years of fighting may have resulted in a toll of war dead approaching one million. The economic cost ... may have already exceeded $500 billion...'[14] It is also true that 'non-Opec developing countries (the 25 least developed nations of the world included) ... bought US $64 billion of foreign arms from 1970-1979.'[15] Seen from this perspective, therefore, there is no reason why Third World countries could not become open territories for all kinds of human miseries. As a result of these and other external and internal factors, poverty, hunger, disease, together with their closest ally, illiteracy, have become the distinct features of degraded social conditions closely associated with most African, Asian and Latin American countries.

As we pointed out earlier, Third World peoples are not

only limited to the continents of Africa, Asia and Latin America. They exist all over the world including Western Europe and North America. Those people whom this author would like to refer to as 'Third World of the First World' are the poor who languish below the poverty line in the midst of incredible material riches. Most North American native people (who call themselves the 'first nations') and the great majority of people of African origin who live either in Europe or in North America would probably fall in this category. Third World people, to this author, whether they belong in Europe, North America, Africa, Asia or Latin America (no matter what colour they are what language they speak) are those who suffer most as a result of being excluded from the mainstream of society and denied the right to equal opportunity to be what they want to be (and not what others want them to be). These people are surely in need of adult education programmes specifically designed to serve them as weapons in their protracted struggle for a 'cultural action for freedom', to use the words of Paulo Freire.[16]

True, Third World countries are politically free and hence are able to hoist their national flags. The unfortunate part of the whole freedom scenario is that these countries are still under the tight economic grip and political influence of the former colonial powers. Former colonial powers are still enjoying the economic products of their political and military presence in the Third World. A typical example of this is revealed in a recent interview the executive director of the International Monetary Fund gave to the Toronto Star. He said that the 'poor countries owe rich countries between US $750 billion and $1 trillion' (Toronto Star, 16 October 1986, p.E-3). Furthermore, Third World countries are under the rule of corrupt and often politically inept and irresponsible dictators, who enjoy a life of western affluence while the masses of the people under their regimes suffer from an incredible material poverty and a hopeless feeling of an uncertain future. These kinds of leader, in the words of Julius Nyerere of Tanzania, are 'looters in their own country', who make capital accumulation and development impossible in the Third World.[17] But the masses of the Third World do not seem to question why and how such things are happening (for they lack the proper knowledge) let alone take decisive political measures against such 'leaders'. This is so partly because written and other media systems are effectively used to cover up the wrong-doings instead of exposing the corrupt administrative and political practices.

The quality of educational and cultural infrastructures the colonial rulers and their ideological detachments (the missionaries) had left in the Third World are astoundingly inadequate. According to Rodney, 'of the total revenue collected from taxing Africans', for example, 'in French West Africa, only 4.03% was utilised on education'. In the British colony of Kenya, 'as late as 1946 only 2.26% of the revenue was spent on African education'. In Uganda, as late as 1959, the very few 'lucky' Africans who were able to go to school had to receive abysmally low quality education. For instance, the ratio between the educational expenditures of Ugandan European and Ugandan African was 186 to 11 which means nearly 17 Africans were expected to learn at an amount spent for one European.[18] Not only the level of education was very low, but the number of Africans going to school was very few: in the whole of what was known as French Equatorial Africa, which embraced such countries as present-day Chad, the Central African Republic, Gabon and Congo-Brazzaville, only 22,000 school children attended schools in 1938.[19] In that same year, according to Rodney, the number of school-goers in the whole region of what was known as French West Africa was only 77,000 out of a total population of 15 million.[20]

It is also worth mentioning the fact that modern (western) education in former colonies has been used as one of the most effective instruments for making neo-colonialism a workable system. In connection with this, Martin Carnoy, an American author, has clearly pointed out how education in many Third World countries has best served the neo-colonial interests of former colonial powers by citing some concrete examples from Third World realities. In Carnoy's view, the so-called 'modern education' (which he calls 'education for domination') would mainly help in maintaining the neo-colonial status quo. Thus he explains:

The schools are an extension of the metropole structure, just as are the economy, polity, and social structure. As long as the national bourgeoisie in its colonial rule dominates the domestic pyramid structure, we can expect that the school will prevent liberation on two levels: liberation from the definition of culture and development by the high-income imperial nations,

287

and liberation from the domestic pyramid structure.[21]

Carnoy has even gone to the extent of shedding some light on how educational reforms in the United States from 1830 to 1970 were used as instruments of 'internal colonialism' or a domestic means of 'social control'.[22] On top of this, investing 'too much' on formal schools (in the Third World) by ignoring adult education programmes seems tantamount to contributing to the training of a 'new' breed of white-collar local masters for peasant cultivators of the predominantly rural Third World countries.

So far we have documented a few of the problems that do and will continue to hamper socio-economic and cultural development in most regions of the Third World. Here, not only do we want to suggest that the masses in the Third World need to pull themselves out of the grinding jaws of poverty and the debilitating effects of famine, disease, illiteracy and exploitation, but also we want to argue strongly that these tasks will not easily be accomplished without a carefully designed adult education/literacy programmes or, in the words of Paulo Freire, a truly liberating 'Pedagogy of the Oppressed'.

ADULT LITERACY AND REVOLUTION: THIRD WORLD INITIATIVES

In the first part of this chapter we have seen how over 80 per cent of Africa is still behind the 'iron curtain' of illiteracy. This is an indication that illiteracy is rampant in many Third World countries. (Here illiteracy should not be seen only as the 'disease' of the 'Third World'. Even in the technoligically advanced (western) societies - where people should not only become literate but also 'computer literate' -illiteracy is said to be not only on the rise but spreading at an alarming rate.)

Mention should also be made here that widespread illiteracy usually means widespread famine, unsanitary conditions (hence the spread of preventable diseases) and, most importantly, widespread oppression and exploitation. One could deduce from this that in societies where higher rates of illiteracy exist female members of society (whose number, for instance, accounts for over 50 per cent in Africa) and cultural and ethnic minorities not only suffer most from the debilitating effects of illiteracy but also receive the heaviest economic and social blows resulting from being illiterate. Hence, it is not only socially sensible but also politically and economically essential to provide adult (literacy) education if we are truly seeking a better future for the multitude of adult illiterates of the Third World. Adult literacy/education is also highly necessary for the fostering of harmonious and peaceful living between peoples as well as for the maintenance of a healthy environment which is long overdue in most parts of the the Third World. It is with this view and concern in mind that we are going to probe 'Third World' initiatives in adult literacy/education.

As has been pointed out earlier, the Third World really needed a powerful economic locomotive that would pull it out of the long tracks of poverty, illiteracy and easily preventable diseases. Obviously it was 'modern' (western) education which was seen as the key to development in the Third World towards the end of the 'decade of decolonization' (1960s).

Within the same decade, however, it became quite evident that western education was in virtual crisis in most of the European and North America cities.[23] Nevertheless, most Third World governments went ahead with expanding western education in their respective countries as they were convinced that that was the only alternative they had in filling up the horrendous educational and cultural gaps left behind by the colonial powers. In spite of all the anticipated difficulties and weaknesses which could result from transplanting western education into Third World social and economic settings, newly formed national governments decided to go ahead with it since many of them were of the opinion that without western education they would not realise their dreams of creating Third World adaptations of 'little Englands', 'little Frances', 'little Hollands', 'little Belgiums', 'little Spains', etc. This is not, however, to suggest that there were no Third World governments or leaders whose main aims were entirely oriented to the immediate fulfilment of their peoples' needs. Certainly there were Third World leaders who were not interested in realising false dreams of using Europe as their models of development for their countries. This group of leaders sought 'modern education' because it was obvious to them that there were no adequately trained scientific and technological personnel among the local people who could run the affairs of their governments and be able to disseminate scientific and technological know-how to their predominantly unschooled masses. The dreams of such genuine leaders were not to meet unrealistic 'needs'. In the words of one prominent adult educator, 'peasants, workers, housewives, needed to be informed, influenced, taught new skills and socialized, to enable them to participate in the process of development'.[24]

Among the problems faced by most leaders of the newly independent Third World countries in fulfilling the aspirations of their peoples were: acute shortages in financial and material resources for the quick provision of universal primary education for school-age children, shortage of highly trained teachers and scientific and technological equipment deemed necessary for 'modern' schools, etc. The other paradoxical phenomenon which occurred in many Third World countries was the lack of employment opportunities for even those graduates of the few formal schools. This was a clear indication of the fact that the newly transplanted 'western education' which had its own inherent problems soon proved unresponsive to the local problems of the Third World. In short, 'modern education' soon became a part of the very problem it sought to resolve. The problem was also coupled with the unrealistically high expectations of the graduates of the academically-oriented secondary schools to find 'white-collar' jobs which were obviously in short supply in the predominantly agrarian and peasant economies of the Third World.

We indicated earlier that there has always been a close relationship between literacy and power and literacy and revolution in human history. We also said that literacy has always been a powerful weapon which helped in bringing about desirable socio-economic and political changes for illiterate and poor peoples when steered by forces committed to the liberation and prosperity of the broad masses. Thus the Soviet Union could be seen as the first country which recognised the power of mass literacy and relied heavily on formal and non-formal education campaigns (including literacy) to change the face of Tsarist Russia into a peoples' 'Union of Soviet Socialist Republics'. Elizabeth Moos writes on the results of the emphasis and importance accorded to education by the Soviet Union:

Transformation of [the Soviet Union], a backward, largely agricultural country to a great industrial power and one of the leaders in scientific achievement was possible largely because of the concentration on education.[25]

The People's Republic of China is another good example where adult education was widely made available and mass literacy campaigns were launched as part and parcel of the overall socio-economic and political revolution that took place since 1949 the year in which China was declared a People's Democratic Republic. In that year the rate of illiteracy in China 'was reported to be 85% among the total adult population and as high as 95% in the rural areas of the country'.[26]

It is worth noting here that both Mao and the Chinese Communist Party drew invaluable lessons from the educational experience of the first socialist country - the Soviet Union. Since the Party saw literacy as a major vehicle for revolutionary (Marxist) ideas, it made all efforts possible to free the over 80 per cent of Chinese people from illiteracy. The Communists, who had launched a series of campaigns in the liberated areas before 1949, conducted another nation-wide campaign in the 1950s which was instrumental in the decline of the rate of illiteracy from over 80 per cent in the early 1950s to less than 10 per cent in the early 1980s.

After independence and after drawing their lessons on how much education and literacy had helped in transforming the USSR from a primarily agrarian country into an industrial world power, a few Third World countries attempted to establish adult (literacy) education programmes for their predominantly illiterate masses. Such efforts have been and are more conspicuous in those Third World countries where some kind of political and economic reforms or revolutionary changes have taken place. Cuba, Ethiopia, Guinea Bissau, Mozambique, Nicaragua, Tanzania, Vietnam, etc., are countries where highly noted and influential campaigns have taken place.[27] Here I want to examine two initiatives, one in Latin America, the other in Africa.

Nicaragua

With an estimated population of about three million, Nicaragua is the largest of Central American countries in terms of area. This is a country which became a shining star of the 1980s in terms of its mass literacy campaign conducted mainly as a result of the devotion of the Sandinista government which came to power only in 1979 after chasing the corrupt regime of Somoza into exile.

The Nicaraguan National Literacy Crusade which was often referred to as the 'second war of liberation', was organised with the aim of turning the country from a battlefield into a large school of literacy education. Hundreds and thousands of young Nicaraguan men and women who had, in the past, taken up arms and gone to the hills to fight against the Somoza regime, were once again invited to pick up textbooks and pencils as their weapons and go back to the same mountains, this time to fight another equally dangerous enemy - illiteracy. The determination of the campaigners in their response to the national call could be measured by the words of one Nicaraguan woman who said, 'We've freed ourselves from the ruthless tyranny of Somoza and his national guard and now we must free ourselves and brothers and sisters in fields and factories from ignorance.'[28]

The Nicaraguan Literacy Crusade, according to Carlos Tunnermann, former Minister of Education, was not only intended to do away with the 50 per cent rate of illiteracy which existed in Nicaragua before the campaign. The Literacy Crusade, which covered a period of six months, March through August of 1980 (turning the whole country into one large literacy school), had a broader socio-economic and political goal. The Literacy Crusade, as the 'second war of national liberation', had the goal of liberating people 'to be full human beings, conscious people empowerd to build their own future'. The former Minister, in an interview given to Philip Zwerling, adds that literacy education was a means to an end and not an end in itself. Thus he elaborates:

> The attainment of literacy was not simply the gaining of an academic skill, but the empowerment of a people who became aware of their reality and gained the tools, reading and writing, to affect and determine their future. The Literacy Crusade was not a pedagogical undertaking with political effects; it was a political undertaking with pedagogical effects. It was a political mobilization with political goals. In only two countries in Latin

America have such literacy Crusades been undertaken: in Cuba and in Nicaragua.[29]

The Nicaraguan Literacy Crusade, sometimes referred to as
a 'war on ignorance' and 'the cultural insurrection',
according to Maxwell, 'maintained the same organization,
strategy and tactics of the war of liberation against
Somoza'. She maintains that the 'Brigades [of literacy
campaigners] were organized into some six battlefronts used
by the FSLN [the Sandinistas] during the war of
liberation.'[30] It was these 'Brigadistas' with a total number
of 60,000 in cooperation with the 'Peasants' Literacy Army',
the 'Urban Literacy Guerillas', and the 'Workers Literacy
Militia' that made it possible to bring down the illiteracy
rate from 50 per cent in 1979 to 11.8 per cent in 1980 - an
official estimate acknowledged by UNESCO.[31]

Ethiopia

This is a country that claims to be one of the oldest centres
of human civilisation. In the more than 3000 years of its
recorded history, Ethiopia has never been colonised by a
European power (except the Italian occupation attempt of
1936-41), unlike most African and other Third World
countries. Despite its immense natural resources and
historical heritage, the country remained a land of many
paradoxes: the country prides itself on its antiquity and long
history of independence and yet over 85 per cent of its
peasant population remained prisoners of a feudal system
until the 1974 revolution: this is the only sub-Saharan
African country which developed its own alphabet and
accumulated a literary tradition over 1500 years old.
Unfortunately, however, over 90 per cent of its population
remained behind 'the heavy curtain of illiteracy' alien to
their own literary heritage until the 1974 revolution. This
same country used to be referred to by agronomists and
economists as the future 'bread basket of Africa and the
Middle East' until the famine, that dissolved the whole world
into tears, turned parts of the country into graveyards for
hundreds of thousands of Ethiopians who starved to death
because of food shortages.

Actually, it was the university student unions who
initially began adult literacy in Ethiopia. The University
Students' Union of Addis Ababa in 1965 started a paper

known as Tagel (struggle) which became the sole voice of the oppressed masses and began serving as a vehicle for the dissemination of 'new and progressive' ideas to the general public (mainly the poor). However, students soon came to realise that the poor could not benefit from the students' paper since they lacked the basic skills of reading and writing. Therefore, according to Edouard Trudeau, a Canadian Jesuit missionary, establishing community service clubs, literacy centres and schools for the children of the urban poor and the unemployed of the city of Addis Ababa became top priority in the students' agenda. True, the students' initiative was insignificant in terms of reducing the rate of illiteracy when compared to the activities of other voluntary and religious organisations: 'Their importance ... lies not in the scale of the programmes [they offered] but rather in the fact that they expressed the conviction that literacy education was central to meaningful political and social change in the country.'[32]

Two separate literacy campaigns were undertaken in Ethiopia after the feudal regime of Emperor Haile Selassie was overthrown in 1974. The first one launched as a component part of a campaign of 'Development Through Co-operation' was launched in 1975-76 involving the participation of about 60,000 senior secondary and all university students (including this author) plus their teachers. The 'Provisional Military Government of Socialist Ethiopia', locally known as the 'Dergue', sent the students (sometimes referred to by peasants as the 'children of the Dergue') to 397 districts all over the country. The campaign, which cost, the nation about US $21 million, registered tremendous achievements as a result of the commitment shown by student and teacher campaigners. Here are some of their results:

1. 4.5 million literacy primers and books written in five major Ethiopian languages were distributed and about a million peasants became literate;
2. 206 new clinics and 158 new primary schools were built;
3. a total of 5,537,000 poor peasants were organised in 19,314 associations;
4. 63,500 tribunals and 55,000 'defence committees' were organised (mostly against the wish of the military government).

The second and the biggest literacy campaign ever in

the history of the country was officially launched in 1979 after the establishment of a national body known as the 'National Literacy Campaign Co-ordinating Committee (NLCCC). The campaign started with the ambitious target of completely eradicating illiteracy from Ethiopia by 1987 – a target which soon proved to be impossible to achieve. However, it has succeeded in bringing down the level of illiteracy from 90 per cent in 1974 to 37 per cent in the first half of the 1980s. The success of the campaign in achieving this result is partly attributable to the material and financial contributions of the Ethiopian people mobilised by mass organisations and religious institutions such as Political Study Forums, the All-Ethiopian Trade Unions, the All-Ethiopian Peasants' Association, the Ethiopian Teachers' Association, the Ethiopian Journalists' Association, the Urban Dwellers' Associations, Revolutionary Ethiopian Women's Associations, Revolutionary Ethiopian Youth Associations, the Ethiopian Orthodox Church, the Ethiopian Mosque, etc. Some of the major achievements of the second national literacy campaign are:

- over 20 million male and female adult illiterates and over a million literate people were mobilised under the popular slogan 'every illiterate Ethiopian shall learn, and every educated Ethiopian shall teach!';
- a generous contribution of about US $20 million was made by the general public which covered nearly 60 per cent of the campaign expenses from 1979 to 1983
- over 20 million publications and books written in 15 different Ethiopian languages spoken by about 95 per cent of the population were distributed free of charge;
- over 6000 reading centres (rural libraries) have been established where new literates can obtain follow-up reading materials.

CONCLUSION

The major aim of the author, is to underline the fact that the Third World badly needs greater adult literacy/education than ever before. Nearly two dozen senseless regional wars (a third of them in Africa) are being fought in the Third World most of them triggered by the sheer ignorance and irresponsibility of the political and military leaders of those countries which are trapped in a tragic cycle of destroying their badly needed human and material resources to the extent of making the reinstitution of peace and development a virtual impossibility. As was stated earlier in this chapter, the Iran-Iraq war alone has become a nightmare in the Third World. Hence, the Third World needs relevant adult education with the help of which peoples of different countries will learn about each other, and about the vicious and insidious behaviour of the sponsors of war in our world.

Famines, diseases, and of course their closest ally, illiteracy, make the Third World their final stronghold. It is up to the masses of the Third World to decide whether to get rid of the main causes of poverty, diseases, famine etc., once and for all, or remain with the economic and social ills for ever. But, before people are expected to make such choices, they need to be freed from the shackles of illiteracy so that they see the cause effect relationships of the socio-economic and political problems of their respective regions. Here, adult education is needed not only for its traditional role of preserving the old values and knowledge; adult education in the Third World has a special task of facilitating the creation of new social values and knowledge.

Literacy programmes like the ones sponsored by UNESCO in Africa and the rest of the Third World should never be viewed as failures even if they have only limited success. Here we may fail to produce a 'scientific way' of quantifying the positive results of those 'failing literacy campaigns'. Nor can we present arguments that match the criticisms of those area experts who want to measure the successes/failures of literacy campaigns only in terms of quantifiable figures. But to this author the very possibility of causing a change of attitude in favour of 'modern education' for the adult and ageing members of society (not only for school-age children) is in itself a great success, the financial value of which is very hard to estimate. The real result of such campaigns comes only in the shift of attitude of peoples which we may see only after years or decades of literacy campaigns.

In this era of scientific/technological and media revolution the world is increasingly becoming smaller and smaller in that people living in one corner of the world can no longer afford to keep quiet while their fellow human beings are suffering from tragedies of any kind in an other corner of the world. We have seen one good example of this when practically the whole world responded when drought and famine brought many Ethiopians and other Africans to the brink of death. This means that educating all corners of the world is technically possible if the world leaders have the will to cooperate in making our world a planet of human joy, peace and development.

A lot of explaining the problems of illiteracy and the relapse into illiteracy needs to be done through a close cooperation between adult educators of the Third World and those of the technologically advanced societies. We need to present a strong case that emergency aid for Africa and the rest of the Third World should not be limited to food handouts. Because, as the Paddocks have correctly put it, Third World nations are also 'hungry for education, for health, for housing, culture' and in general for the twenty-first century. We have to prepare ourselves for reducing the tensions that will definitely exist between those who are enjoying the fruits of the twenty-first century and those who bitterly resent the fact that they are left behind still to suffer from the wounds of earlier centuries. We need to remind people that we have to respect pledges we have made on several UNESCO and other international forums that 'literacy is the right of every human being'.[33]

Fellow adult educators whose homes happen to be on the 'luckiest side of the world' must understand that without their help no mass provision of adult literacy/education is possible in the Third World. Without their help adult educators in the Third World cannot emerge victorious over such human tragedies as pollution and environmental degradation, population explosion, desertification, and the very recent human catastrophe, AIDS. Without mass literacy, without adult education we are excluding the illiterate millions from being our partners in the twenty-first century. We adult educators of the 'First', the 'Second' and the 'Third' Worlds have no time to waste. Let us rise up and unite in rebuilding and strengthening such important organisations as UNESCO, UNICEF, WHO, etc. Without such organisations we have no solid base on which to start creating a sense of belonging to one family, of all human beings sharing one country - Mother Earth. As responsible adult educators we are not expected only to help in protecting the human family from man-made catastrophe: through providing a liberating and unifying education to the masses we need to avert the shameless campaigns of war and destruction perpetrated by a few arrogant and shortsighted figures who are currently enjoying temporary positions of international significance.

REFERENCES

1. P. and W. Paddock, Hungry Nations (Boston: Little, Brown & Co., 1964), p.18.

2. M. Beloff, 'The Third World and the Conflict of Ideologies', in The Third World Premises of US Policy, revised edition (San Francisco: The Institute for Contemporary Studies, 1983), p.21.

3. M. Carnoy, Education as Cultural Imperialism (New York: David McKay, 1974), pp.233-306.

4. S.E. Finer, 'The Military and Politics in The 3rd World', in W. Scott Thompson, The 3rd World Premises of US Policy, pp.76-7.

5. UNESCO/UNDP, The Experimental World Literacy Programme: A Critical Assessment (Paris: UNESCO, 1976).

6. IDRC, The World of Literacy: Policy, Research and Action (Ottawa ICAE, and IDRC, 1979), p.5.

7. The World Bank, World Development Report 1983 (Washington DC: Oxford University Press, 1983).

8. A. Angelopoulos, The 3rd World and Rich Countries (New York: Praeger Press, 1972), pp.15-16.

9. The World Bank, Accelerated Development in Sub-Saharan Africa: An Agenda for Action (Washington DC: 1981), p.1.

10. H.S. Bhola, Campaigning for Literacy: A Critical Analysis of Some Selected Literacy Campaigns of the 20th Century with a Memorandum to Decision Matters. Report submitted to UNESCO, 15 April 1981, p.6.

11. Ruth L. Sivard, World Military and Social Expenditures (Washington DC: World Priorities, 1980-83) p.6.

12. Ibid., p.24.

13. Ibid., p.5.

14. Abbas Alnasrawi, 'Economic Consequences of the Iraq-Iran War', Third World Quarterly, Vol.8, No.3 (July 1986), p.869.

15. R. Sivard, World Military and Social Expenditures, p.16.

16. Paulo Freire, Pedagogy of the Oppressed (New York: Herder and Herder, 1970), p.205.

17. P. Enahoro, 'Interview with Nyerere'. Africa Now, (December 1983), pp.98-125.

18. W. Rodney, How Europe Underdeveloped Africa, 4th Impression (London and Dar-es-Salaam: Bogle-L'Ouverture Publications and TPH, 1976), p.265.

19. Retta Alamayehu, 'Literacy for Work: A Comparative Study of Literacy. Campaigns in Tanzania and Ethiopia', MA thesis (McGill University 1984), p.8.

20. Rodney, How Europe Underdeveloped Africa, p.265.

21. Carnoy, Education as Cultural Imperialism, p.72.

22. Ibid., pp.156-270.

23. P.H. Coombs, The World Education Crisis: A Systems Analysis (New York: Oxford University Press, 1968).

24. H.S. Bhola, Campaigning for Literacy, p.19.

25. Elizabeth Moos, Soviet Education: Achievements and Goals (New York: National Council of American-Soviet Friendship, 1967), p.5.

26. Bhola, Campaigning for Literacy, p.108.

27. B.L. Hall and J.R. Kidd, Adult Learning: A Design for Action (London: Pergamon Press, 1978).

28. Canadian Action for Nicaragua, The Nicaraguan Literacy Crusade (Toronto: Action Print, 1982), pp.2-6.

29. P. Zwerling and C. Martin, Nicaragua: A New Kind of Revolution (Westport, Connecticut: Lawrence Hill & Co., 1985), p.67.

30. Jane E. Maxwell, 'Adult Education in a Revolutionary Setting: A Study of the Nicaraguan Popular Basis Education Program', MA thesis (University of Toronto, 1982), p.116.

31. UNESCO, Statistical Yearbook (New York: UN Publications, 1985), pp.16-19.

32. Alemayehu, 'Literacy for Work', p.84.

33. UNESCO, Literacy: The Right of Every Human Being (Paris: UNESCO, 1978).

Conclusion:

Radical Adult Education

Tom Lovett

The whole discussion about adult education and social change, about the role of adult education in popular social movements is intelligible only in relation to the question of purpose; as Tawney indicated, it rests on a particular view of the nature and capabilities of men and women and the sort of society which would assist their development.

Education that aims to promote, strengthen or support a social movement has to adjust any notion of relevance to the aspirations of the movement: it has to be relevant to the kind of society the movement is trying to achieve and to the campaigns alaong the way, rather than to existing social circumstances. It has to attract and hold students who have these aspirations, and it has to provide intellectual stimulation which deepens their understanding and enhances their efforts.

However, as the chapters in this book illustrate, social movements rarely have unitary objectives. They comprise widely disparate aims, united for tactical reasons. As Johnson, Armstrong and Westwood indicate, the early British labour movement contained the disagreement between radical populists and precursors of socialism; between those who wanted a Marxist education and those concerned with an 'objective' education; between those concerned with a traditional, and often reactionary, view of women's education and those who fought for a truly liberating education for women.

Radical social movements today are composed of similar incongruous elements and concerned, in some respects, with resolving similar problems and contradictions. One of the problems is whether to create a genuine alternative radical model of adult education which can survive without long-term financial support from the state, or to attempt to change existing educational institutions. In practice the result is usually a combination of the two with alternative education initiatives cooperating with

300

'institutional guerillas'!

Another problem is that collective efforts at adult education provision, with people involved in organising and directing the programme, often result in programmes which are concerned with lifelong learning and an emphasis on individual development and advancement. A third problem is that attempts to provide a sustained, intellectually stimulating programme for 'activists' can become vehicles for second-chance education and social advancement. The working out of these problems is, as Armstrong reminds us, to be engaged with the dialectic of the contradiction, and it is in this process that the development of the antithesis, that praxis begins to take shape.

As the chapters in the second half of this book illustrate, this is a process engaging the attention of adult educators in a wide range of contemporary social movements. Many would argue that radical social change is only possible if those involved in this process can reflect on their action and develop a coherent, alternative vision of the future and a strategy to achieve it.

However, such activists are obviously and under-standably concerned with practical knowledge and know-how. There is no unfathomable gulf between the latter and a grasp of underlying principles which would enable them to manipulate their practices and surroundings in pursuit of planned objectives. But neither is there any immediate or necessary association of the two. Education has however a large and indispensable role to play in that mediation.

The long-term criteria for such an educational programme could then be set in relation to a general purpose and a subsequent set of questions. What is to count as progress and as development? What will be the future of industrial society and of social class? What new institutional arrangements can be developed to ensure democratic participation and control in society? How can we protect our environment and ensure the future of the global village? What new economic arrangement will rid us of the Third World both abroad and in our own midst? What can we do to enhance the possibility of world peace? How can we ensure genuine liberation and equality for women and other oppressed groups?

These are large questions and it is unrealistic to imagine that radical social movements will purposefully come together to address them. However, as the concluding chapters indicate, adult educators are involved in such

301

movements and they have links with each other, nationally and internationally. They have the opportunity to pursue such matters and to learn from, and assist, each other.

As their experiences confirm, such radical adult education involves some notion of what it is to be educated not in a universal sense, but in relation to some implied or explicit social objectives. It cannot prosper under conditions where the educator has lost all sense of where we should be going. Education that is mounted by adult educators who throw up their hands and declare that the future is wholly uncertain, that any scenario is as valid as another, are as guilty as those who, without any opposition or struggle, cooperate in attempts to link education more effectively to government views of what society 'needs'.

The question - what is the social purpose of adult education given the reality we confront and the future we expect? - can then be answered in terms which affirms the right of men and women to challenge that reality and shape their own future. That process will be greatly assisted by the development of radical educational perspectives and accompanying movements and networks concerned to offer a different set of social and educational objectives and a vision of a new society based on equality, fraternity and social justice. Hopefully the analysis, and the illustrations of practice offered in this book, will make some small contribution to that process, nationally and internationally.

Index

Index

Index

United Auto Workers 278
United States
  adult education 270,
  275-6; Finnish 122-5;
  institutions 270; through
  worker-ownership 269-80
  Highland Centre 160
  Industrial Workers of the
  World (IWW) 120-4
  militant Finns in 120
  Work People's College
  114, 118, 120-5
  workplace democracy in
  269-70
  see also Black Panther
  Party
university
  adult education for
  unemployed 256-7
  extension movement 45-
  6, 48, 63-4, 247-8
  transdisciplinary studies
  214-15
uranium mining issue 203-8,
  211-13, 217-22
Useful Knowledge Societies
  4

Vanek, Jaroslav 279-80

Warden, Benjamin 22
Webb, Catherine 70
welfare state 91, 142
whaling 216
women
  black 197
  divisions among 196-7
  domesticity 68-70, 74-6
  education of 15, 17, 59-
  60, 63, 65-8, 75, 183-4,
  235-6; emancipatory 80;
  1919 report 77-8
  equality of 174
  guerrilla action by 194
  in adult education 188-

90, 193, 195
  in 19th century 59-60,
  62, 64-5; in social
  services 68
  in 1980s depression 182-
  3
  lecturers 19-20
  left's attitude to 182
  liberation of 141-2, 181-
  2, 191, 197, 199-200
  suffrage campaign 67,
  68-70, 72, 75
  Third World 288-9
  unemployed 182;
  education for 254
  violence against 166, 183
  wages 70
  workers 74-5, 78
  working class 197
  see also Cooperative
  Women's Guild; feminism
Women's Education Centre
  195
Women's Institutes 77
Women's Labour League
  (WLL) 67-9
Women's Liberation
  Movement 195, 199
Work Peoples' College, US
  114, 118, 120-5
worker ownership of means
  of production 263-4, 274
  education through 264-8,
  274-5; in USA 269-80
  Mondragon initiative
  267-8
  principles of 277-9
Workers' Educational
  Association (WEA) 46-
  53, 55, 64-5, 150, 186-7,
  190, 193, 236, 247, 266
  drift to middle class 224
  trade union courses 230
  women in 66-7
Workers' Educational Trade